DRINKING ARAK OFF
AN AYATOLLAH'S
BEARD

DRINKING ARAK OFF AN AYATOLLAH'S BEARD

A JOURNEY
*Through the Inside–Out Worlds
of Iran and Afghanistan*

NICHOLAS JUBBER

DA CAPO PRESS
A Member of the Perseus Books Group

The author is grateful for permission to quote from
A Poem by Nadia Anjoman, translated by Mahnaz Badihian.

Map designed by Sally Maltby

Designed by Trish Wilkinson
Set in 11.5 point Minion by the Perseus Books Group

First Da Capo Press edition 2010

Library of Congress Cataloging-in-Publication Data

Jubber, Nicholas.
    Drinking arak off an ayatollah's beard : a journey through the inside-out
worlds of Iran and Afghanistan / Nicholas Jubber. — 1st Da Capo Press ed.
        p.   cm.
    Includes bibliographical references.
    ISBN 978-0-306-81884-4 (alk. paper)
    1. Iran—Description and travel. 2. Afghanistan—Description and travel.
3. Jubber, Nicholas—Travel—Iran. 4. Jubber, Nicholas—Travel—Afghanistan.
5. Firdawsi. Shahnamah. 6. Iran—Social conditions—1997– 7. Afghanistan—
Social conditions—21st century. 8. Social conflict—Iran. 9. Social
conflict—Afghanistan. I. Title.
DS259.2.J83 2010
915.504'544—dc22   2009048191

Published by Da Capo Press
A Member of the Perseus Books Group
www.dacapopress.com

Da Capo Press books are available at special discounts for bulk purchases in the
U.S. by corporations, institutions, and other organizations. For more information,
please contact the Special Markets Department at the Perseus Books Group, 2300
Chestnut Street, Suite 200, Philadelphia, PA 19103, or call (800) 810-4145, ext.
5000, or e-mail special.markets@perseusbooks.com.

10 9 8 7 6 5 4 3 2 1

For my mother
and in memory of Sylvia Jubber

Contents

Photographs follow page 175.

Preface

In June 2009, President Mahmoud Ahmadinejad of Iran was re-elected by a landslide.

Or, to put it another way: in June 2009, hundreds of thousands of people marched through the streets of Tehran, demanding a recount.

This, after all, is the land where there are always two sides to the story.

As usually happens in Iranian history, the demonstrators were suppressed: knocked down with chains and batons, pepper spray and gunfire, carted off in SUVs, and in some cases tortured or killed.

And, as usually happens in Iranian history, they found subtler, more secretive ways of expressing their outrage. They voiced their opinions on social networking Web sites and uploaded protest songs. They released green balloons from their rooftops, declaring their support for the defeated candidate, Mir Hossain Mousavi, who had chosen green—the color of Islam—as his emblem. And one day they gathered in large numbers in downtown Tehran around the statue of a medieval poet and tied a green scarf around his neck.

That poet was Ferdowsi, whose *Shahnameh*, or *Book of Kings* (an epic completed 999 years before the demonstrations), tells of the many rulers who, like President Ahmadinejad, dismissed their opponents as "dirt and dust"—and usually wound up as the victims of a coup or a popular uprising.

This is the story of my journey in Ferdowsi's world, both past and present, a few years before the protests broke out. It was a time when the presidency was passing from the ineffectual Mohammed Khatami to the volatile Ahmadinejad; when across the border Afghanistan was dipping its toes, hesitantly, in a new democracy; while in neighboring Turkmenistan the world's oddest dictator was nearing his last breath.

In the summer of 2009, images of the demonstrations would burst onto news screens around the world. But they were hardly new. Iranians had been protesting for much of the past decade. And, as the statue in the green scarf in downtown Tehran quietly underlines, their leaders had been abusing them for longer.

DRINKING ARAK OFF
AN AYATOLLAH'S
BEARD

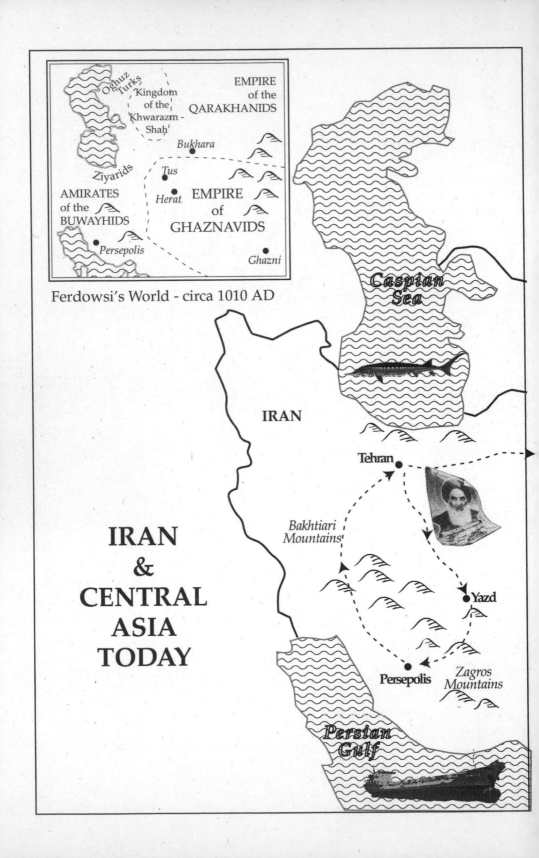

Ferdowsi's World - circa 1010 AD

EMPIRE
of the
QARAKHANIDS

Oghuz
Turks

Kingdom
of the
Khwarazm -
Shah

Ziyarids

Bukhara

Tus

Herat

EMPIRE
of
GHAZNAVIDS

AMIRATES
of the
BUWAYHIDS

Persepolis

Ghazni

Caspian
Sea

IRAN

Tehran

Bakhtiari
Mountains

Yazd

Persepolis

Zagros
Mountains

IRAN
&
CENTRAL
ASIA
TODAY

Persian
Gulf

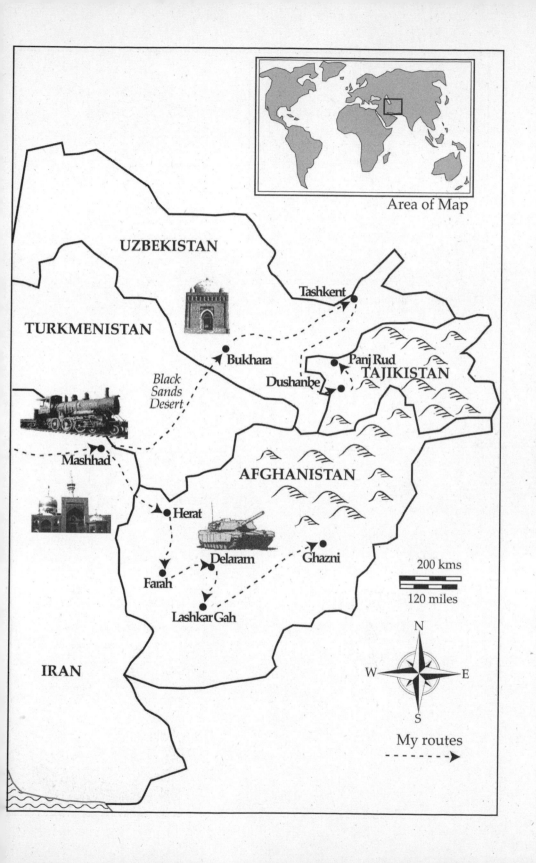

Area of Map

UZBEKISTAN

TURKMENISTAN

Tashkent

Bukhara

Panj Rud

Dushanbe

TAJIKISTAN

Black
Sands
Desert

Mashhad

AFGHANISTAN

Herat

Delaram

Ghazni

Farah

Lashkar Gah

IRAN

200 kms

120 miles

N

W   E

S

My routes

"Tavana buvad har ki dana buvad"—"All who had power had knowledge"

—WRITTEN ON THE GATE OF TEHRAN UNIVERSITY, FROM FERDOWSI'S *SHAHNAMEH*

Prologue
Mashhad, Eastern Iran. September.

"Oh. My. God."

One glimpse is enough to rip out my optimism—like someone came along and extracted it with a knife.

The bus is the last in its row, each more battered and less brightly painted than the one before, its roof more heavily crushed by boxes and buckets strapped on with string, and a larger pool of water rising around the wheels to trap them in a glue of mud. All the buses in the station look decrepit, but this one is a parody of the rest. It looks like the worst bus in the world.

A man is standing over me, wrinkling his nose at my ticket. It turns out he's the driver.

"Why do you go to Afghanistan?" he exclaims. "You think this is a country for tourists?"

His laugh is throaty and thoroughly disconcerting. Had the old man behind me not set his arm on my shoulder, I might be making a dash for the bus back to Tehran.

"I am a traveler like you," he whispers.

This man has skin like walnut bark and wears a gray waistcoat over his knee-length shirt, under a brimless woolen cap that looks like it's been woven from his beard.

1

"I have been on a pilgrimage," he continues, "to the Holy City."

"You are a *Hajji*?* You've just come back?"

"No, no, no!" His teeth gleam gold between his parched lips. "I went thirty years ago. I couldn't afford to go now!"

His small gray eyes shine through the creases of his skin. He seems to be kind, so I decide to stick with him.

"Afghanistan is a good country," he says, poking his nose between the headrests in front of me—we have settled inside the bus now. He squinnies his brow for a moment, before adding, "It *was* a good country."

"When?" says a man in an ocean-colored polo shirt who's taken the seat across the aisle from mine. He looks like he should be on vacation in Hawaii.

The *Hajji* looks up, frowning, then in a burst of inspiration he declares, "In Kaiser Wilhelm's day!" He raps the headrest as he explains, "There was a train."

We wait an hour for movement. When it finally comes, there is a terrible groan underneath us, as if some wild beast has been stretched out under the chassis, then a *tick-tick* as the engine rattles to a stop. Is this bus not even capable of forward propulsion? But I can hear a noise swelling around us, suggesting another cause for our pause. Gingerly, the *Hajji* lifts a pleated nylon curtain to peer through the window. I notice an anxious expression creeping across his face.

"*Mujahideen*," he whispers.

A wave of sunlight washes through the door: a swamp of flailing limbs, enormous beards, long torn gowns. Boxes fly down the aisle; burlap sacks pile on the seats and around the steps in the middle. Buckets clatter on top of them, all the way up to the Formica ceiling, as do more sacks, plastic bags, and finally—shunted through the door, defying the tiny space that's left—a Honda motorcycle.

"They are fighting men," whispers the *Hajji*. "Do not say you are a foreigner."

---

* *Hajji* is the honorific title given to any Muslim who performs the *hajj*, the pilgrimage to Mecca.

All of them are dressed in baggy trousers and knee-length shirts—the traditional Afghan costume known as *shalwar qameez*. I bought a set for myself only yesterday, knowing I would need it in Afghanistan's troubled south, but I haven't put it on yet, so it will be easy to identify me as an outsider. Hiding my tell-tale Roman-scripted notebook in the overhead rack, I excavate an enormous green-jacketed hardback out of my pack. It's the only Persian book in my possession—the language not only of the Iranians whom I'm leaving, but also of a large number of the Afghans among whom I'll be traveling. Tooled across its spine—a gorgeous cluster of golden dots, elaborate curls, and long barbed stalks—is the word *Shahnameh—Book of Kings*.

"*You* are reading *that*?" asks the *Hajji*, his gold teeth flashing in his gasp.

The man in the ocean-colored polo shirt, whose name is Wahid, is more proactive.

"Here," he says, leaning across the aisle and reaching for the book, "give it here."

He turns its pages delicately, and familiarly—as if he's caressed these very pages in the past—and when he comes across a verse he likes, his mouth expands to the size of a tea saucer:

Mayaazaar muri ke daneh kash ast	*Oh stamp not the ant that is under your feet*
Ke jaan daarad u jaan e shirin khush ast.	*For it has a soul and its own soul is sweet.*

The *Hajji* smiles, his eyes as bright as his gold teeth, repeating the verse in a whisper, as if to memorize it for himself. I have come across plenty of poetry aficionados in Iran—on a few occasions I've even attended poetry circles where traditional instruments were played as people recited from their favorite authors. But I was advised not to expect this sort of thing in Afghanistan. "They are murdering brutes" was one of the less cryptic descriptions I heard. So to watch polo-shirt-wearing Wahid, his eyes glued to the pages and his lips quivering to the rhythm of the thousand-year-old words, is hugely reassuring. Maybe the Afghans won't be as formidable as I've been warned.

We are near the border. You can tell because the landscape is growing less and less friendly. A medieval traveler would have known the "abundant fruit-trees, streams and mills" spotted here by the great Muslim globe-trotter Ibn Battuta in the fourteenth century. But now the fertility has dried up. Low-slung mud-brick farmsteads slumber behind bald fields and mountain scarps scissor the sky like dragon scales. As the Afghan border draws ever closer, even these features grow scarce. It's as if the land is stripping itself of possessions in preparation for bandit country.

I had spent eight months in Iran before I finally set out for Afghanistan. Eight months of incredible comfort with the kindest of families in a gated house in North Tehran. For more than half of this time, I was actively planning a journey to Afghanistan—a grand old romp through that distant and seemingly treacherous land. But whenever I was on the verge of setting out, something astonishing would happen: I would stumble, quite by chance it seemed, on an absolutely unavoidable reason to delay. *Well, there's a film festival coming up in Tehran and my host's daughter has been teaching me all about the Iranian film industry, so it would be a crime to miss it. . . . Oh, I should really go and visit the eighth imam's footprint. . . . And what about the Quran museum, where the nation's Supreme Leaders (the Ayatollahs, Khomeini and Khamenei) have been embroidered on velvet, composed out of wheat, or depicted in oils by an armless war veteran who paints with his mouth? . . .*

Even when I did finally set out, I decided not to let my fellow passengers in on what I was up to.

"If you tell the Afghans your plan," said my host in Tehran—his brown owl-like eyes gleaming with the warning—"they will tear you to pieces!"

So I'm keeping my mission under wraps, hidden in my backpack, and when they ask me what I am doing here, I only give them a vague indication of my route.

"I suppose," I say, when the *Hajji* asks me, "I want to find out if Afghan and Iranian culture have much in common."

"Oh yes," he says excitedly, "we are the same. We are both Aryan, we have the same poets—Hafez, Ferdowsi, for example—and our music is also similar."

"No we're not!" declares Wahid, stamping his foot on the runner. "You know what we call the Iranians? You know?"

His mouth twists into a scowl and he screws up his nose, preparing me for the most offensive put-down in history.

"We call them," he announces, "sandwich-eaters!"

It isn't quite the slap-down I was anticipating, although it makes sense—given all the sandwich restaurants I've encountered on the Iranian streets. Afghans, as I will learn, do not generally indulge in "Westernized" snack food, preferring to stick to their traditional dishes.

"They aren't tough like us," continues Wahid. "They don't know what it means to be a man!"

As if to underline his point, he drops the green-jacketed copy of the *Shahnameh* directly onto my lap. It's hard not to be winded by the direct plunge of a 1,500-page weight—but I dare not utter a sound, lest he decide I'm another sandwich-munching sissy. Now, drawing closer to me on the seat, he appears to be continuing his test of my physical endurance, by squeezing my shoulder under his paw. His face, however, is turning softer, his eyes lighting up with a new thought.

"Mind you," he says, "have you been to Shiraz?"

"Yes."

"The women!" He chuckles, looking round to check the *Hajji* isn't listening. "I went to Shiraz," he whispers. "I thought I was in paradise!" He squeezes my shoulder even harder, before drawing back to his seat, shaking his head as he adds in a loud voice, "a country of sandwich-eaters!"

I'm not the only one who's been trying to delay the inevitable. The driver is in no hurry to reach Afghanistan himself—a few miles before the border, we stop at a roadside canteen. Buckwheat grits are scooped onto tin plates as men hunch over the tables, while the women wait patiently on a veranda outside. Sitting among them are an old man trilling on a *ney* flute and another with a bandaged stump for a leg, who stretches out a hand for alms. It's the musician who is receiving the most attention, but neither has the crowd for long. At the hoot of the air horn, they turn into a scrum and charge the bus, where the boxes and buckets already clinging to the rusty bars of the roof are now jostled by a cooker, a metal safe, and a dozen gas-pump poles.

"I walked across this border once," says Wahid, as we watch the last few parched kilometers of Iran in the window. "It was in the war. When the Russian tanks came to Herat I decided to escape. I walked over the mountains for a day and a night and came out on the other side."

"Where did you go?" I ask.

"Germany. I lived there for twenty years. Now I'm back in Afghanistan but I still have business with Germany—I sell secondhand BMWs in Kabul."

He leans toward me, his sharp eyes peering through the glare of sunlight coming from the window.

"Where in my country do you want to go?" he asks.

"Well," I whisper, "I really want to go to Ghazni." I'm referring to a city on the other side of the country, roughly between Kandahar and Kabul, which was once the fulcrum of Afghanistan's mightiest empire. "Do you think it's possible?"

"Ghazni?" His voice has turned to a gasp. "But that's in Taliban country."

One of the *mujahideen* has overheard us. His beard is dangling over the headrest in front of me as he studies my face, like it's a map for hidden treasure.

"You can't go to Ghazni," he says.

"But I've *got to*!"

The *Hajji* leans forward, his chin snug in the crook of his hands: "There is no reason he can't go to Ghazni. I am from Ghazni myself. In Ghazni it is secure. It is the road *to* Ghazni that is the problem."

Sweat is dripping off my brow and trickling down my glasses—although I'm not sure if it's been caused by my anxiety or the heat. The driver is sweating too; he dabs his face with his handkerchief, having braked to allow a policeman inside.

"Anyone who has a passport," says the policeman, "get down."

Apart from Wahid and me, everyone stays put.

The border post is a vast encampment, spread across the scrub desert. A dozen UNHCR* buses are parked outside makeshift tents, near the mud-brick customs huts, which spew out a crowd of Afghans in their baggy trousers and long shirts. They aren't much taller than me, but they look enormous, enlarged by their beards and the hauteur with which they stride. I feel like an Oompa-Loompa at a convention for giants.

"Come on," says Wahid.

He hangs an arm over my shoulder, as warmly as a lover, leading me to a hut where an officer in a navy uniform is sitting behind a wooden counter. The officer's face is impassive, his thumb pressed down on the business end of his Kalashnikov (otherwise known as an AK-47).

"You are a child of where?" he asks.

"Britain." I want to say "Great Britain," but giants and Kalashnikovs have whittled down my national pride.

He seizes my passport, thumping his stamp onto my Iranian visa.

"That's Iran," I say.

He snatches the passport back, stamps the right page, and throws it directly at my head.

Back at the bus, a problem is brewing. A relay of *mujahideen* are carrying bottles and bowls of water to cool down the radiator, while the driver and a lackey are bustling under the chassis, hammering away with the contents of a toolbox. As I watch them at work, I'm struck by the thought that we might end up having to stay here all night.

"It is in the hands of God," declares the *Hajji*, his palms raised and his gold teeth catching the last flashes of the dying sunlight.

---

* United Nations High Commissioner for Refugees.

I crouch down on the tarmac beside him, too nervous to enjoy the attention I'm receiving from the *mujahideen*. But I'd better make their acquaintance, that much is becoming clear—because one of them is flicking through the pages of a familiar green-jacketed hardback. He's picked up my copy of the *Shahnameh*—the thousand-year-old epic Persian poem, which I had left on my seat.

"This is yours?" he asks, one heavy brow inching up his forehead.

I nod firmly—remembering what Wahid said about Afghan toughness, I don't want the *mujahid* to think I'm a pushover:

"You have read it?"

"Of course! It is the story of my country."

The book is presented on his outstretched palms, as if he were an upmarket waiter offering a rare delicacy.

"You are a foreigner," he declares, probing me with his gaze.

"Well . . ." I stall, scrabbling in my head for some way of avoiding the inevitable answer, before succumbing at last: "Yes, I suppose I am."

"So why do you read *Shahnameh*? You want to know how we defeat our enemies?"

I'm puzzled. Are we talking about the same book? The same *thousand-year-old* book? Sure, there might be a lot of battles in it—in fact, there are times when you wonder if there is ever going to be anything else. But the warriors of the *Shahnameh* fight with bows and spears and occasionally an ox-headed mace—it's not exactly the stuff of modern-day warfare.

"Because," he says, "if you read *Shahnameh*, you can understand why we will never let foreigners rule our country."

He is communicating a view I have often heard in Iran and will hear again in Afghanistan. It's a view of the *Shahnameh* as more than just a collection of tales—a living, breathing entity; the most accurate account available of the psyche of the Persian-speaking people (in this case, meaning the Persian-speaking Afghans as much as the Iranians).

Our conversation is interrupted by a whoop—a joyful trilling all around us. The bus is ready to move! The *tick-tick* of the engine transforms into a confident, definitely-making-progress rumble, to which the *mujahideen* respond with a declaration of the Doctrine of Divine Unity: "There is no God but God and Mohammed is the messenger of God." They recite it at the same pitch as English soccer fans chanting a winning score: not so much one–nil as One God. Why are they so happy? To our right is the same craggy mountain that's refused to budge ever since I arrived in Khorasan,* while on the other side are mud-brick slums, soldiers sitting on tires, and square metal cargo containers—brought over during the Cold War and now doubling as shops.

At the edge of a village, a crowd is milling around a man whose knee-length shirt is flecked with blood. The cause of the blood, I assume, is the car behind him—it's been concertinaed by a truck lying sideways on the road, although he could just as easily have been wounded by one of the Kalashnikovs that are carried as copiously as iPods in London: unattended on the steps of domed mud-brick houses, in the laps of men sipping tea, resting against the cargo containers.

It's dark when we pass a copse of towers the shape of smokestacks. Where are the lights? There was more luster in the smallest Iranian village than there is now in Herat—Afghanistan's second largest city. A taxi drops me at a crossroads called Flower, where the Taliban used to hang its "criminals"—musicians, drinkers, intellectuals, lovers. . . . In the lobby of the Hotel Mowaffaq (which means—for reasons that must have been clear an awfully long time ago—"successful"), scallops of plaster are peeling off the walls, as if the building is protesting its name.

After a brief skirmish with the keyhole, I step inside a chipped door to find a bare, rugless room. There are cracks across the walls, a hole concealed by newspaper, and bedding so stiff you could probably sell it to a sculptor and pass it off as rock. Outside my window, the dogs are already starting to bark.

Compared with the comfort I've enjoyed for the past few months— a warm bed in the coziest of houses in the most affluent part of

---

* The name of this region on both the Iranian and Afghan sides of the border.

Tehran—this is like falling through a trapdoor and ending up in the bowels of hell. I can hear a metallic clicking under my bed, but I don't have the spirit to find out which particular species of creepy-crawly is lurking down there, waiting to feast. I drop my backpack on the floor, sprawl across the bed and close my eyes. . . .

PART ONE

ᴄᴧᴩ

IRAN

"May the glad noise of revels long ring out!
Perish the sanctimonious and devout!
Be their patched frocks and azure gabardines
Trod in the tavern by a drunken rout!"
— *THE RUBAIYAT OF OMAR KHAYYAM*

1

The Inside-Out City

Tehran. Eight months earlier: January.

"Turn it up! Turn it up!"

Sina's voice was bouncing around the car. We were racing up the Jordan Highway, one of Tehran's most horn-honkingly overactive thoroughfares, under the icy peaks of Mount Alborz and the high-rise tower-blocks, buffed by the afternoon sunlight. Curly brown ringlets were shaking as he nodded to the beat, beaming out of the window of his friend Mustafa's Peugeot 206.

"This is the best place for listening to music!" he exclaimed.

He turned toward me while simultaneously thrashing about to Persian electro-pop recorded in California.* Forget about trying to find a nightclub on the street: If you want to dance in public in Iran, you have to do it on wheels. Out here on the highway, we were going too fast for the Morality Police to catch us.

When we slowed down, creeping along with the traffic, Mustafa turned down the music and opened the window. The smell of diesel wafted through; you could taste it and see it too, hovering over us like some amorphous, mythical beast, feeding off the mobile kilns that pass in Tehran for cars. Driven by Iran's two most abundant natural

---

* There are so many ex-pat Iranian musicians producing pop and distributing it back home through under-the-counter sales and Internet downloads that their community is known locally as "Tehrangeles."

13

resources—petrol and testosterone—they went the wrong way down one-way streets, U-turned, ignored the red lights, and covered each other with dents. It was absolute mayhem—in fact, it was the only public space in which strict regulations failed to hold. But it wasn't just the cars. The motorcyclists were too fast, the mobile fruit-cart pushers were too slow, and you never knew when a bus would come careening down its contra-flow.

Now, as the traffic reached gridlock, people were spilling between the cars. Mustafa reached out, dropping some banknotes into an old woman's pot of wild rue,* and the smell dissipated the diesel stench, promising to keep us safe from the Evil Eye. On the other side of the car, a young woman, shivering in the winter chill, held a baby in one arm as she stretched out the other for alms, while a flower seller darted between the vehicles and a small boy carried a bucket of water to wipe down people's windshields. The traffic jam had turned into a bazaar.

"*Jigaret bokhoram!*" cried Sina, when he spotted something he liked in the next lane. Literally: "I want to eat your liver!"

I could never get over the cannibalism of this classic Persian phrase—which he was actually using to express his admiration.

A young lady—two-tone lipstick and bubblegum-pink handkerchief-sized headscarf—was gazing out of the car next to us. Ripping a piece of paper out of my notebook, Sina hurriedly scribbled something onto it before rolling down the window and passing it across.

"What did you write?" I asked as we pulled ahead.

"Eh!" he exclaimed with a grin. "It's just my phone number."

We swept back into the highway steeplechase, and once again my friends were swinging their shoulders to the plastic beat.

"I want this girl to call me now!" said Sina. "When I listen to this music, I want *all* the girls to call me!"

That evening we were cruising the highways. On another occasion we were on foot. This time Sina came prepared—he'd written his number several times over, so he was able to stuff it into the

---

* *Esfand* or wild rue is a strong-smelling, herbaceous plant burned in many traditional ceremonies in Iran, whose fumes are said to keep away evil spirits.

hands of passing girls as we strolled down Valiasr Street, the major road that cleaves Tehran from north to south.

"But how do you know they'll *want* your number?" I asked.

Sina laughed, his large brown eyes flashing as he shook his head. I think he found it hard to believe that anybody could be such a novice.

"Didn't you see the way they move their headscarves? If they make it open it means they are interested. You just have to look, if you use your eyes you can see the signs."

Occasionally, all the number exchanges would reap their fruit, and he would receive an invite to a party. He would empty out his tub of gel, spray himself with Dolce & Gabbana, and give his best shirt to his mother or sister to iron (although his sister, Tahmineh, would usually grumble, she always ended up doing what he'd asked). Mustafa would turn up in his Peugeot, shiny from a recent wash, and we'd set off for some house up in the hills or a soundproofed basement in the concrete labyrinth of the Ekbatan district.

Gliding across the threshold of one such venue was a group of young women, buckled in trench coats and wrapped up tight in their headscarves. It was raining on this particular evening, so the men were all dripping as we stepped into the checkerboard hallway, but thanks to their scarves the women were untarnished. A few moments after they were in, bare legs and arms were out, and they were nuzzling their chins to their shoulders or flicking their glossy, un-rained-on ringlets, all coy glances as a dozen young bastions of hair gel and pluck competed to pour them a drink. Our ears pounded to the Black Eyed Peas, then DJ Ali-gator (an ex-pat Iranian now based in Sweden), followed by the Turkish superstar, Tarkan, while our eyes were locked to the belly-button rings catching the web of light from a teardrop chandelier: round, oval, butterfly-shaped, and one with tiny beads that swung on the barbell as its owner danced.

Parties like this take place every night in North Tehran, charged not only with the usual chemicals you would expect at a gathering of twenty-somethings, but the added intensity of what might happen if the authorities turn up. Sometimes there will be a rap on the door and a bearded officer will be standing outside. Depending on his mood, the partygoers' excuse ("Officer, peace be upon you, we're celebrating the birthday of the blessed imam's holy sister!") and how much they can offer as a remuncration, he will either let them off with a caution or bundle them into an SUV to spend a night behind bars.

No such visit had broken the party so far tonight. At the back of the flat, in the kitchen, a few people were gathering to talk away from the music. Some of them were discussing the latest escapades of the pop star Britney Spears. A couple of others were gossiping about an Iranian soap actress who had broken up with her fiancé. Struggling to keep up with the fast pace of their chatter, I pulled up a stool at the breakfast counter and sipped my vodka.

"So you're the English boy!" said a voice beside me.

I turned, peering through the fug of smoke and eventually located her: a young woman in extremely high heels, a black miniskirt, and a white collared shirt with a necktie draped over her shoulder (the latter was a deliberate act of rebellion—they are banned from state offices and storefronts, as a symbol of Western decadence). She offered me a Pleasure Light cigarette, took a sip of my vodka as I was fiddling with the Zippo, and asked what I was doing here. I talked about a book I'd written—I thought it would impress her but she just shrugged, her shoulders catching the light as they rose.

"It was about the past," I said, "so now I want to look at the present."

"Then Tehran is exactly the right place to be." Mischief was glimmering in her eyes as she drew on her cigarette. "You will find it is a very modern city. We have the most traffic accidents, and the worst smog . . . and the most heroin addicts, of course!"

She was laughing. She tipped the rest of my drink down her throat and leaned toward me.

"But it isn't all bad," she said. "We also have the biggest number of Internet bloggers outside America—so even if we are choking to death and overdosing, at least we are telling the world about it!"

We sat together for a while, me with another vodka and she with a glass of red wine.

"It's what our poets always drank," she pointed out, adding with a droll smile, "and it always makes me think deep thoughts!"

Among these thoughts, it transpired, was a disapproval of my plans.

"So what about the history?" she asked, leaning toward my cupped hands to light another cigarette. "You don't want to write about that too?"

"Well . . ." I hesitated, looking into her eyes, sparkling on either side of the flame. "I suppose . . . I want to find out what's going on today."

Again she was laughing. "So you obviously don't know what this song is about?"

I turned an ear toward the dance floor. It sounded like thrash metal—crashing drums and manically plucked guitar strings, although the singer had a strangely soulful baritone, drawing you into the whirlpool of noise. It was impossible for me to make out the words: Not only was the drumbeat too loud, there was the rush and thrum of people's feet and bodies as they crashed against each other and the roar of the more excited men, chanting over the lyrics, not to mention the frailty of my Persian, which at this stage was lost outside a simple one-on-one conversation.

"I wish it was as easy as you are thinking," she said, sliding off her stool and flashing me one last smile, "but you know, the past times and today, they are like a tortoise and its shell. Even if you can pull them apart, it is not a good idea."

I was still trying to work out what she meant, testing her words in my head, enjoying the tang of my first Persian riddle, when I felt an arm on my shoulder. Beaming over me, with dance sweat dripping down his curls, was Sina.

"Hey! Why are you alone?" he exclaimed indignantly. He grabbed hold of my arm, towing me back into the living room. "You know," he said on the way, "I think my baba would like this song."

"Why?"

His father was a wonderful and in many ways very eclectic man. But he wasn't exactly what you'd call a heavy metal band's target audience: a middle-aged academic, specializing in ancient Persian folklore. The idea of him turning up at this underground honky-tonk, taking off his homburg, and leaping about to the beat was utterly fantastical.

"Because," said Sina, "the words they are singing are from *Shahnameh*."

"You mean . . . ?"

"*Shahnameh*."

"You mean the one from a thousand years ago?"

"Of course, Nicholas! What else?"

"No, it's just . . . well, where I come from, it's just . . . medieval poems and pop music, they don't usually go together all that much."

"Really?" Sina wrinkled his nose, as if I must have been spawned in some kind of barbaric hellhole. "Well," he said, "poetry is poetry, isn't it?"*

He didn't stick with me for long; his eye was on the dance floor. Leaping in among the dancers, he shook his hips beside the girl I'd been talking to a few moments earlier, whose movements were slightly restricted by the enormous spike heels on which she was perched.

I turned back to the kitchen, where people's glasses were being replenished from an ice-packed bucket of Central Asian vodka, and as I reached for another refill, I tried to make out the thousand-year-old words, spiraling over the ripple of the guitar and the clash of the drums.

◇

I had been in Iran for several weeks when I first bumped into Sina—several weeks of studying the Persian language at an institute connected to Tehran University, staying at a cramped hostel on a street full of tire stores and mechanics' workshops. It wasn't exactly the time of my life. I'd heard about all the underground bars and black-market

---

* Medieval Persian poetry has a habit of turning up in Iranian pop lyrics. Banyan and Manizeh, the Sonny and Cher of 1950s Iran, had a hit when they sang a poem by the tenth-century minstrel Rudaki, while the rock band O-hum, which is big on the Iranian scene today, uses the mystical verses of the fourteenth-century poet Hafez in its songs and has even released an album named after the poet—*Hafez in Love*. In this case, the band was called Kahtmayan and had made a point of their enthusiasm for Ferdowsi's tenth-century epic.

pop records, and I was eager to find them. I suppose I wanted to be able to say what a hip, happening place Iran really is, how there's a pop band in every block and a bottle of bootleg vodka under every shop counter. But here I was, waking up to the roar from the traffic and the recorded calls-to-prayer from the mosque next door, stepping onto a street where the air was so filthy you might as well have been pressing your lips to the exhaust pipe of one of the ubiquitous pickup trucks.

If Tehran was a person, then for me it was one of the "thick-necks" who manned its bazaars. Pockmarked with potholes, scabbed with scaffolding, its wounds bandaged up by sheets of canvas, it was as pretty as its pinups—the gray-bearded ayatollahs,* who look down on the people from the billboards and the sides of the smog-stained apartment blocks, often accompanied by slogans from the Quran, which are repeated on the girders of overpasses and the fence of the National Bank. You tear down the highways, crammed into a creaking Paykan—where you're squeezed so tight you're pressing thighs with a woman you're not even supposed to talk to. You step out and straight into a *joob*—one of the narrow street-side channels that carry water down from the mountains—and sprain your ankle. You turn up late for your class, where your fellow students are mostly from the Korean embassy, so it's quite hard to follow what they're talking about in the mid-lesson break, and the teacher is so formal you still don't know her name. And she tells you the city is wonderful, the country is wonderful, everyone is happy. *Well, it doesn't look like it from here.*

But there was a magical world under Tehran's cold, austere surface, and when I met Sina that world came bursting out to pull me inside.

"Excuse me, sir, you would like a program?"

It was hardly an unusual question—coming from an usher. But as I turned toward Sina for the first time, there was a warmth in his

---

* Literally "sign of God," the rank of ayatollah is the highest in Twelver Shiism, given to experts in Islamic law and philosophy.

face I hadn't come across so far. By the time he'd shown me into a vinyl seat halfway down the auditorium, I had already told him more about myself than anyone else I'd met in Tehran. And I had learned more about him too.

"You see that lady in the blue headscarf?" he said, his grin sparkling in the splash of the house lights. "She's a pleasure-daughter!"

"What do you mean?"

"Oh, sir, I'm not saying she's like the women you get on the street—the ones who chew gum and smoke outside—but she's kissed at least two of the directors here, and a few months ago one of the actors did her. My friend Fereydoun, he did her too. Although I must tell you, sir, Fereydoun's done everyone—he's got a cock like an Arab!"*

It was hard to believe he was actually saying these things. With his patrician nose and curly brown hair, he looked like he could probably make a living pretending to be a Greek statue. He was far too dignified to have spoken so racily—look at him now, smiling sweetly at the lady in the row behind me, pressing a hand to his chest in the traditional Persian manner, as if he's a eunuch at the court of the ancient shahs.

"I have to go now," he said when the house lights came up at the end. "I am meeting my girlfriend and I want her to give me a blow job."

"This is . . ." I tried to remember the name he'd mentioned. "Mira?"

"No, she's my other girlfriend."

"Oh, you've got two?"

"No."

---

* This is the one detail in which Iranians tend to compliment their neighbors across the Gulf. There's an old Persian joke about Arabs leaving three tracks in the sand, which Sina was fond of repeating. As will become clear over the ensuing pages, there is no love lost between Iranians and Arabs and even this example (similar to the white man's joke about black men) barely hides a Persian perception of Arabs as a race of beasts, several rungs down the evolutionary ladder from the refined and courteous Iranians.

"Sorry . . . I'm a bit confused."

"I have six girlfriends."

"Well . . . You must be busy!"

The show I had been watching was a folklore concert—partly organized, I later learned, by Sina's father. I think the performers were good—I have a vague memory of some excellent Turkoman lute players and a pantalooned Baluchi tribesman with a tambourine—but Sina is my abiding memory of that evening, and of the next day. I'd given him the name of my hotel, but I never expected him to turn up at my door, telling me to hurry up and pack my stuff.

"Come on," he said, "again, come on! I told my baba about you and he says I must bring you in front of him."

As the shared taxi dodgemed up Valiasr Street, under dirt-smirched concrete and the winter plane trees, the talk was all about his father: how he'd once been seized by the Revolutionary Guard and thrown into prison, how he had a personal dealer to provide him with his vodka (which usually arrived in the back of a taxi), how he had been friends with a famous writer who was suffocated during a spate of murders in 1998.

A black metal gate announced us with a squeak, the loose branch of an apple tree nudged us along, and the chipped tiles of the entrance balcony tipped under our shoes. Ahead of us, standing inside the mosquito-net door of a flat-roofed house were the figures of Sina's parents. But they were quickly superseded by the extraordinary vision behind them.

Sitting at the kitchen table, her dyed blond hair dusting her bare knees as she applied pink polish to her toenails, was Sina's sister. She had several things I'd missed over my first few weeks in Iran—bare hair, flowing over her shoulders in what seemed like reckless abundance, bare shoulders, bare knees, and—as she stood up to greet me—a strip of bare midriff. I had to concentrate just to stop myself from staring, so I turned to my freshly unshod feet, which prompted Tahmineh to do the same.

"You need new socks," she said.

"Oh . . . yes." A big toe was peeking out, like an underground creature sticking its head out of the earth. "Whoops!" I added, curling my toes and trying to stop my face from turning the color of a barberry. As I would soon learn, Tahmineh might not be particularly keen on the government's dress-code rules, but she had plenty of rules of her own—and scruffy dressing was a definite no-no.

After several weeks on the public side of Iran, without a peek behind its secret, private walls, the Professor's house was a different world. It was proof that the old Persian saying, "A man within his own four walls is like a king in his own dominion," still holds. Outside, there were ayatollahs on the billboards and the screams of a million car horns; men in baggy trousers and women in bags, whose faces were as likely to be covered by a white surgical antismog mask as a full-on veil. But inside the house, the solemn, commanding world of outdoors was replaced by the forbidden sight of women's hair, the forbidden sound of a woman singing on the tape deck (this was Googosh—an Iranian icon, whose ballads were Sina's mother's favorites), and the forbidden taste from a bottle of Akband vodka. The house was a treasure trove for all that was prohibited in public.

Even the decor had a whiff of the unlawful—from the print of Darius the Great (a shah from the sixth century BCE, whose name was blacklisted from birth certificates in the wake of the Islamic Revolution of 1979) hanging in the living room to the walnut bookcase with its pile of white-spined under-the-counter paperbacks. If you were a member of the local morality police—the *basijis*—you would be clicking your tongue all the way down the corridor. You'd be flaring your nostrils at the poster of a bare-headed actress flapping over the desk in Sina's bedroom, as well as several pairs of black-market Calvin Kleins. And if you took a few steps farther down the corridor into Tahmineh's room, you would find your outrage very difficult to keep in check when your eyes settled on the pile of banned pre-revolution DVDs under her dressing table (not to mention a pirated copy of *Star Wars: Revenge of the Sith*—although, to be fair, most of Princess

Padme's scenes had been cut, presumably to stop any young men from getting overly excited by her cinnamon-bun hairdo).

After the shock of all this illicit material, you'd probably need one of the Professor's stiff drinks just to recover (and maybe a few bank-notes to help you forget this painful ordeal). And maybe you could tuck into one of Khanom's (or "Madame"—the name by which I always addressed Sina's mother) delicious meals too. Even this would be completely different from anything you could expect outside. You might find rice and chicken kebab in the street-side eateries (along with the ubiquitous sandwich stores), but not like this—with red barberries and saffron threads, the meat oozing with juice and sea-soned with lemon and pepper. It made the dry, rubbery food sold outside all the more unappetizing.

This contrast with the austere Iran of outdoors illustrated how the country had been turned inside-out by the revolution. For the better part of three millennia, Iran was ruled by shahs, or kings. They came in different forms—from the balloon-crowned pre-Islamic emper-ors to the Mongols in their owl-feathered headdresses, the Safavids in red plunger hats and turbans, and the extravagantly mustached Qajars, who gave themselves sumptuous honorifics like "Asylum of the Universe" and squandered the state funds in Parisian brothels; to the last two kings, the Pahlavis, who decked themselves in military medals and bought up the US arms industry.*

But in January 1979, the last of these rulers, Mohammed Reza Pahlavi, self-titled "Light of the Aryans" and "King of Kings," fled the country with the best of his jewels and a clod of Iranian earth. All at once, like a flipped coin, the culture over which he had presided was switched for the "other side" of Iran's identity. His father's mausoleum was dynamited and replaced by an Islamic seminary, and the street

---

* The name Pahlavi was taken from the word for the ancient Persian language, un-derlining the dynasty's emphasis on Iran's pre-Islamic heritage and disregard for Islam. The latter would be one of the principal causes of the dynasty's downfall.

that had been named after his dynasty was renamed after the twelfth Shia imam, Valiasr.* Americans, who had enjoyed diplomatic immunity, were expelled, while a man who had been expelled by the shah took his place as the country's new head of state. That man was Ayatollah Ruhollah Khomeini, whose broadcasts—which only months before had been sold on black-market tapes under the counter—now replaced royalist propaganda on state TV. It was a revolution in the most literal sense. A turning-around.

Going down	Going up
mini-skirts	headscarves
family protection law	polygamy
pop music	mourning songs for the Prophet Mohammed's grandson
neckties in public offices	beards
women in advertisements and on bicycles	women being hanged for adultery
Tintin (and especially his heavy-drinking comrade Captain Haddock), along with other examples of Western "cultural decadence"	Mickey Mouse (who, along with other Disney characters, is all over the Tehran bazaar: on carpets, cushion covers, towels); one offshoot of the diplomatic impasse is that there's no need to pay copyright duties
streets named after royalist or Western figures, like Cyrus the Great Street and Churchill Street	streets named after Islamic figures, like Ayatollah Beheshti Highway and Dr. Shariati Street, along with more spurious "anti-imperialists" like Bobby Sands Street, named for the Irish hunger striker

---

* Who disappeared in the early tenth century. He was the only one of the twelve Shia imams—all of them descendants of the Prophet Mohammed—who wasn't killed. They were all persecuted by the caliph (leader of the Sunnis) of their time, and denied what the Shia considered to be their rightful rank. As a result, the Shia—who represent more than 90 percent of Iran's population—are known for their suspicion of authorities.

Yet few of the newly forbidden activities were lost. People still drank alcohol (and became experts at making their own), still listened to pop music, still wore ties at home, and still watched American soap operas or prerevolutionary romances thanks to illegal satellite TV. They remained, as so much of the "new" identity had before them, hidden behind the walls that divide the parallel worlds of public and private.

That first evening with Sina and his family, there was one almighty obstacle to my being accepted.

"My son," announced the Professor, his back erect, at the head of the table, "tells me you are a child of England."

Oh dear . . . Just when I thought I was doing so well! I admitted that this was indeed the case and waited for the subsequent pause to end . . . And waited . . .

The hiatus was interrupted, finally, by the squeak of a stifled laugh. I looked up, to see Tahmineh burying her head into her brother's shoulder.

"Tahmineh-dear!"

A distinguished mop of silver hair crowned the Professor's high forehead; underneath it was a pair of large owl-like eyes that swallowed you up whenever they turned on you.

"If you have something to say," he continued, in the tone of a commander-of-all-he-surveys, "you must have the courage to say it."

Tahmineh dropped her head into her hands and kept it there, leaving Sina to explain:

"She calls you the Old Fox. That is our name for the English. Because they are cunning and they brought in the mullahs. We have a proverb—if you look under a mullah's beard, you will find the words 'Made in Britain.'"

"Oh . . . ," I said, with a weak smile.

I was offered a second helping and a third, followed by a sticky pastry and a glass of tea in a filigree holder made out of silver. Everything was piping hot and served with the utmost courtesy—this, after all, was Persia, the land famous for its codes of politeness (it's only "Iran" when you get into politics and the really bad stuff). But it wasn't especially hard to feel the chill coming from the other end of the table. Especially when the Professor—glaring at me like a living glacier—decided to lecture me on how the British had ruined his country:

"And what did he want, I ask you! What did he want? Freedom and equality!"

He was talking about Mohammed Mossadegh, a great figure in Iranian history—especially to liberal intellectuals like the Professor— and its prime minister in the 1950s. Despite his habit of attending to state business in his pajamas and bursting into tears whenever he made a particularly impassioned speech, Mossadegh managed to pass a Free Press Law and to nationalize the Anglo-Iranian Oil Company—thereby confirming himself as a hero to Iranian nationalists. The last of these achievements put the wind up Winston Churchill, who was so enraged that he told the Americans Mossadegh was about to become a Communist. President Eisenhower, never one to overlook a rumor of the reds, took the bait. The CIA was dispatched: Bribing the thugs in the Tehran bazaar when they realized fair play wouldn't work, they stoked a coup and forced Mossadegh out.

"The British preferred the shah, of course," continued the Professor, "because he was in their pocket! And when he wouldn't play their game anymore, what did they do? They pushed him out so they could bring in the onion-heads! You don't believe me, child? Then do you never wonder why the ayatollahs are always traveling to London for their medical operations?"

It was clear, from the furrows over his brow and the continuously icy glare, that I would need to find a way of ingratiating myself. Scanning the room for something to work with, I latched onto my chance and bided my time. When supper was over, I sidled up to the Professor. My plan was ready and if it didn't work, then I doubted anything would. In stumbling Persian and my politest voice, I declared:

"Your books . . . for me . . . are a fascination."

It mightn't have been the best expressed Persian sentence of all time—but it certainly worked! In a moment, we were standing next to the walnut bookcase, the Professor drawing out thick, vinegary-smelling tomes, tooled and gilded on the spines, and piling them into my arms as if I were a walking book cart:

"Now, this is Farabi—wonderful man, he went around in disguise so he could interview the princes at their courts, and if you look at the instruments in his *Great Book of Music*, many of them are still played a thousand years later. . . . Ah! I am sure you have read *this* one. . . . No? But it is *My Uncle Napoleon*, it is one of our most famous comedies, and *Savushun* by Simin Daneshvar. It has been reprinted sixteen times. . . . No? And . . . "

"Oh, well, I *have* read some of *that* one," I said.

Trying to show that I wasn't a complete donkey-brain, I pointed to an enormous green-jacketed hardback on the top shelf.

"The *Shahnameh* of Hakim Abu'l Qasim Ferdowsi," I read, to prove my point.

"You know it?"

The Professor's owl-like eyes were sparkling; all the ice in his expression had melted.

"I read some of the stories in England," I said. "I like them."

"Ah, but did you read them in Persian? You must read them in Persian. Look around us. Look, child!"

The sweep of his arm was taking in the whole of the room—from the bookcase to the TV set to the sofa on which Sina was lying, stretched out like a length of rope, to the Professor's favorite armchair—a walnut-armed Louis XVI, with several of the brass tacks missing from the splat.

"Because of this book," he said, tapping its cover, "because of this book we are Persian. Without it—poof!" He lifted a hand, driving it through the air to illustrate a sudden disappearance.

"Now tell me, child," he said, tugging my arm toward the sofa, "how long do you intend to stay in Tehran?"

I told him my course would keep me here for about six months.

"Then," he declared, "you will stay with us. As long as you are in Tehran, you are our guest."

I looked toward the bookcase and said a silent thank-you. Those piles of leather-bound, crinkly edged, yellowing paper—and above all the green-jacketed one on the top shelf—had nudged me toward the best accommodation upgrade of my life.

2

The Most Persian Persian
Tehran. February/March.

Over the course of that winter and spring, I saw how the Professor's family negotiated the contrast between the different worlds of inside and out, and became used to negotiating it myself. I would address taxi drivers as "sir," never shake hands with a woman outside, and keep mum about the latest joke on the Supreme Leader's opium habit . . . until I was indoors. I learned how to dart like a bullet through the traffic and, when I needed a lift, how to haggle with a driver whose car was still moving; how to walk home at night without falling into the *joob* canals, and how to do so when I was too drunk to risk calling a taxi.

The contrast between public and private was most visible in Tahmineh. Inside, she rarely concealed her arms or midriff, but if she stepped outside the mosquito-net door, she always wrapped herself in a knee-length trench coat (the standard uniform for young women—although Tahmineh's was the right size for a twelve-year-old) and covered her hair with a brightly patterned headscarf, her fringe carefully sprayed to curl out underneath.

"Eh baba!" she laughed when the Professor suggested one day that her choice of headscarf might attract trouble from the authorities (it was the size of a handkerchief). "If God wanted women to hide our hair, why did he make it longer than men's?"

Sina and the Professor also changed their clothes when they were inside, taking off their trousers and schlepping about in loose cotton pajamas, although Sina, who was pretty casual about such things, could just as easily be seen in his black-market Calvin Kleins.

"But Nicholas," he would object, when I persisted in wearing my khakis, "those trousers are for outside. You cannot be comfortable!"

This contrast between inside and out was reflected in the Professor's own professional experience, which had been turned on its head by the revolution. As the weeks went by, we got into a habit of talking together over a postsupper glass of arak* or vodka (or, when money was tight, the Professor would produce a bottle of industrial ethanol—the only alcohol sold openly in Iranian mini-marts—and mix it with lemon juice. "It has an excellent taste!" he would announce, somewhat unconvincingly, on those occasions). It was one such evening that he told me how his career had been shaped by political events.

"Before the revolution, you know what I was doing?" he said. "I was a rising star of our civil service! Ha! But when those onion-heads came to power, I said to myself, 'Can you work under this system? Of course not!' So I decided to study the history of my country and save our culture before it eats the dust."

Even when he emerged in public, he was pushed back under the surface: intermittent teaching jobs at Tehran's universities were canceled when the authorities got hold of poems he had published and came knocking at his door.

"I had the honor of spending forty days in jail," he explained, to the tinkle of the ice in his vodka glass. "They put a blindfold on me and made me sit in a cell with a dozen other gentlemen. My wife was expecting Tahmineh at this time, so I worried I would be too late. I worried a lot, I am not ashamed to tell you this, and do you know

---

* A colorless, distilled alcoholic drink. Although arak is usually made with anise, the Iranian version has to be different, of course, so it's made with raisins. It's one of the cheapest drinks available on the black market, and as a result it tastes like something you should put in your car, not your mouth.

how I comforted myself? I turned to stories. Stories I remembered from my childhood, stories that have been with me all my life. For example, you know the story of Bizhan? It is in *Shahnameh*; he is thrown in chains in a deep pit because of his love for the daughter of the king. Well, I thought of this story—I thought of others too, many stories, and they gave me comfort at this time. Then, after forty days, they let me out and that same week, what do you think happened? My daughter was born!"

Tahmineh was in her room, listening to her music. If she had seen her father's smile as he uttered this last sentence, she could never have doubted his love for her. To him, this coincidence was proof that, however nasty the mullahs' regime, there was enough goodness in the world with which to fight them. It enabled him to look back on his prison experience not as some scarring ordeal but as a proud moment that set him alongside his heroes in a brotherhood of victims.

"If you never went to prison," he said another evening, "you are nothing."

We were in the living room this time, sitting on the sofa, while Sina channel-hopped between MTV and the soccer.

"But I was not only in prison under the mullahs," the Professor continued. "The shah was also an enemy of the bright-thinkers. The things he would do to people who disagreed with him! You know, the Savak* arrested many of my friends. Of course, these mullahs are monkeys, but they are not the first."

To the Professor, tyranny was a constant in the country's history. When his friends—scholars, magazine editors, a novelist—came over for poetry discussions and cake, they would back him up. There were stories of cruel censorship, forcing a book through a dozen variations to toe an ever-shifting government line; of cells full of cockroaches and urine; of someone's niece, who had disappeared and was believed to be holed up in the dreaded Evin prison; of beatings at demonstrations either side of the revolution; and of an elderly poet who had been shot by a firing squad under the shah.

---

* The shah's secret police.

But there was a crucial difference between the tyrants. When Aya-tollah Khomeini, flying back at the end of the revolution in 1979, was asked what he felt to be returning to his homeland after a fourteen-year exile, he gave a stony-faced reply: "nothing." In contrast, the shah, leaving the country only a week and a half earlier, stooped to pick a handful of Iranian soil before boarding his plane.

"Even if the shah was bad," said the Professor, "at least he *believed* he loved Iran. But these onion-heads, they want the Middle East to be one great Muslim empire, like it was in the time of the caliphs. To them, Iran means nothing, just like Khomeini said."

The Professor and his family represented a particular kind of Iranian—against the government, but certainly not hoping the shah would come back; proud of Iranian history and lukewarm to the religion they out-wardly professed.

"Most Iranians are spiritual," he once told me, "but does this oblige us to attend the mosque every Friday and perform the fast in Ra-madan? Of course not! These things are external rituals, they are not what matters."

The Professor rarely talked about religion, but he frequently talked about being Persian. If I wanted to get in his good books, all I had to do was repeat the phrase "Farsi shirin e"—*Persian is sweet.*＊

＊ The terms "Persian" and "Iranian," often used interchangeably, can be tricky to de-fine. "Persian" was coined by the Macedonians in the fourth century BCE, from "Fars" or "Pars," the name of the province in which the capital stood at this time, which they took to account for the country as a whole. To the natives, however, the land was always "Iran"—from "Aryana Vaejah," "land of the Aryans." As the scholar Richard Frye puts it, "Aryan, with an approximate derived meaning 'noble, lord,' seems to have been the general designation of these people speaking Indo-European tongues or dialects, who migrated into the lands between the Ganges and Euphrates rivers at the end of the 2nd and the beginning of the 1st millennium BCE." The name "Persia," however, stuck in the West until the early twentieth century. It was Reza Shah, father of the last shah, who introduced "Iran" to the outside world.

An imposing 6-foot-3 ex-Cossack trooper, known in the army as Reza Maxim for his expertise with the British machine gun, he seized power in a British-backed coup in 1921 and turned into the ultimate nationalist snob. He banned people from pho-tographing camels (because they might provoke associations with the Arabs), ripped

"The Persian culture," he liked to say, "is the most important culture in this part of the world. Maybe if you are a religious fanatic you will disagree, but otherwise you cannot argue. We have poetry, we have music, we have philosophy! And medicine also—in fact, without the Persians, the history of medicine would be a disaster."

He would dip into his walnut bookcase, introducing me to his favorite writers—most of whom were dead before the bubonic plague: Ibn Sina (known to the West as Avicenna), who produced the *Qanun* or "Code" of Medicine—the seminal medical text not only in the Middle East but in Europe too until the 1800s; the scholar Abu Raihan al-Biruni, who proved that light travels faster than sound and argued that the earth moves around the sun more than five hundred years before Copernicus (as well as, among his other observations, pointing out that flowers always have three, four, five, six, or eight petals but never seven or nine); the bawdy poet Abu Dulaf al-Khazriji, who suggested that beggars should stoke the sympathy of the crowd by inserting porridge up their rectums (so it oozed out as the suppurations of a wound) and whose company included "every person avid for copulation, for vulvas and anuses indifferently." Together, these extraordinary

---

up the power of the mullahs, and when people protested the brimmed hats he wanted them to wear or his banning of the veil, he had them shot. By insisting on his country's name as "Iran," he was trying to evoke the image of an older civilization, part of a campaign in which lines from the national epic, the *Shahnameh*, were quoted at his coronation ceremony, ancient heroes were invoked at military parades, and an academy was set up to purify the Persian language. Ironically, rather than calling to mind an older civilization, in the West "Iran" tends to evoke the country in its postrevolutionary, theocratic phase—the modern-day Iran, while "Persia" is associated with a less threatening, magical land—a place of silk carpets, wine-drinking poets, and fluffy cats. So the meaning of the terms has flipped: Many people who oppose the regime of the mullahs—the Professor among them—now prefer to think of themselves as Persians, to distinguish themselves from the official regime. Evolving from its original sense, the term "Persia" now suggests, for many Iranians, the land they would like it to be, and the land they believe it once was.

Throughout this book, "Persian" will be used in this sense, the sense in which it is used by people like the Professor—to describe the non-Islamic side of the country, its culture and history, and "Persian" will denote anyone who speaks the Persian (or Farsi) language (which includes not only most Iranians, but also many Afghans and the Tajiks of Central Asia) as their mother tongue.

authors expressed the amazing eclecticism of the medieval Persians—specifically, of the late tenth and early eleventh centuries, when this region was fizzing with more far-reaching ideas than the rest of the world put together.*

Figure 1: Persian Egg-Heads of the Late 10th/Early 11th Century

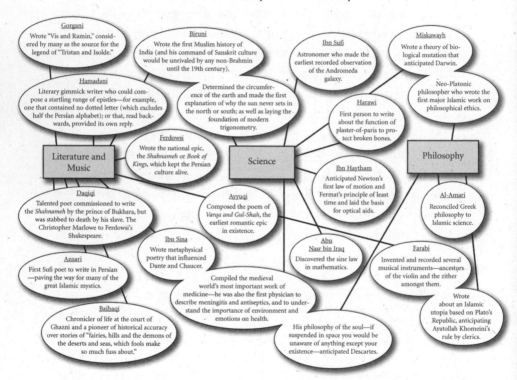

---

* To put the achievement of this era in context, it's worth noting how backward the West was at this time. While Britain was a forest of stinking tribesmen, where street lamps and carpets were a long way off and dysentery was treated with a recital of the *miserere me deus* and a bowl of boiled mugwort, the people of the Persian-speaking world were perfuming themselves with ambergris, lit their way with kerosene, had been weaving carpets since the Bronze Age, and were analyzing tuberculosis, measles, and even cancer in ways that would take Europe several hundred years to match. We tend to look down on the Middle East now, but the achievements of this time show how much we're indebted to the medieval Persians (and Arabs too, whose accomplishments are similarly staggering). Equally, many Iranians today insist on "basking proudly in Rostam's reflected glory," as the twentieth-century writer Jalal al-e Ahmed

Many of the Professor's books were poetry collections, spanning the gamut of Persian literature, from a blind medieval minstrel called Rudaki to Forough Forrukhzad, a heroine to thousands of Iranian women who was killed in a car accident in her early thirties. The Professor would quote from these poets at the dinner table, pointing out the particular genius of the Persian language for rhyme ("Bush mush!" he would say to prove this point. "(President) Bush is a mouse!"; "Anar e bustan, anar e pestan!"—"Pomegranate of the fruit garden, pomegranate of the breasts!")—and this wasn't because he was an intellectual, it was because he was Persian. As the film director Abbas Kiarostami puts it, "Poetry in Iran pours down on us, like falling rain, and everyone takes part in it." Even Ayatollah Khomeini had been known to pen the odd couplet, composing mystical verses influenced by the medieval Sufi poets. Among his lines—somewhat surprising given the system he imposed on the country—is the following: "Open the door of the tavern before me night and day, / For I have become weary of the mosque and seminary."*

Coming from a society in which poetry is often perceived as elitist and out-of-date, it was hard for me to recognize its importance to Iranians. But each time I heard a taxi driver, stuck in congestion, soothing his frustration with a quote from the mystical medieval poet Hafez, or the Professor's wife, reciting from Forrukhzad while she was hanging up the laundry, another piece of my skepticism would be nibbled away. What had appealed to me at first about Iran was all the parties— the drink, drugs, and flirting—because they reminded me of home. It's a way of saying, "Look, they're just the same as us!" But the longer I stayed in the country, the more I was drawn to what made them . . . themselves. And foremost was their love for poetry. Over the coming months, I would hear verses recited in grocer shops, at the sauna, in a

---

put it (referring to a character from Ferdowsi's *Shahnameh* to symbolize the tendency to dwell on long-ago achievements), overlooking the failure to match these feats in more recent times. Both perspectives could do with more balance.

* Published in a collection called "A Jug of Love: Eight Ghazals of Imam Khomeini." The "forbidden" imagery is a common convention in mystical Persian poetry, emphasizing the importance of internal belief over outward appearances.

university dormitory. And I would realize that Iran isn't ayatollahs and headscarves and nuclear centrifuges. It's a butcher reciting verses from the national epic in his village shop, as everyone crowds around to listen, not caring at all if they will have to wait for their meat.

The Professor wasn't alone in emphasizing the "national" over the "religious" culture. Several musicians, like the popular DJ Div or the band Kahtmayan, used pre-Islamic stories and characters in their songs. It was a way of marking themselves as rebels, against the status quo, but it was also a way of exploring their national identity—an issue, as I was to learn, that was very important to many young Iranians.

It was at the New Year (celebrated—with more logic than the Roman calendar—on the spring equinox) that this identity came to the fore. According to the tenth-century scholar Biruni, "It has been the custom of this day to sow around a plate seven kinds of grain on seven columns, and from their growth they draw conclusions regarding the corn of that year, whether it would be good or bad." The custom is retained, even in the cities: For several weeks leading up to the festival, Khanom was tending a tray of wheat sprouts, which she kept on top of the fridge, and in accordance with tradition, a table was set up in the living room, under the print of Darius the Great. In keeping with the theme of "seven," it contained seven items beginning with the Persian letter "sin" or s: an apple (*sib*), a sweet pudding called samanu, a clove of garlic (*sir*), a vinegar bottle (*serkeh*), a jujube fruit (*senjed*), a handful of sumac berries, and the tray of sprouts (*sabzi*).

The festival, known as *Nowruz* or "New Day," was celebrated long before even Biruni was around, which is reflected in one of its most significant rituals: On the Wednesday before *Nowruz*, known as "Red Wednesday," people set off firecrackers and leap over flames. I was itching to see this ritual, so Sina took me to a school playground, where a set of seven small fires had been stoked. Smoke was puffing at Spider-Man sneakers and singeing the odd sock as a gang of small boys chanted the traditional phrase "My red for your yellow and your yellow for my red." The yellow is the chanter's weariness, while the red signifies the power of the flames, which he hopes will refuel him for the coming year (although none of the boys, prancing over the flames and setting off Russian petards to scare the girls, looked like they were in need of an energy boost).

"We have been doing this since before the Arabs attacked,"* said the father of one of the boys, passing around a plate of pistachio-flavored nougat, "since the time when we were Zoroastrian. We had a great love of fire because it can purify things, so on this day we brought out anything rotten from our houses and put it on the fire."

"What do the mullahs think of it?" I asked.

"Oh, who cares? Sometimes they try to stop it. One of the ayatollahs made an announcement, he said it is un-Islamic.** But why should we listen to them? This is the problem in our country, we act like sheep and let ourselves be pushed around by people who aren't true Iranians."

I was intrigued by the way he identified so closely with Zoroastrianism—a religion founded more than a millennium before Islam. Growing out of native folk beliefs, Zoroastrianism developed from the older veneration of nature its customs of worshipping in front of a fire and leaving the dead on mountaintop towers to be eaten by vultures. Equally striking was his dismissal of the ayatollahs as un-Iranian. Like many Iranians who were fond of the native culture, he despised the ayatollahs' emphasis on Islamic traditions. It was an attack, as far as he was concerned, on the country's identity—an individuality drawn principally from its pre-Islamic heritage.

"I do not consider this a good thing," said the Professor, when I talked to him about the Red Wednesday ceremony.

I was surprised: I had thought he was keen on the pre-Islamic motifs—after all, this was the subject of his research.

"They are doing it for negative reasons," he said, "to announce to the world they are not standing beside the mullahs. They jump over the fires but if you ask them about Zoroastrianism they will be unable

---

* He was referring to the Arab invasion of the seventh century CE, which brought Islam to Iran and destroyed the Persian empire.

** This was Ayatollah Safi Golpaigani, who insisted in a speech that "superstitious customs such as Red Wednesday do not befit the dignity of the Muslim people of Iran."

to answer you. And if they are interested in Red Wednesday, then please tell me, where are the other old traditions, like the boys spoon-hitting or *Hajji* Firuz?* What these young people are looking for is an opportunity to gather in large numbers—so the boys and girls can exchange their telephone numbers."

The Pahlavi shahs exploited the pre-Islamic motifs to strengthen their power; the same traditions were being harnessed now by the powerless youth, hungry for the opportunities the mullahs' regime was denying them.

I think the Professor was only partially right. I talked to a lot of young Iranians about the pre-Islamic motifs, and most of them expressed little interest in, or knowledge of, the historical background. But a surprising number of them did. For every three youngsters who treated Red Wednesday as a dating game, there was always one who wanted to tell me about the story behind it. Typical of these was Mehrdad, a twenty-year-old music student, who unbuttoned his shirt to show a metal figure resting on his chest.

"This is the *faravahar*," he said.

It was a bearded man with wings and a disk around his waist, hanging from a silver chain around Mehrdad's neck.

"It is the Zoroastrian symbol," he said. "I am Muslim, that is my upbringing, but I am Iranian and this is more important for me. Iranians are Zoroastrians—we have only been Muslim for a few hundred years, but Zoroastrianism is natural to us. It is connected to being Iranian because it has a love for the sun and the mountains and trees, and these are all important things in our culture."

In Britain you might hear of the odd pagan cult or a ritual in a Wiltshire field, but it's hardly mainstream. Nor are views like Mehrdad's in Iran—because if he were to express them in public he could be accused of apostasy, which is punishable by death. But he was far

---

* Traditionally, "spoon-hitters" would be young boys who dressed up in cloaks and visited people's houses during *Char-shanbe Suri*, to be given sweets and nuts, like trick-or-treaters in the West. *Hajji* Firuz was a man dressed in red satin and a blacked-up face, who would dance in the streets with a tambourine and a trumpet. He is spoken of as an "Iranian Santa Claus."

from alone in wanting to celebrate the pre-Islamic culture—it couldn't be kept down, not even when it came to the biggest of all the country's Islamic ceremonies . . .

"Look!" said Sina one cold night at the end of February. "You want to go and see?"

Leaning over the balcony railing, it was hard to work out what was going on. The black metal gate was acting as a screen—all I could make out behind it were the tops of brightly colored feathers and the curved iron tongues of a processional standard. It was the sounds that were drawing us out—the thunder of a bass drum, growing louder with every beat, and the chanting of the men.

"You see!"

Sina was grinning as the gate closed behind us, his head already buzzing with pickup lines.

"This is what happens on *ashoura*," he explained, nodding at a row of girls wrapped in black cotton on the other side of the road. "The girls from the strict families are given permission to go outside because it's a holy day, and they are hoping they will find a boyfriend."

He dug a hand into his pocket, drawing out a piece of paper with his phone number, and cast his beam on the girls—he'd been expecting this. Even if it was a religious festival, it was still a large gathering, and in Iran, all large gatherings involve the number exchange. That night, Sina swapped details with three girls (a modest tally by his standards, although it made up for the loss of two of his girlfriends in the last fortnight). But, having accompanied him on every conceivable variation of the Tehran pickup tour, I found my attention was drifting from the girls; this time it was the men who engrossed me.

They were all wearing black trousers and shirts. They formed rows behind the standard, some of them carrying metal chains, which they gripped on short wooden handles and struck hard against their backs.

"Oh Imam Hossain!" they cried, to the rhythm of the drum, "oh Imam Hossain!"

There is no figure in Shia Islam as popular as Imam Hossain. He was as ubiquitous in Tehran as Ayatollah Khomeini: strung up on the roadsides and outside government buildings, painted onto the sides of apartment blocks, and raised over the marquees where the mourning songs were sold. He was usually depicted face-on, blood pouring from his forehead: a reference to his death on *ashoura*, the tenth day of the Islamic month of Mohurram, in 680 CE. It was the defining moment in the schism between the Shia and the Sunnis,* when Imam Hossain, a grandson of the Prophet Mohammed, was besieged along with his entourage on the plains of Kerbala and struck down by the forces of the caliph Yazid. They were "treated in such a way as never in the whole world the worst criminals have been treated," narrated the scholar Biruni. "They were killed by hunger and thirst, through the sword. They were burned and their heads roasted, and horses were made to trample over their bodies." The caliph, on the other hand, "celebrated a feast, and gave banquets and parties, eating sweetmeats and various kinds of confiseries."

The standard (known as an *alam*) is based on those carried on the battlefield, traditionally signifying the presence of the ruler. A verse from the Quran wove an openwork inscription around it, while fantastical metal beasts hung down around the lustrously bearded image of Imam Hossain.

A stocky man was buckled to it, lifting it like Atlas as he towed the procession forward. We followed them down a series of backstreets, between smog-blackened, plaster-dripping walls, across the City Park and under a motorway tunnel where the traffic, amazingly, stopped to let them pass. Black bunting fluttered over our heads in the bazaar district as we converged among other groups, one of which was followed by a pickup truck full of sheep. A couple of the sheep were being dragged off the truck and onto the street, where they were held down by burly men with rolled-up sleeves. The light from a lamppost struck the edge of a knife, sparkling on the drops of blood growing

---

* A schism that began in the immediate aftermath of the death of the Prophet Mohammed and revolved around who was his true successor—his son-in-law Ali or his companion Abu Bakr. It was the latter who was chosen, but Ali's followers resented this, and when Ali was murdered, after becoming the caliph himself, his cause fell to his sons, Hasan and Hossain.

on the pavement, which spread around us and trickled down between the cracks in the paving stones.

A man on a motorbike had parked near one of the sheep corpses. He knelt down, dunking his fingers in the blood, then dabbed it on his rearview mirrors.

"You know why he is doing that?" asked Sina. "He thinks it will give him good fortune."

And it wasn't just bikers. Others did the same to the bumpers of their cars, dipping their fingers like Christians at a font and anointing their vehicles with mumbled words of prayer.

"We are doing this for Imam Hossain," said one of the men, gripping his chain in his hands. "He was a good man, the best of men."

But the "chain-hitter" next to him was more ambiguous about whom they were honoring.

"It is not only Imam Hossain," he said, "it is also Siyavash. Before we became Muslims we did this for Siyavash. Now we do it for Imam Hossain, but in my heart I am thinking also of Siyavash."

"Siyavash?" I asked.

I was puzzled. I'd read about Siyavash many times—he was perhaps my favorite character from all the Persian myths I'd absorbed over the past few weeks; but I was sure he was not a figure who would fit easily into an Islamic festival, so I wasn't surprised when the first man told me to ignore him.

"Siyavash is a myth," he snapped. "Imam Hossain is real; that is much better."

It was too late—he couldn't rub out what the other man had said: "Siyavash." It was like a magic word, fracturing the surface of *ashoura* like the cracks through which the sheep's blood had been trickling, pulling out the ghosts of Iran's pre-Islamic past to stand alongside the great figures of Shiism.

"Siyavash," I kept saying, repeating the talismanic word. "Siyavash. Siyavash! He said Siyavash . . ."

But Sina was looking serious for once, squeezing my shoulder to shut me up.

"Don't say it so loud," he whispered. "Some people don't like it."

"But he said . . ."

Siyavash was a pre-Islamic prince, a mythical character who has no place in the Quran. If he lived, it was nearly three millennia ago, probably in Central Asia. To toss his name into a Muslim festival is like turning up at a Christmas vigil and talking about Thor. But the same connection was made again, just a few days after *ashoura*, when I met the acclaimed theater director Pari Sabery.

She was an imposing figure—her eyes shining under the wisps of gray hair that peeked under her black headscarf. In the café underneath the City Theatre, she sat down in front of a poster for a play she'd directed about Siyavash's story only a few months earlier.

"Imam Hossain is like Siyavash," she explained. "Their blood purifies us."

THE TALE OF SIYAVASH

Blessed with the sort of looks to make a woman melt like ice near a fire, Siyavash is the most sought-after of princes. Somewhat too sought-after, in fact. His stepmother invites him into the royal harem and offers him a lot more than a glass of rose water. He flees from her embraces, but she cries rape, tearing her garments and slashing her cheeks with her fingernails, and with the help of a witch she blames Siyavash for causing her to miscarry. There is only one way the prince can prove his innocence: He must ride his horse through a tunnel of flames.*

"When Siyavash rides his horse through the fire," said Pari Sabery, "it cannot touch him, because he is an innocent and pure human being. He is perfect."

This innocence is Siyavash's trademark, singling him out and exposing him to the manipulation of others. Sent out to lead the Iranian army

---

* Some people trace the fire-jumping tradition of Red Wednesday to this story (although there are a number of other theories on the source of that custom). Whether or not it's a direct descendant of Siyavash's challenge, it certainly shares the same ancient Iranian belief in the redeeming power of flames. Before he spurs his charger, Siyavash is convinced the fire won't harm him, because it reflects the will of the Almighty.

against its rival, the Kingdom of Turan, he manages to secure a truce. But his father, wary of Afrasiyab, the wily Turanian king, demands that he break his word and fight. This is something Siyavash cannot countenance. Instead, fed up with all the machinations, he decides to live on his own, building himself a city on the Turanian border. He lives there in peace, at least until Afrasiyab's jealous brother accuses him of plotting to take over the kingdom. Afrasiyab rides out to attack, but Siyavash knows what's coming—like Imam Hossain after him, he can see his own future. He burns his treasury, sends his horse away, and sets out to meet his fate. Grabbed by the hair, he is thrown to the ground, a bowl placed under his chin and his throat cut "as if it were a sheep's."

The story of Siyavash is told by the poet Ferdowsi in the *Shahnameh*— an iconic story still remembered by many Iranians. Long before the *ashoura* festival there were mourning rituals for Siyavash, which are mentioned by the tenth-century historian Narshakhi in his "History of Bukhara" (the Central Asian city in which Siyavash was legendarily said to have lived).* It is more than a coincidence, I think, that Ferdowsi was writing soon after *ashoura* was first publicly commemorated. The earliest records place it in 963 CE, when the poet was in his twenties (before then, the Shia were persecuted and unable to mark their holy days in public, but around this time a Shia dynasty called the Buwayhids wangled their way to control of the Sunni caliph in Baghdad). Shops were closed, women blackened their faces and tore their clothes, while the mourners beat their faces as they marched.

"The Shia people," noted the scholar Biruni, "lament and weep on this day, mourning over the protomartyr in public."

Standing on the pavement with Sina, watching the slashing of the knives on the sheep's throats, their blood and their shiny white intestines glowing in the lamplight, I thought of Ferdowsi's description:

---

* Sir Richard Burton, the great nineteenth-century explorer, was one observer who thought "the wailings for the death of Siyavash" had been "transferred to the pathetic tales of Hasan and Hoseyn," while the prominent Iranian scholar Nodushan Eslami told me that both Siyavash and Imam Hossain recall an earlier tradition, "a mourning for the death of spring—of rain and trees."

Siyavash, the martyr prince, grabbed by the hair and thrown to the ground, his throat cut "as if it were a sheep's." And I thought of the man who said he thinks of Siyavash "in my heart."

It wasn't the only pre-Islamic detail peeking out through *ashoura*'s Islamic surface. The beasts hanging from the processional standards included winged bulls like the creatures carved at the ancient shah's city of Persepolis, in western Iran. Imam Hossain's father, Imam Ali (the Prophet's son-in-law), was presented on several banners with a flame-maned lion behind him, inadvertently suggesting the old royal symbol and the Zoroastrian importance of the sun (rather than the Islamic motif of the moon). And most significant of all was a shrine I visited, up a copper-colored cliff on the outskirts of South Tehran, where women tie rags and offer prayers outside the iron-grilled mouth of a cave.

"This is where Bibi Shahrbanu came when she was escaping from the Arabs," said one of them—a young woman in floral printed voile, whose tears were threatening to put out the candle she was holding.

She was talking about the daughter of Yazdagird III, the last pre-Islamic shah. According to tradition, Imam Hossain took her as his wife after the Persian empire had been crushed; but the night before the siege of Kerbala, knowing she was pregnant with his son, he sent her away.

"When the Arabs came to catch her," said the caretaker, offering me a glass of tea and a boiled sweet in a recess behind the shrine, "Imam Hossain had told her to cry out 'Yahu!' which means 'oh God' in Arabic, and then God would save her. But her Arabic wasn't very good, so she cried out 'Ya kuh!' instead (which means 'oh mountain!') and she was eaten by the rocks."

It's a surreal tale that captures the ambiguity of Iran's Islamic identity. Taken by Islam, the daughter of the shah fails to be absorbed by the Arab culture. She retains her Persian language up to the end and is rescued by the old Zoroastrian symbol—the mountain. This Zoroastrian connection is made even stronger because, before Bibi Shahrbanu was honored here, this spot marked a shrine to Anahita, the Zoroastrian water angel (which is why, according to some theories, Bibi Shahrbanu came here—to pray in a place long venerated by her ancestral faith). It's her offspring who make this shrine so important to Muslim Iranians today: Her son would become the fourth Shia imam; so from her blood—the blood of the ancient Persian shahs—come the remaining imams, reconciling the "alien" faith of Islam to the native Persian tradition of kingship. Through Bibi Shahrbanu, Islam is Persianized and made palatable to the wider Iranian population.

"Is the story of Bibi Shahrbanu important for you?" I asked the caretaker.

He put down his tea and nodded, gripping the fingers of one hand in the fist of the other.

"Of course it is! Through Bibi Shahrbanu, Iran and Islam are one."

Together, these festivals (the Zoroastrian *Nowruz* and the ostensibly Islamic *ashoura*) showed that, bustling behind the screen of the mullahs' particular brand of Islam, there is a thriving native culture. Many Iranians, especially young, middle-class ones like Sina, were fed up with all the religion the authorities had forced down their throats—they wanted a different way of seeing themselves, a way that could distinguish them from their hated overlords. And there was one man, above all others, who stood at the heart of this identity. . . .

"There he is!"

One afternoon in early spring, when the crocuses were starting to come out in the parks and fresh white asphodels were filling up the glass florists' shops on the roadsides, the Professor met me outside the Literature Faculty of Tehran University. Taking off his homburg and holding it in front of him, he stood, in a respectful bow. Above us, sitting cross-legged on a cushion, with the end of his turban draped over his shoulder, was the poet Ferdowsi. If he didn't happen to be made out of bronze, you might imagine he was sitting in a teahouse, ready to recite one of his tales.

"So is he your favorite poet?" I asked.

"Favorite?" The Professor snorted. "Favorite has nothing to do with it. Look at him, he is more even than a poet, he is . . ."

He stopped for a moment, as if he needed to work this one out.

"He is . . . the most Persian Persian who ever lived. Yes, that is it— the most Persian Persian. Do you understand?"

"I think so."

There was a bench nearby. The Professor lowered himself onto it, holding the armrest as he looked at the poet.

"In your culture," he said, "people do not remember poetry, do they?"

"Well, some people do."

"But not everyone. You see, child? In Iran, *everyone* remembers poetry. Everyone can remember lines from Ferdowsi, for example. This is why he is so important! Without him, we would not speak Persian. Without him, we would have no history, no heritage. Without him, we would be like all the other countries the Arabs attacked—we would be extinct! An Iranian, a Persian speaker, would be the same as a dodo or a Phoenician. People would talk about it as if it was something from the past."

As I stood looking at the bronze poet from a thousand years ago, it was as if I were watching him come to life. As if his toes were starting to twitch inside those curly-ended shoes and his lips were quivering over his long twisting beard. Without this extraordinary figure from the past, Iran would have no present. Which made him more important to the country today than any other aspect of its culture. Because Ferdowsi and his *Shahnameh* represent the national cultural DNA.

"He was a farmer from the east of our country," said the Professor, "a province called Khorasan, near the border with Afghanistan.*

---

* He was a *dehkan*, a member of a squire class that traced its ancestry back through the centuries. "The *dehkans*' houses were libraries," according to *Ustad* (or "Master") Homaioun, founder of the Ferdowsi Seat at Kabul University, "and their minds were full of the customs and heritage of ancient Iran." Nizami of Samarkand, the poet's first biographer, wrote in the eleventh century that he "enjoyed an excellent position, so that he was rendered quite independent of his neighbors by the income which he derived from his lands." Among these neighbors were a fellow poet, Asadi of Tus, who specialized in "strife" poems about opposites (such as the moon and the sun, the land and the sea, and, in one controversial work, the Persians and Arabs), and the reciter Abu Dulaf, who accompanied Ferdowsi on his journey to the court of Sultan Mahmud.

He saw that our Persian culture was in decline—ever since the Arabs invaded, they tried to make us speak Arabic and even if they didn't succeed, many Arabic words became stuck in our language, like mud on your shoes when you have fallen in the dirt. So he decided to do something about it. You have to understand who this man was! He loved everything that made us Persian. He loved drinking wine, he loved our literature and our history, he loved the land, the mountains, the rivers, the sun. Oh yes, he was a Muslim—but more than that he was Persian! So for thirty-five years he worked without stopping, purifying the language all the way to its roots and collecting the legends and the history of the days before the Arabs came, the time of the shahs. Then he took his book, the *Shahnameh*, to the richest lord in this part of the world—Sultan Mahmud of Ghazni."

The Professor looked at me, his owl-like eyes expanding, his face lengthening like a shadow at dusk.

"The sultan had offered him a gold dinar for every couplet—well, he had toiled so hard he had lost all his wealth—his farm was no more than a few empty fields. So he traveled all the way to Ghazni, a journey of many days across the most dangerous lands, he presented the *Shahnameh* at Sultan Mahmud's court, and do you know what happened?"

He was still looking at me, his thick dark brows building arches over his eyes, his furrows filling up with bold lines of shade.

"For sixty thousand couplets, for forty years' work, for the greatest poem in our language—did Sultan Mahmud give him what he promised? Ha! He gave him a single sack of silver!"*

At this, the Professor drummed the arm of the bench and, throwing back his head, exploded. It was a laugh, but one consisting less of mirth than a raw, maniacal anger. Several students, coming out of the Literature Faculty, stopped their chatting and turned to look at him, blinking in the sunlight and not daring to approach.

---

* This is generally reckoned at 20,000 dirhams. Because of the lack of silver at the time, it is difficult to confirm exactly what this amount was worth, but it was certainly no more than one thirtieth of what Ferdowsi was originally promised. According to the contemporary historian Baihaqi, an elephant would have cost five times as much.

"Ferdowsi was furious!" he continued. "He went to the bathhouse and he threw away the money. He gave half of it to the bath attendant, and the other half to a sherbet-seller. Then he asked for one more look at his poem, and he wrote something in the back."

A rueful smile crossed the Professor's face, his eyes even brighter now as a defiant chuckle crept out of his mouth.

"Those words he wrote, how they made Sultan Mahmud boil! He told his soldiers, 'Find that poet and trample him under my elephants!' But Ferdowsi could not be found—he was gone."

"What were the words?" I asked.

The Professor nodded slowly, looking up at the statue with an expression of such intensity it was as if he were channeling the spirit of the poet himself. After a deep breath, the words of Ferdowsi's wrath came bursting out, in such a thunderous tone that several of the students walking past stopped to listen:

Agar shah ra shah budi pedar	*If only your father a true king had been*
Besar bar nahadi mara taj e zar	*Then wouldn't your gold on my head have been poured?*
Vagar madar shahbanu bedi	*And as for your mother, if she'd been a queen*
Mara sim va zar ta be zanu bedi.	*Then I would be sunk to my knees in your hoard.**

There was a long silence between us, punctuated by the Professor's deep breaths, as I took in the age-old insult—the king derided

---

* And there are more than a hundred couplets of equally bitter vituperation in the published version of Ferdowsi's satire (although scholarly doubt has been cast on their authenticity). During the course of the satire, Ferdowsi derides Sultan Mahmud for his lack of sense, justice, or honor, but mostly he has a go at his parentage—a subject on which Mahmud was especially sensitive, since his father had been a slave. But he was somewhat more successful than the majority of slaves usually are, taking over his master's realm (which amounted then to little more than a chunk of eastern Afghanistan) and expanding it to incorporate much of eastern Iran. Under Mahmud, it would become the largest empire ever controlled from what is now Afghanistan.

for his low birth. So much of what I'd learned about Persian culture so far (the concern for birth, reflected in the ancestry of the Shia imams; the tradition of poets being crowned with gold) seemed to be evoked in these lines, along with something else I would learn more about in the coming weeks and months—the anger of a poet spurned by the ruling regime. Some of the students were still looking at us, drawn by the power of the Professor's recital, but at last they moved on.

"You see?" said the Professor. His smile had fallen and in its place was a gentler, sadder expression. "He worked hard all his life and what did he ever get from the world? When people say we have troubles, I tell them, bright-thinkers in this country, we *always* had troubles! Look at Ferdowsi!"

Shaking his head, he pressed down on the arm of the bench to pull himself up. Then, holding his hands behind his back, he slowly made his way toward the university gates, whispering to himself as we walked: "the most Persian Persian who ever lived."

3

The Snake-Shouldered Tyrant
Tehran. March.

I was falling in love with all things Persian. With the food—the marinated kebabs, the rice speckled with barberries, the hot stews full of okra or spinach, the boxes packed with crunchy, syrupy, pistachio-sprinkled pastries that guests always presented when they turned up for dinner. With the language—its long, drawn-out vowels suggesting a languorous, philosophical people, while its compound words were earthy and resonant—like "earth-apple" for potato, or "fire-fountain" for volcano. I was falling in love with the music—the traditional orchestras (I loved going along to concert rehearsals with a friend of Sina's who was a flautist, matching the sounds to their instruments—the sigh of a horsehair bow sawing across a *camancheh*; the copper rattle on a giant *duhul*, a drum as big as a truck tire, beaten with a large wooden rod by a woman in a turquoise gown; the hoot on the *neyanban*—the Iranian bagpipes—as a man in a sailor suit blew into an inflated goatskin) or the endless spirals and unworldly melodies of the late Fereydoun Farughi on the Professor's favorite CD.

Most of all, I was falling in love with the wonderful family who, with classic Persian generosity, had welcomed me into their home. Sina would always have some new activity to set out upon—fishing at the Karaj Dam, taking the cable car up Mount Alborz (often with a lemonade bottle filled up with vodka), or setting off for the forests of Mazanderan, where a friend of his had a house in the hills. We would grill the lamb on the slope and warm ourselves up with a log fire, while playing blackjack over glasses of arak. There would be afternoons at the house when the Professor's literary friends turned up, sharing jokes and the verses of poetry that spilled out of their mouths as easily as the crumbs of pastry falling down their lapels; or evenings of frustration trying to beat Tahmineh at backgammon. "I carried!" she would holler each time she won (which was almost always). And every so often the Professor would tell me to put on my best shoes for an evening excursion.

"No more questions, child!" he snapped on one occasion, when I asked where we were heading.

Khanom and Tahmineh were waiting on the balcony in their best headscarves (Tahmineh's was a knockoff of a Hermes), and Tahmineh was teasing her brother for his getup.

"Don't you have a clean shirt?" she asked with a sniff.

"Eh!" he retorted, stiffening his collar between his fingers. He threw back his head, which was the one item of his apparel that was always immaculate—wherever he went, he always wore enough wax on top to make a candle.

Our taxi rattled around a cypress tree on a traffic roundabout and screeched under the webbed green leaves of the plane trees. Perhaps we were off to the Rudaki Music Centre, or was there a poetry recital at Vahdat Hall? But nobody would tell me this afternoon's destination until we arrived.

"I saw this show once before," announced the Professor, leading us through a chain-link gate toward the small, ungainly concrete building ahead of us. "In fact, the composer is an acquaintance of mine. I believe you will enjoy it—*if*," he added, with an arch of his brow, "you English have a heart."

Bursting out of a billboard above us was a flame-haired beefcake. Two horns were spiking out of his helmet, while an ox-headed mace swelled in his hand. I'd spent long enough under the Professor's roof to recognize him—Rostam, the most popular figure in Persian legend, whose feats include plucking the liver out of a ferocious monster called the White *Div*, slaying a dragon, and disguising himself as a merchant to sack an enemy fort. To be a champion worthy of admiration in this region, you need the cunning of Odysseus and the strength of the Incredible Hulk.

We were on the steps of a small theater in the center of town, where the red velvet curtain was about to rise for an operatic performance of Ferdowsi's most popular tale—"The Tragedy of Rostam and Sohrab."

"Don't you know this story?" asked the Professor as we took our seats. "It is the most famous of them all."

I told him about the English poet Matthew Arnold, who composed a loose translation of the tale in the nineteenth century. Coming across Arnold's atmospheric version at university was my first experience of the *Shahnameh*—filling my head with a sumptuous land far closer to the world of Shakespearean drama than the Iran I would see on the news.

"Ha!" said the Professor, with a wry smile. "You English took all those other things from us, why not take our stories too!"

Just like the rest of the world, going to an Iranian opera is as much a social as a cultural experience. While Rostam was strutting about in his double-horned helmet and dancers in brightly colored bodices were sashaying around the court of the far-away kingdom of Samangan, Sina and Tahmineh were introducing me to their friends in the row behind us. To anyone who saw us, the only charitable explanation would have been that we had recently acquired eyes in the backs of our heads and were showing off our new abilities (although the whispering might have hinted at our less than absolute concentration on the show).

"See that guy there," whispered Sina, nodding to a fellow with bushy eyebrows, "he's the best one to know if you want to smoke ganga. Eh! And you see that girl there? . . . No, not *that* one, the one to the left. Don't stare, Nicholas, just look! She's going out with the guy two rows behind, the one who's reading the note she just passed him. But she's also going out with the guy in front of us, the one whose head is so big he's blocking the stage. . . ."

Tahmineh was being especially vocal: A couple of times she even received a tongue-click from Khanom ("I think you spent the whole performance gossiping with your friends," she said later, adding pointedly, "I don't suppose you want to share any of this gossip with the rest of us?"). The only time in the first act that Tahmineh appeared to be paying attention to the stage was when she tugged at my arm.

"That's me!" she whispered.

She was pointing at the crepe-gowned heroine floating to the front, whose name she shared—a princess who falls in love with Rostam and gives birth to his son. As the hero approached her, Princess Tahmineh glided toward him, her long uncovered hair cascading down her back. Wait a moment . . . Uncovered hair? Cascading? But that's impossible, or certainly illegal . . . There could only be one possible explanation for such an illicit act of strumpetry. Oh yes! Like all the other characters, Princess Tahmineh was a puppet.

For all the chatter, it was hard not to be won over by the score: It had an oomph from the off. The woodwinds conjured a playful, romantic atmosphere, complemented by the ripples of the strings, while in the court scenes the horns made a ceremonious grab for the harmony. Warbling up the arpeggio like a ringdove, Princess Tahmineh declared her love to Rostam, who hurled it back in a rumbling baritone, their voices washed by the soft caressing waves of the strings.

Marionettes may not exactly be ideal for a story full of battles, but these were no Thunderbirds: They moved around with an extraordinary agility, bending at the elbow and performing jumps and pirouettes, and when the action required a mass mobilization of troops, the use of shadow play added to the spectacle. Slowly, we were all drawn into the story: By the time Rostam was locked into a fight with his son, we were transfixed.

The duel had come about because Rostam, shortly after impregnating Princess Tahmineh, decided to head back home. His horse had been found, which was his main priority—so what was the point in hanging around? But this being the fertile world of myth, a child had been conceived. His mother named him Sohrab, and when he had grown to manhood, he was determined to meet his stay-away father.

Only one option could bring him close—fighting in the army of Iran's mythical enemy, Turan. Fate—which has a major role in most Persian myths—drove father and son toward a tumultuous reunion, which was set on course when the shah (infuriating Rostam, who was binging on wild horse) ordered his champion to tackle the new enemy threat.

The baritone of Rostam thundered against the tenor of his son, the tension rising to the fall of the pitch. Swooping up the accelerando like a bird up a thermal, the strings conjured an atmosphere of imminent danger. The kettle drums rolled in, the trumpets sounded, the drummers' beats became the crunch of the soldiers' boots and the crescendo of the chorus's chant became the pace of the march, as the armies of Iran and its enemy, Turan, assembled for war. Neither Rostam nor Sohrab knew who the other was, but Sohrab appeared to be the more likely winner, throwing his father to the ground and raising his dagger to cut off his head—until Rostam made a cunning appeal:

> In wrestling you cannot bestrew your foe's blood
> The first time his back is laid out in the mud;
> But throwing him twice, now endowed with the name
> Of one like a lion, you slay without blame.

I looked at the Professor. His back was straight but his lip quivered as his head inched forward. He knew Sohrab would let Rostam go, and Rostam would pray to God to increase his strength; he knew the heroes would fight once more and this time Rostam would throw his son. He knew that Rostam, still unaware he was fighting against his own flesh and blood, would drive his sword through the younger man's chest. Even though he had heard the story many times before, he still turned to Khanom with a shake of his head, as if to say, "Why must it be like this?"

The shadow screen rose and Sohrab's head lifted as he faced his killer.

"My father, on knowing I've died / Will seek to avenge me," he gasped, declaring his father's name: "Rostam."

This is the most famous moment in Persian literature—a moment I would hear throughout my travels in the Persian-speaking world—by an eighteen-year-old boy in the mountains of central Iran, reading the tale in a nasal, mystical voice over a leather-bound edition of the *Shahnameh*; by a man with a drum between his thighs in a traditional athletes' hall; by a swordsmith in Afghanistan, sitting near the oven where he melted his metal. The moment when Rostam, the mightiest of all Iran's legendary champions, realizes what he has done and collapses over the corpse of his slaughtered son.

"Come, child," said the Professor, leading me into the lobby after the show to introduce me to the composer.

He was called Loris Tjeknavarian—an Armenian-Iranian, with a tuft of tousled white hair like a lick of ice cream. As we shook hands, I could feel the crowd pressing around us. I clearly wasn't going to have long with him, so I asked him why he had chosen to score this story in particular.

"This," said Tjeknavarian, "is *the* story. The most famous in Persian literature, the most spoken about, the most popular."

The lobby was heaving now, and Tjeknavarian was quickly lost in a wave of admirers. It was hard to disagree with him. After all, the puppets had received a standing ovation, and there had been a gleam in the audience's eyes as the final aria was being sung. Even Sina was impressed.

"Eh, Nicholas," he whispered on our way to the taxi, "you know what I am thinking? I'll bring my girlfriends to this show. They will love it!"

"Not if you bring them all at the same time!" I said.

"No, no!" He laughed. "You think I'm stupid? But the show is on for a few weeks; I will bring them one after another."

The images of the brightly dressed puppets stayed in my head for weeks. The Professor was right—I *did* enjoy it. And I started to wonder why this story, a story written half a millennium before Shakespeare, could draw such a large, admiring crowd. Did it say something about what it is to be a Persian today?

A few days later, Sina took me up the Alborz mountain. A friend of his was making a "clip," a video for a pop song he would be releasing on the Internet. He had a terrific, melancholy voice, low and gruff, like all the pleasure had been picked out of it with a scalpel. He sat on a wooden fence under a judas tree, its bright white flowers mixing with the cherry blossom scattered on his shoulders, crooning across the mountain while someone filmed him on a digital camera. As we sat waiting for the next take, the guy in charge of the microphone asked me what was the most exciting thing I'd seen so far in Iran. And it wasn't the parties I mentioned, or the drinking sessions up in the hills. It was the puppet opera of "Rostam and Sohrab."

"This is a good answer," he said, nodding his head over the mike. "If you understand Ferdowsi, you understand everything about what it means to be Iranian."

I looked at him in surprise. This was the sort of sentiment I expected to hear from someone like the Professor—but not from a student barely out of his teens, who was usually to be found toking up between takes. Was he right? I'd come here to find out about the present, but I was becoming mesmerized by Ferdowsi and his blood-splattered poem. I wondered if the *Shahnameh* really could shine a light on contemporary Iran; if the best way of getting to grips with this strange, secretive country might be through the unlikely binoculars of a thousand-year-old epic.

The story of "Rostam and Sohrab" gets going when Rostam is welcomed into the house of the King of Samangan, practicing the hospitality code that is still a feature of Iran today (it was exercised, for example, by the Professor in inviting me to stay, and I would experience it on numerous occasions around the country). In the story, Rostam is ordered to fight against Sohrab by the shah but at first he rebels, going so far as to tell the shah he's "fit for a madhouse." Like the Professor, railing against the current regime, Rostam is a typical Persian, unhappy with a cruel and incompetent authority.

On the other hand, he is the older figure, deceiving the idealistic young upstart with a false rule (*In wrestling you cannot bestrew your foe's blood / The first time his back is laid out in the mud* . . .). This rings true with many young Iranians today, unhappy with the "tricks" of the old bearded men whose faces appear on the billboards above them. As the translator Dick Davis puts it, Rostam is a "trickster hero" (on other occasions, he disguises himself as a merchant to sack an enemy fort, uses the help of a mystical talking bird to overcome an apparently invincible opponent, and lies about his name). Iran is hardly the "Splendide Mendax" it was branded by Lord Curzon in the nineteenth century, but a country in which shopkeepers push aside your pay until you've offered it three times, or dinner invitations are issued when everyone knows they will have to be refused—a country, that is, in which insincerity has its own ritualized code,* is one in which a clever hero is likely to be cherished. "Every particle of the world is a mirror," wrote the poet Mahmud Shabustari; "In each atom lies the blazing light." Ferdowsi's story is one such mirror. Its frame might be old-fashioned, but if you look carefully into the glass you can see today's Iran reflected back.

~~

"Come on, Tahmineh-dear!"

I could hear Khanom as I stepped out of Sina's room—she stretched the long vowel of "*jaan*," or "dear," as if it were a lasso to draw her daughter back toward her. But Tahmineh was already approaching me in the corridor: She wasn't going to be swayed.

"You will have to tell us one day," said Khanom. "They only ask because they care about you."

She was holding the kitchen phone against her apron—I guessed she had been talking to one of the many aunts who were always ringing up for family gossip. But Tahmineh wasn't going to be caught out by any cheap tricks: This, after all, was the girl who was invincible at backgammon, even against her father.

---

* This is known as *taarof*, or "offer," and while it is uniquely Persian, it corresponds to politeness codes common in other cultures—for example, the tendency among middle-class English people to say "Oh, I shouldn't" when they're keen for another slice of cake, or the "Have a nice day" ritual of the Deep South.

"Your shirt is missing a button," she said to me—it was a common tactic of hers to point out other people's dishabille when she was backed into a corner, and I was a hapless target. "Mama—Nicholas wants a needle." There was a loud chuckle, the bang of her door, and she had disappeared.

A few minutes later, while I was trying to work the needle through a spare button, I could hear the sound of Googosh, Iran's favorite diva, singing in her rich, fruity soprano. Her most popular songs were recorded before the revolution, when she was the country's number-one style icon. But even though they predated Tahmineh's birth, she played these songs as often as the more recent hits by stars like Binyamin and Arash. Like many young Iranian women, she looked on that earlier era with the rose-tinted nostalgia of never having lived through it, and no one, as far as I could tell, represented it for Tahmineh as much as Googosh.

"I think she's beautiful," she said, when a friend of hers was mocking her for not being more familiar with the new "in" acts. "She always dresses in an interesting way," she explained, "and she was at her best when our country was good."

It was only when I saw her film collection that I realized why Tahmineh looked on the earlier era with such affection. She would watch the films in the evenings, when she came back from her acting classes (or more recently, rehearsals—for a play based on Persian literature's most famous romance, which I was looking forward to seeing in a few weeks' time). Tucking her feet under an armchair in front of the TV, she would dig a spoon into a tub of ice cream. Some of the films starred the B-movie heartthrob Mohammed Fardin, famous for playing hard-drinking, hard-playing heroes in black-and-white boy-gets-girl adventures. He could rip off his shirt and dive off a bridge as easily as he could break into song or flirt with a woman in a tiny dress whose car had just broken down.

"I love Fardin!" Tahmineh exclaimed one night, when the Professor was criticizing the "Fardin cinema" for being crass.

Trashy these films might have been, but when characters in current soap operas had to wear the veil even in kitchen scenes, the films of

Fardin were a glimpse of a more fun-loving, but still Persian-speaking, world.

The films of Googosh were more complicated. The ones I saw were all tearjerkers that were attempting to engage with the social problems of Iran under the shah. In one of them, Googosh played a young woman who discovered she was pregnant and traveled to Tehran with her boyfriend to get an abortion, staying at the house of an opium addict. For Tahmineh, however, far from being a gritty account of prerevolutionary Iran's social problems, the film was about one thing above all, which set it apart from any film made since the revolution: It was all about the hair.

"I wish I could look like that," she announced during one scene, in which an abandoned Googosh, sporting a glorious golden bob, was sprinkling her flat with tears.

Living in a country where films were so strictly censored, Tahmineh had adopted a censorship of her own—so she could pick out from any film she watched precisely the qualities she was looking for.

<hr />

"Nicholas, come!"

The Professor was standing by the walnut bookcase, sliding back the glass door to take out his copy of Ferdowsi's *Shahnameh*.

"I know just the story to start with," he said.

The puppet opera wasn't alone in drawing me toward Ferdowsi. Many other incidents had pushed the epic closer, nudging it up time's narrow corridor.

A friend of Sina's who had been hoping to avoid military service by paying a $10,000 bribe, had only been able to produce the necessary funds when it was too late. "Like the elixir that came after Sohrab's death," sighed his father. He was using a popular proverb, referring to a potion that Rostam is given in Ferdowsi's story, but only after it's too late to save his son's life. When I mentioned this encounter to the Professor, he exclaimed, "Ha! You *see*—you are starting to understand. *Shahnameh* isn't just in that book in the bookcase—it's *everywhere*."

Now, while Khanom was hard at work in the kitchen—fashioning a giant ball out of several pounds of ground lamb—the Professor was setting his copy of the *Shahnameh* on the glass table in the living room. It was the same green-jacketed volume that, many months later, I would show to my companions on the bus to Afghanistan. The so-called Moscow edition, it has a hundred lines to the page, and more than 60,000 verses in total: four times the length of the *Iliad* and the *Odyssey* combined.

The Professor leaned forward eagerly, like the pages were pieces of cake and he was greedy to gobble them up, licking a finger each time he turned them. As I sat down beside him, the smells from the kitchen—the buttery rice, the garlic and parsley, a tingle of turmeric—were seeping into the living room—a teaser of the meal to come, adding their aroma to the atmosphere of the verses.

Strictly speaking, the *Shahnameh* is a chronicle: the story of fifty kings, or shahs, from the prehistoric Gaiomart to Yazdagird III, whose defeat at the hands of the invading Islamic army in the seventh century CE brings the Persian empire to its calamitous end. Although the shahs would be revived many years later, there is no need, in the minds of many Iranians, for their reigns to be chronicled—they are simply repeating the original cycle, right up to their demise at the hands of the "Islamic army" of the ayatollahs.

In many ways—especially in the mythical first half—Ferdowsi's epic takes place in an unfamiliar world. A world that is flat and supported on the horns of a bull, where a dragon is just as likely to swoop over your head as a buzzard and demonic *divs** are always lurking in wayside ruins. It's a brutal world, where troops become so caked in blood "that none knew another until they had bathed"; but it's also a sensuous world, where tulip-cheeked princesses smell of jasmine and ambergris and the sun shines "like the ruby of Badakhshan." For the English-speaking reader, these tales evoke the legends of King

---

* The *divs* are horned creatures, usually depicted with shaggy, spotted coats, who battle against the heroes in many of the ancient Persian legends.

Arthur, the epics of Homer and the magic of *The Lord of the Rings*.
Many of the storylines have a familiar ring to them: the youth Zal,
brought up Mowgli-like in the wild; the hero Rostam, who has to perform a series of labors like Hercules; the prince Siyavash, tempted and
slandered by his wicked stepmother, like Joseph by Potiphar's wife;
the nearly invincible Asfandiyar, whose eyes are his Achilles's heel.
The best stories transcend the national history for a global appeal, so
it's no wonder they have traveled so far and wide—entertaining the
courts of Mughal India (where Emperor Akbar was advised by his
chief minister to read them), painted in miniatures that now hang in
Windsor Castle and the National Library of Russia, filmed in Central
Asia, retold in the novels of the Nobel-winning Turkish author Orhan
Pamuk, and most recently printed in comic books in California. But
in the principal homeland of the *Shahnameh* itself, they have been
out of favor ever since the Islamic Revolution.

When the mullahs came to power in 1979, Ferdowsi's epic was an
inevitable casualty. Under the Pahlavi shahs, it had been recited on
television and at coronation ceremonies; papers were delivered on it
by an acting prime minister; and in 1929 a government edict forbade
the teahouse storytellers from reciting anything else. It was as public
as a poem could be. But in the wake of the revolution, Ferdowsi's
bronze statue was taken off its plinth in Tehran, his tomb was attacked, and the *Shahnameh* was written out of the school curriculum.
There were even reports of copies of the epic being burned in the
streets. Like so many other pleasures in Iranian life, the *Shahnameh*
had gone private.

What turned it into a pariah? Well, the title didn't help. *Book of
Kings* isn't the best choice if you want to get on with the regime that's
just pushed the kings out. Under the Pahlavi shahs, the *Shahnameh* had
been the official state poem, endorsed by a regime that fired on demonstrators in the nation's holiest shrine, tried to ban the headscarf, and
whose secret police once raped a leading mullah's daughter (and forced
the mullah to watch by burning his eyelids with cigarettes). A regime
that used every opportunity to associate itself with the sort of kings
Ferdowsi was writing about—most ostentatiously in 1971, when the

shah celebrated the so-called 2,500th anniversary of the Persian monarchy at the ancient palace complex of Persepolis. Serving foie gras and stuffed peacock to the likes of Nicolae Ceaucescu and the Duke of Edinburgh, pouring the Chateau Lafite into Limoges crystal and decorating the air-conditioned hospitality tents with Italian drapes, the shah was fueling the mullahs' argument: that he was more interested in abroad and had lost touch with real Iranian values.

There is another critical reason for the mullahs' antagonism: The *Shahnameh* doesn't celebrate holy men fighting for God. Ferdowsi's heroes are national—not religious—champions, men who fought for king and country. And even when God is invoked, he isn't the God of Islam. Ferdowsi might have been a Muslim living in Muslim times. But his stories are not.*

They are, above all, the stories of the Zoroastrians—the faith that preceded Islam and grew out of the folk religions of Iran's earliest history. In this sense, the *Shahnameh* offers an alternative account of the country to the Islamo-centric narrative of the mullahs, an account whose greatest strength is that it grew out of the very roots of Iranian civilization. By preserving these Zoroastrian and pre-Zoroastrian stories, Ferdowsi shows that Iran doesn't just mean Islam. He keeps alive many of the traditions that Islam succeeded, and shows that Islamic culture—of which the *Shahnameh* is the supreme poetic

---

* This is underlined by a story told by Ibn Ishaq, the Prophet Mohammed's first biographer. One Nadr bin Harith, a member of the same tribe as the Prophet, had picked up tales "about Rostam the Hero and Isfandiyar and the kings of Persia" (the same tales that would later make their way into the *Shahnameh*) and narrated them at the assembly in Mecca. Nadr used his stories to mock the Prophet, claiming, "By God, Mohammed cannot tell a better story than I and his talk is only of old fables which he has copied as I have." And it was Nadr who appeared to have won their rivalry—the Prophet was forced to flee to Medina, while Nadr gained a high position in Mecca. But the last laugh would be the Prophet's. Condemning the "man who buyeth an idle tale, that in his knowledge he may mislead others from the way of God," he captured him at a pivotal battle, at the wells of Badr in 624 CE, where Nadr was one of only two prisoners to be put to death. Several hundred years before Ferdowsi was even born, the tales of the *Shahnameh* and the Quran were already vying for attention.

achievement—is not as exclusive as fanatics on either side of East-West warmongering would have us believe. Pushed underground by the mullahs, hidden in the subculture with pop music and alcohol, the *Shahnameh* became a symbol of what the mullahs are not. This was underlined to me by the best-selling author and scholar Nodushan Eslami, over tea and slices of melon one afternoon in his elegant North Tehran apartment.

"The government," he said, "has been against the *Shahnameh* because they are more interested in Islam than Iran. But for the young generation today, Ferdowsi is more alive now than ever before. They are very curious about Ferdowsi and they consider the *Shahnameh* as a symbol of Iranian nationality and independence."

Ferdowsi's epic was spread too thickly across Iran's cultural landscape to remain underground—and as impatience with the current regime was growing, it was breaking out.

"You understand?" asked the Professor, leaning over the living room table as I gripped my forehead between my fingers.

The thousand-year-old diction wasn't exactly a pushover, so I was dependent on his modern translation.

"One day it will strike you as fast as if it was in your own language," he said, with a gentle smile.

I was grateful for his optimism, although I knew my Persian would never reach that level. But there was something intriguing about the attempt. Over the coming weeks, I would take part in many similar sessions with the Professor. I enjoyed them as much for the bond they gave me with this remarkable man—in the absence of Ferdowsi, the most Persian Persian I ever met—as for any insight they offered into the linguistic nuances of the poet's verse.

Today we were looking at the first of the great tales in the *Shahnameh*—the story of a villain called Zahhak (who, like many baddies in Iranian culture, is an Arab). Once the prince of a Bedouin tribe, he has sold his soul to the devil and now has a couple of snakes writhing out of his shoulders. At first alarmed, he slowly grows accustomed to this dramatic change in his body. The snakes have an exacting diet: Every day, without fail, they must feed on the brains of two young men. Whatever vitamins this sustenance provides, it's just what you want if you're a megalomaniac—strengthened by his surreal appendages, Zahhak marches out from the Arabian desert, taking over the Kingdom of Iran and splitting the shah in two. The people cower before his snake-swollen prowess, and for a thousand years he is their hated ruler, draining their youth to satisfy the appetite of his sinuous shoulder pads.

"You understand this?" said the Professor, hurriedly lighting up another Bahman cigarette, as if he needed to soothe himself from the calamity he was reading. "Maybe Zahhak never lived; it is too long ago to know for sure. But we can feel that it is true because we know what it is like to suffer under tyranny."

He jerked his chin at a newspaper on the table in front of us, which was carrying a photograph of Ayatollah Khamenei, in his heavy black turban and oversized glasses. Towing an ashtray across the table, the Professor set it on the paper, so the Supreme Leader's solemn gaze was slowly obscured by the mound of his ash.

I tried to be skeptical. A monster with snakes in his shoulders? *Puh-leeze.* But the puppet opera had loosened Ferdowsi's epic from its medieval chains; it was lunging forward through time, insisting on its place in the present. I thought of the girl at the party a few weeks ago: "The past times and today," she had said, "they are like a tortoise and its shell." Any lingering doubts were slowly being smothered. And after an encounter with Sina's friend Reza—a ponytailed artist with a fondness for smuggled scotch—I would never doubt the significance of the *Shahnameh* again.

⁓

Reza's place was an anomaly: the kind of hideaway that showed how distinct Iran's public and private worlds could be. It was in the heart of the bazaar district, the most conservative area in town, where machine-produced carpets displayed the profile of the Supreme Leader and fortune-telling parakeets picked out medieval verses to tell your fortune. The street itself was a crumbling alley where the pipes were as caked in lime scale as the rolling shop-fronts in rust. An intercom crackled above a chipped stoop and if you stood there long enough your head would be gunked in plaster. Then up, around the newel post, up the stairs, and through a door with splashes of paint on the jamb like multicolored spit—and finally we were in.

People came to Reza's for a release, to unwind, to listen to music and drink and share jokes, knowing they would never be caught. Persian House would spin on the stereo as a dozen young men swung under a Chinese paper lantern. The smoke from a water pipe would shroud Sina's head while he tamped down the charcoal with a pair of rusty tongs. Ring-pulls would crack on 330ml cans of "London" gin (made in Turkey but labeled "London" because that was the most popular brand, just as whiskey was called "Scottish" even if it wasn't); a Yamaha would twang to someone's riff, or someone else would toot on a flute; and occasionally there would be a peal of female laughter and a headscarf or two hanging on the hook by the door.

"Hey, Nicholas, you know what you're drinking?" asked Reza, approaching me through a curtain of smoke and placing a can of "London" gin in my hand. On my first appearance at his flat, we had joked about the can's alleged provenance and from that moment on, "London" gin became my drink.

"Thanks!" I said.

I took a swig, then grabbed a Maz-Maz crisp and dipped it in a pot of yogurt, before accepting a roll-up from Mustafa. No one was going to say the British don't know how to party!

Drinking behind closed doors wasn't particularly hard to get used to: It took me back to the monastic boarding school where I was incarcerated as a teenager. Once again I was ruled by men of the cloth, wasn't allowed to drink or have any liaisons with women. When I visited Reza's, I was a schoolboy again, hiding out behind the fire escape, where my friends and I used to guzzle our bottles of cheap Cinzano, watching out for the monks or one of the wilier lay-teachers—who looked on such activities with only a little more mercy than the *basijis* of Tehran.*

There was another reason why going to Reza's made me feel like a naughty schoolboy. Because even though the Professor liked a drink himself, he was far from liking Reza.

"That painting boy!" he huffed one afternoon when he had whee-dled out of Sina where we were headed.

"Baba doesn't like Reza's uncle," explained Sina, having assured his father we would be giving "the painting boy" a wide berth. "He thinks Reza has a bad family. Now come on, Mustafa, let's go to Reza's!"

Reza's uncle was a high-profile artist who had been a friend of the Professor's before the revolution. But he'd accepted several commis-sions from the regime to design a set of murals that were displayed in prominent places in the center of town—all red-headbanded *basijis* and long-bearded ayatollahs. As far as the Professor was concerned, he'd sold out. The scorn the Professor poured on Sina's friendship with Reza was something I would encounter on several occasions—and it would have a massive impact on my Iranian experience a few weeks later.

If I felt like a rebel going to Reza's, it was he who really carried it off. Most Iranian men wore their hair short, but Reza's crashed down his neck and splayed across his shoulders. Bearish stubble prickled his chin, which hung low on a pale face where the light of a smile rarely flickered. His work, which was scattered around the flat—half-finished plaster-of-paris busts tottering between the cutting mats and canvas boards leaning against the walls (among which was a sketch for a poster of one of Tahmineh's plays)—shared the same sadness etched on his face.

---

* I only met the *basijis* once. I was sitting with Sina on the roof of Mustafa's Peu-geot, slurping up bowls of wheat groat porridge from a street stall, when we were approached by a couple of *basijis*—the brown-shirts of the ayatollahs' Iran, who are often spotted tearing down the highway on their motorbikes. They ticked off Mustafa's girlfriend because her headscarf was red and told us we should all be at the mosque. "Why are you so polite to them?" I asked. Sina and Mustafa shook their heads as if I was crazy. "You don't know?" said Mustafa. "They carry knives and chains, and if you don't show them respect, you get cut."

It was on this occasion that I took a good look at them. A couple of drinks had left everyone else on the floor (as usual they drank with one clear purpose—to knock themselves out as quickly as possible—and achieved the feat in half an hour.) But Reza and I were more accustomed to alcohol—he as an artist and me as a Brit, so we climbed up a wooden stairwell for a look at what he called his studio, where he kept all his finished paintings.

"If your heart really wants to see," he said, his loosened hair swinging across his shoulders and the treads creaking under his feet, "then I will show you."

At the top of the stairs, a naked bulb cast a dim glow around a small, shabby room, where the first noticeable feature was a frayed carpet lying under a clay prayer tablet.

"Is this where you come to pray?" I asked, half in jest.

"Actually, yes."

Reza's expression was serious, even though his breath reeked of gin.

The paintings were set against the walls, sometimes two or three together, many of them united by a shared motif: a bird. Small and sparrowlike, they appeared in a series of wintry scenes painted in thick, dark oils on canvas boards, looking out of a window set among spindly trees or sitting on a branch beside a mosque.

"The bird represents *me*," said Reza. His soft maroon eyes were fixed to the bird as he added, in his most disenchanted voice, "because I am divided from society."

Somehow—maybe it was the length and pallor of his face, which gave a certain conviction to what he was saying—he was able to carry off this introspective angst. I think it was partly because of the political dimension, which he explained as we sat down on the floor, nursing our cans.

"You heard about the 18th of Tir?" he asked.

He was talking about a square in the city center, where thousands had raised banners over a week and a half in the summer of 2003.

"They sent in the *basijis*," he explained, "because they're tough and everyone's scared of them. They had clubs and knives and they cut some of the women on their hands and faces, and they took some of us—hundreds of us. I was in prison for ten days, in solitary confinement. They came into my cell every day at least two times, and they beat me."

"Will you demonstrate again?" I asked.

His eyes fell to the wood-paneled floor, his face dappled by the light from the bulb.

"I always demonstrate," he said, "through my art. If you go to a demonstration, it's dropped the next day and nothing comes of it. But art . . . it can last."

He slid back down the stairs in search of more booze, leaving me alone with the paintings. I'd had enough of all the birds, but as I sifted through the boards there was one picture that struck me—and not just because it was avian-free.

Two black forklike stakes rose up beside an ethereal figure—a mass of copper-colored metallic coils that spiraled around each other and framed a domed shape curving inward like a snake's head. The impression was alien and hostile, the circular motion suggesting powerful sophistication and the spikes on the end of the stakes conveying an atmosphere of danger. But there was something familiar in the form—the towers on either side of a dome.

"You know what this is?" asked Reza.

He was standing behind me as I stared at the painting, two fresh cans in his hands.

"I can't say it publicly, of course," he added, "so I have to say it in symbols. The towers are the minarets and between them is a dome. It's a mosque."

Here was something genuinely, dangerously rebellious. It wasn't just the hostile atmosphere of the painting; it was the name Reza had given it—a name that, had he presented it in public, would have gotten him arrested.

"I call this picture *Zahhak*," he said.

As soon as he uttered the name, I could feel the breath sweeping up my throat. Zahhak—the evil prince with the snakes in his shoulders: the tyrannical ruler from the story I had read with the Professor.

It was only now, as I looked at Reza's painting, that I realized how alive Ferdowsi's thousand-year-old epic actually is. Because this was the first time I saw a story from the *Shahnameh* brought to life for today—to explain the way people were living *right now*. Its significance to the present wasn't simply a matter of interpretation—it was the whole point of the painting.

By calling it *Zahhak*, Reza was sending out a clear message. To many Iranians, the mullahs, like Zahhak, are draining the Iranian youth (most directly in the eight-year war with Iraq in the 1980s, when Ayatollah Khomeini encouraged as many young people as possible to be "martyrs" and exhorted women to bear more children for the battlefield) and many consider the mullahs to be "Arabs"— as Zahhak is—because they are more interested in Islamic culture than in the indigenous Iranian traditions.*

Reza wasn't using Ferdowsi's tale to make himself look clever, or as a gimmicky nod to the past; he was using it because it illustrated just how badly the Iranian youth have been let down by their leaders. Because Ferdowsi's tale, a thousand years after it was written and many more thousand since it was set, has a powerful contemporary resonance.

As hatred of Zahhak spreads across the land of mythical Iran, an underground resistance movement is formed, led by two unlikely heroes. The first is a blacksmith called Kawa, who strips off his leather

---

* An example of this attitude was expressed when I was in a taxi one afternoon with Sina. Noticing the enormous mural of Ayatollah Khomeini on a nearby apartment block, I said jokingly to Sina, "your blessed leader," knowing what his response would be. "Blessed?" The driver's eyes looked demonic in the rearview mirror. "He was no Iranian, he was Arab. All these mullahs are Arabs! They came here with fire and sword hundreds of years ago and since then they haven't left us alone." He was referring to the Arab invasion of Iran in 637 CE, when the Persian empire was destroyed—an event that many Iranians are still unable to forgive. Among the booty won by the Arabs on that occasion was a flag known as the *drafsh-i Kavyan*, the legendary leather apron raised by a blacksmith called Kawa to rouse the people against Zahhak, which was traditionally carried by five Zoroastrian priests at the head of the Persian army.

apron, sticks it on a spear-point, and raises it as a revolutionary flag. Much as in the 1979 revolution, the bazaaris turn against the king. The second hero is the noble-born Fereydoun, whose father was killed by Zahhak and who is eager for revenge. Marching on Zahhak's palace, supported by Kawa and the rioting bazaaris, he smashes the heads of Zahhak's guards and binds the tyrant with lion-hide straps, to be locked for eternity in a cave under Mount Damavand—the now-dormant volcano that tapers to the north of Tehran.

"Hopefully," said Reza, as we stood looking at his canvas, "we can find a new Fereydoun and drive those fathers-of-bitches away."

I thought he meant getting rid of the mullahs altogether. In fact, I would later discover that he had a more complicated relationship with the theocracy; but that evening, as he poured the gin and we clinked, I remember the giddy feeling of having stumbled across something magical—a rope dangling into the past. It was there in Reza's flat, with a can of "London" gin in one hand, that I became conscious of what a mighty figure Ferdowsi is in the Iranian psyche. And it was there, in Reza's flat, that the seeds of my mission to Afghanistan were sown.

4

In the Land of Fire

Iran. April.

"You're drawing a cat?" asked Sina.

I was sitting over the desk in his room, with my pencil on a sketch pad. It was a map of Iran, in fact—but there was something unmistakably feline about the form. Its ears were poking into the Caucasus, while Afghanistan, tellingly, was coming out of its rump. Given the volume of secondhand goods sent across Iran's eastern border every day, that was appropriate.

I was drawing the map to work out the places I wanted to visit—my term at the language institute was coming to an end, so I would have plenty of time to tour the country. At the top of my list was Yazd—a desert city famous for a minority community who, I imagined, would be able to lift up the curtain on the roots of Persianness.

"You must go to Fars as well," said Sina.

"Really?"

"Yes, of course, Nicholas! This is where all the most important shahs were. The Achaemenians, the Sassanians . . . The ones when Iran ruled the whole world. So—when shall we leave?"

"We?"

I had been planning on going it alone. But Sina's term at law school was about to end too and his enthusiasm was infectious. One afternoon on the cusp of summer, when the desert outside Tehran was baking to the texture of an overcooked pie crust, we set out on a sleeper train for Yazd. Sharing our cabin were a couple of chain-smoking soldiers, who offered us their Bisotun cigarettes and puffed out of the window with us as we tried to identify the stars over the Great Desert. The soldiers had a hip flask, which they'd filled up with what tasted like a combination of orangeade and whiskey. It was one of the most disgusting drinks I've ever had, but we still knocked it back, and it gave a certain frisson to the images we saw outside—the silhouettes of the mountains and the egg-shaped domes swelling over the ancient water reservoirs, which ran like veins under the stretched-skin canvas of the sand.*

The best view of Yazd is from the roof of the Friday Mosque. Sitting there browning in the blaze, with our backs to the beige brick dome, we took in the vista: buff and ocher hulks of rock, muscling out of the sandy plain that sweeps back into the city and matches its coloring— its domes, its walls of sun-dried brick, its *badgirs* or "wind-catchers"— vented turrets that suck the air and exhale it into the rooms underneath to keep them cool.

"We stay with Siyavash," announced Sina, striding into a neighborhood of curved streets where groined arches hung over us like hoods and the houses pressed toward each other but were kept from intimacy by their thick wooden gates.

An atmosphere of secrecy whispered through these streets. The mud-brick walls were high and instead of windows there were glass bottles embedded as spyholes, while the wooden doors sported thick brass knockers dating back to medieval times. There were two kinds— one round and one rectangular, so the sex of the visitor could be identified. Approaching the house of Sina's friend, I stepped forward to swing the brass phallus in front of me—but an electric ring stopped me in my tracks. There was a bell and Sina had pressed it.

---

* These reservoirs, known as *qanats*, have been transferring water to Iran's most arid districts since about 800 BCE. A shaft is sunk into the ground, communicating with an inclined tunnel carrying water from the mountains or any other water source. The system was spread to Egypt by Darius the Great and was used by the Conquistadors in the Americas.

"Salaam!" came a gruff call from the other side of the door.

Behind it stood a young man with floppy hair that nearly hid his eyes. The contrast with Sina was striking: Whereas Sina bounded onto the courtyard on the spring of his bonhomie, Siyavash's body language was slow and stiff, and he didn't smile.

"Come in," he said, adding in a strangely abstracted tone, "welcome."

We sat down in a broad, carpeted living room with bolsters to rest our arms. I knew that Siyavash's father had a connection with the Professor, but I didn't know much more. I was intrigued: Siyavash was the first Zoroastrian I had met and I hoped he would teach me about their hidden, secretive world. . . .

THE TALE OF ZOROASTER

A man called Zoroaster turns up at the court of the shah with a brazier of fire from paradise. "Your messenger I am," he tells the shah, "and guide to God." Domed temples are built across the land, in front of the first of which Zoroaster plants a holy cypress tree, while pictures of Fereydoun (vanquisher of the snake-shouldered Zahhak) and other great kings of the past are painted on its walls.

The new faith ripples across the land and Zoroaster becomes its chief priest. But he has a violent end. The army of Turan, in its last gasp before it's crushed for good by the champion Asfandiyar (the heir to the throne and a hero as mighty in his own way as Rostam), sweeps out and converges on the main fire temple, where Zoroaster, along with eighty of his fellow priests, is hurled into the sacred flame he has tended for so many years.

Imagine . . . You're on holiday in Rome and heading for the main basilica. Instead of Catholic priests, crucifixes, and the pietà, you find Zoroastrian priests, or *mobeds*, carrying sacred twigs and worshippers tying prayer cords at the waist, standing around a gigantic urn, reciting prayers in ancient Persian in front of a sacred fire. When you step outside, you see the *faravahar* bird-man, wings outspread, emblazoned over the entablature. You head to any other European city and there, instead of a cathedral, you find a fire temple, instead of the cross a bird-man, and instead of the Virgin Mary a statue of the water angel, Anahita.

Who could have predicted the bumps that tipped Zoroastrianism off the road to global preeminence? That the squabbling Greek city-states would band together to defeat the Persians at Salamis and Plataea? That Constantine the Great would have a vision of the cross at the Milvian Bridge (when the Roman armies were flirting with a Zoroastrian cult, introduced to them by Cicilian pirates off the coast of Anatolia)? That the Arabs would erupt from the desert and grind the Persian empire into the dust? Several times Zoroastrianism was on the doorstep of global domination, but each time it tottered on the step and the door slammed in its face. It is now uncertain whether the Zoroastrians will even make it through another century.

The miracle is that they've made it at all. Persecuted, forced to convert, and sporadically subjected to pogroms, they were reduced to such a desperate condition that, in the 1850s, the French ambassador wrote, "Only a miracle may save them from extinction." The twentieth century brought relief in the Pahlavi shahs' enthusiasm for Iran's pre-Islamic heritage.* But they weren't likely to benefit from a revolution that called itself "Islamic." Ayatollah Khomeini branded their scripture "a harmful book," and his successor, Ayatollah Ali Khamenei, condemned Zoroastrians as "apostates," while strict rules against mixed marriages haven't helped to boost their numbers. So diminished have they become that now they account for less than a single percent of Iran's total population. But even if Zoroastrianism does go the way of the Olympian gods (with whom it was once contemporary), it will survive in the ideas it has given to the wider world.

The most famous Zoroastrians in Christian culture—with all due respect to Freddie Mercury—are the three "magi" who visited Jesus. The latter's halo was inspired by the rings of light that appear above

---

* Under Reza Shah, most of the discriminatory laws against them were removed and a Zoroastrian was appointed deputy prime minister; and under his son, the Islamic lunar calendar was briefly replaced by the solar Zoroastrian version.

Zoroastrian images, and baptism is derived from a Zoroastrian ritual in which children bathed in the rivers; while the water angel, Anahita (known to Zoroastrians as "the Lady"), gave birth to her son Mithra as chastely as Mary would do much later to Jesus, and combined with Mithra and the sun god Mehr to form a trinity that preceded its Christian counterpart by a millennium. Resurrection, Satan, and the very idea of heaven and hell (first transmitted to the Israelites during their Babylonian exile) all have their origin among the Zoroastrians, and Mithra's birthday, which traditionally fell on the 25th of December, was turned by Constantine the Great into Christendom's most popular festival—incorporating the old Zoroastrian customs of candles and a decorated cypress tree.

Zoroaster's ghost might be hard to see, but he haunts Western culture to its core.

Sina hadn't told me a lot about Siyavash, so I didn't have any particular expectations, but he *had* described him as a friend. Which made the coldness of our reception slightly discomfiting. On our first evening, Siyavash didn't even stay in, so I asked Sina if there was a problem.

"Nicholas, you don't expect him to drop everything for us?" he said.

"No, I didn't mean it like that," I protested, shamed by the way Sina had phrased his response. "No, it's just . . . "

But I couldn't work out how to express it: After all the hospitality I'd enjoyed in Tehran, it was hard not to feel we were being snubbed, in some subtly coded but quintessentially Persian way.

When it came to supper, a tray was brought into the guest room by Siyavash's mother, but no one sat with us; so when Siyavash's father asked if we would like to watch TV, Sina and I exchanged a smile. At last, we were being accepted! As soon as we were comfortable, Siyavash's father left the room, and the only interaction we had with the family over the next couple of hours was when his wife brought us tea and a bowl of pomegranates. As I write this I feel like I'm being churlish—they had, after all, allowed me, a complete stranger, into their home. But I did hope it would be easier to talk to them over the next few days.

"What's the connection with your father?" I asked Sina that night, as we lay on our mattresses in the guest room.

"It's baba's folklore work," he said. "Siyavash's father is an expert on Zoroastrian history. He's not actually a historian—he used to be a cameraman for documentary filmmaking, but he's read a lot of books and there are lots of things that only the Zoroastrians know."

The following evening, when I found myself alone in the house with Siyavash's father—Siyavash was at the youth club again, and Sina had gone to an Internet café to catch up with his girlfriends— I decided to try and win him over. There was only one weapon at my disposal. I'd used it once before to thaw a glacial Iranian, and I wondered if the same trick might work again. . . .

"You want to know about *Shahnameh*?"

Siyavash's father put down his glass of tea, his eyes expanding under his thick gray brows.

"Well, well," he said. "I did not expect this. You really want to know about *Shahnameh*?"

"Oh yes, definitely!" I exclaimed.

A few moments earlier, we had been on opposite ends of the room, but now we were so close that I could smell the patchouli oil in his hair.

"There is one important thing you must understand about *Shahnameh*," he said. "It is *our* culture. It is not about Muslims, oh no no. They will tell you it is, but they are wrong! It is about *us*—the Zoroastrians. And it is full of secrets that are only understood by Zoroastrians, because we have a closer relationship to these stories."

Siyavash's father spoke an older version of Persian than I had encountered before, with few Arabic loan-words—closer to the "pure" Persian spoken by Ferdowsi. Instead of "salaam," he said "dorud," the old Persian word Ferdowsi uses. He said "sipos" for "thank you" instead of the Arabic "motashakerram"; and he called children "farzand," as Ferdowsi would have done. These linguistic connections intrigued me, because they suggested a larger link to the *Shahnameh*— and the ancient Persian culture—as a whole.

"Well," said Siyavash's father, "if you want to know how close we are to Ferdowsi and *Shahnameh* you only have to ask our names. For example, my son is Siyavash—the name of a famous prince in *Shah-nameh*. I myself am Manouchehr, the name of a famous king."

In fact, in the week I spent in Yazd, all the Zoroastrians I met took their names from Ferdowsi's epic. Although many of these charac-ters also appear in the *Avesta* (the Zoroastrian scriptures), they are spelled differently there: Siyavash, for example, is Syavarshana. It is Ferdowsi's spelling that has been kept: proof of the epic's popularity with Zoroastrians, over and above their most sacred texts.

"The *Shahnameh* was written to save the real Iranian culture," said Siyavash's father. "It shows a proud, independent people who held on to our culture even when the Arabs attacked. Of course most of them are Muslims now—but they are *not* Arabs."

He pressed a hand on the rug, stroking it through the wine-colored pile.

"Many things," he said, "have stayed the same. They like gardens, they have respect for fire, and if you look at the domes of the mosques you will see they are giving honor to our mountains. You understand? Even if they became Muslim, at least they are still Iranian."

He looked up at me, nodding.

"The *Shahnameh* is still closed," he said. "It has not yet been opened. Only if you take out the Arabic words can you find the true meaning. It is like our Zoroastrian dialect, *Dari*, which includes many words the Muslims cannot understand—which helps us to avoid persecution."

Here was another layer to the *Shahnameh*—a book of secrets, as hard to decipher as the codes of Persian conduct or the occlusive Zoroastrian streets. Once again, Ferdowsi's epic was the key to un-locking other secrets, opening another door on modern Iran. The shell of Siyavash's father's formality had cracked, and for the rest of my stay I was treated with an attentiveness that made me ashamed of the negative thoughts I'd harbored on the first night:

"Your favorite story? . . . No! 'Rostam and Sohrab' is for the masses; the battle with Asfandiyar is much the greater tale! And did

you not read about King Ardashir's vizier? . . . Or the adventures of
Bahram Gur? Or Kai Kavus when he tries to fly to heaven? . . . Or the
wise King Anushirvan? . . . "

Talk like this carried us on trips around Yazd. Driven by a friend
of his, who had an ancient battered Paykan, we visited his old village,
Cham. There, dog roses trailed honeysuckle around the barrel-domes
of the houses and a candle, lit by a sacred fire, bobbed in a pool of
water under an ancient plane tree.

"Everyone is leaving now," he said sadly as a pack of small, well-
groomed dogs followed us down the otherwise deserted street (a
giveaway that this was Zoroastrian territory—although I came across
guard dogs in Muslim villages, it was rare to see them in this condition, since Islamic tradition regards them as unclean; though I did
spot the odd poodle in the handbags of North Tehran fashionistas).

Another afternoon, we crossed the sun-scorched salt desert and
climbed up a mountain slope where lime-painted huts hung from the
cliff like nests in a tree. Near the top, a brace of spear-wielding soldiers
was standing sentinel, embossed on a brass door, which opened to
reveal a marble-floored cavern. The shrine is called Chak-Chak, or
"Drip-Drip," because of the water seeping out of fissures in the rock,
which is said to represent the tears of Nikbanu, a daughter of the last
pre-Islamic shah. Like her sister, Bibi Shahrbanu (whose shrine I had
visited in Tehran), she was eaten up by the mountain, while she was
escaping from the invading Arab army; and the cane she used to climb
to the top became the giant plane tree that soars out of the cavern's
marble floor.

Standing there, under the pink fleshy rock where Nikbanu's legendary occultation took place, we watched the sparks of light on
the damp rock around us, struck by a candelabra hanging surreally
above us.

"If I had a choice," said Siyavash's father, as the light played mag-
ically around us, "I prefer the mountain to take me than to let the
Arabs defeat me."

I could see why he and the Professor were such good friends.

Siyavash himself was harder to thaw. There was little rapport between him and Sina, despite the latter's best efforts; and as for me, I was rarely even able to make eye contact with him. But all this changed after Sina left. He wanted to go on to Shiraz early, to meet up with various friends he was itching to see, and as Siyavash's father had invited me to visit the Chak-Chak shrine the next day, I stayed behind.

That last evening, Siyavash came back from the youth club and asked if I would like to go for a walk.

"My baba told me you are interested in *Shahnameh*," he said.

"Oh yes!" I exclaimed, thrilled at this opening, then settled into a more relaxed tone. "Well, I do really like it, but I'm interested in Iranian culture in general."

"Hmmm."

He placed his hands behind his back, looking at the ground as we paced down those narrow, secretive streets.

"I suppose," I said tentatively, "I'm quite interested to know what it's like . . . for Zoroastrians, I mean. Nowadays."

You could see the sun sliding down to the horizon—a giant pomegranate sucked into one of the "wind-catchers," the last of the light wiped away by the shadows sweeping down the street.

"A few years ago we couldn't even choose our names," said Siyavash. "If we wanted Darius, for example, the government would not allow this because it was the name of a shah. But it is still difficult to get a good job. My uncle works in an office and is suitable for a manager, but they don't give him the job because he is Zoroastrian."

We sat on a ledge and looked down the street. Outside one of the thick wooden gates, a woman in a plum-red headscarf was brushing her doorstep with a handleless broom.

"Why must this woman wear *hijab*?" asked Siyavash. "It is not our religion, it is Islam. But we are forced to do this. And in Ramadan, if we eat in the street, the government arrests us—but we have our own religious fast every month."

He pressed a finger on the ledge, tracing a winding path through the dust. "You mustn't talk to Sina about these things."

"But . . . " I wanted to laugh—surely he didn't think Sina was the same as the people he was complaining about. "Sina isn't really . . . well, he's not *religious*," I said. "He certainly wouldn't support any persecution. They've got a picture of King Darius in their living room."

"You don't understand," said Siyavash softly.

"But . . ."

I thought of what his father had said, about the Muslim Iranians still being "Iranian," still fond of fire and mountains.

"Aren't they still Iranian?" I asked. "Persian, perhaps. Isn't there a shared culture?"

He turned to me, wrinkling his nose, looking at me with small, narrow eyes.

"So why do they attack us?" he asked.

I think that, for Siyavash, there was too much bad history between Zoroastrians and Muslims for him to open up in front of any Muslim—not even one as unjudgmental as Sina. I looked at him and smiled, but there wasn't even the slightest flicker of a smile in response. In fact, in all the time I spent with him, he didn't so much as grin. And yet he was a Zoroastrian—a member of a religion whose prophet is legendarily said to have been laughing when he came out of his mother's womb; a religion once famous for its happiness. "Happiness is a good in itself," wrote the scholar R. C. Zaehner of Zoroastrian philosophy, "and without it the other virtues are sterile." This vein of happiness is what gives Persian culture its sumptuousness, its love of life's finer things—like wine and poetry, music and soft carpets. But there was no sign of this "happiness" in Siyavash's face, nor in any of the Zoroastrians I met in Yazd. "There is no fun in Islam," Ayatollah Khomeini once said, and he'd taken the fun out of the Zoroastrians too.

"You know something else?" asked Siyavash. "If a Muslim converts to a Zoroastrian, you know what they do? They kill him—not the government but the vigilantes. And because the law is Muslim it means the life of a non-Muslim is not as precious. If a Zoroastrian is killed in a car accident, the driver has to pay only half the blood money."

I thought of Ferdowsi. In the *Shahnameh*, he tells us he knew many Zoroastrians, so he would have been familiar with their complaints. At the time, their communities were vanishing fast; for many, life had become so tough they sailed down the Persian Gulf, establishing the "Parsee" community in India. But in some senses, the tenth-century Zoroastrians were a lot better off than their counterparts today. "Zoroastrians (preserve) scriptures, fire temples, and rites from the days of their kings," wrote the tenth-century geographer al-Istakhri, adding, "They maintain their ancestral customs and conform to them." Several Zoroastrians managed to secure important positions—Prince Adud ad-Dawleh of the Buwayhids, the most powerful man in this part of the country at the time, employed Zoroastrians as his treasurer and his physician, and some towns were still run by Zoroastrian governors. And in one particular respect, the Zoroastrians of the medieval era could count themselves lucky. Because if it is hard for them to live in a strict Islamic system today, it's even harder to die in it.

"You remember the Towers of Silence?" asked Siyavash.

We had visited them two days earlier. On the outskirts of Yazd, a circle of mud-brick spun around the crest of a sandy hillock, glowing in the sun like a ring in a forge. Sina had run to the top and pelted us all with sand. It just seemed like a game at the time, but now I remembered how Siyavash had shaken his head, refusing to join in. Maybe he resented Sina for making light of such a holy site. Because this was the place where the Zoroastrians used to follow the *Avesta*'s injunction to lay their dead "on the highest places where corpse-eating dogs and corpse-eating birds shall most surely know it." The Towers were banned by the shah just before the revolution and are now out of use. But there were rumors that not all of them had been abandoned. On the powdery plain outside nearby Ardakan, we climbed through the shored-up doorway of another tower—round and squat and embedded in the sand like a giant stone tube drilled into the earth—where scattered shards of bone lay in the dusty bowl of a circular pit, like pieces of meat in a broth.

"On the third day after death," said Siyavash, "the priests come to the house and say the prayers. Before it was banned, the body would be washed, wrapped in white, and carried to the Tower. The pallbearers placed it inside, they wore special white clothes, and they put the body on a stone. Then everybody went outside and waited for the wild birds to come, except for the guardian of the Tower. The birds ate the flesh and stripped its meat until only the bones were left."

Now the practice is illegal, so the Zoroastrians have to use a cemetery instead. But the Tower, Siyavash insisted, had its uses:

"It's a way to feed the birds, it doesn't occupy much area, and the earth doesn't get dirty. But we are forced not to do this."

"So if you had a choice," I asked, "would you prefer to be buried or eaten?"

"Well, we would be eaten anyway, if not by the birds then by worms. But I certainly prefer the Tower, of course. It is the Zoroastrian way."

As I looked at his earnest expression, I felt I had an inkling of what he was concerned about: The Zoroastrians would lose their heritage. They would be sucked up by the wider Muslim culture, melted down and stripped of their distinct identity. They were one of many specifically "Persian" subcultures I would come across in my travels, all connected in some intimate way to the *Shahnameh*, and all in danger of extinction.

Ferdowsi's epic poem is full of stories about fire: Siyavash riding through a ring of fire to prove his innocence, his son Kai Khusrau taming a land where fire spurts out of the ground (as it still does in nearby Azerbaijan, which is where that story is set),* the prophet

---

* I saw this for myself on a hop across the border later in the summer. Having camped on a hillside in northwest Iran, where the Azeri-speaking locals lit fires and sang songs at the foot of a ninth-century Zoroastrian hero's fort, I trekked farther north to the country of Azerbaijan itself. There, sitting at a teahouse near Baku, I was unable to reply to my hostess's inquiry as to whether I would like honey in my tea, because I was so stunned by the spectacle in front of me: flames, seeping through fissures in the rock, licking the air and framed in the black rings they had singed on the earth. "Oh, it's been like that forever," said my hostess. "No it hasn't," retorted her combative sister. "It's only been there since World War Two." Before that, she explained, the flames had been on the other side of the hill, "but they had to put them out because of all the bombing."

Zoroaster hurled into a holy fire by the invading soldiers of Turan. Nothing symbolizes Zoroastrianism more, and there is none more sacred than the fire of Bahram. It was lit in the time of the ancient kings, drawing the shahs in prayer and kept alive in hidden places after the Arab conquest until it was established, in the medieval era, in Yazd. I was eager to see it. It would be a glimpse of history, of where the past and the Zoroastrian present came together. But there was one ever-so-slightly niggling obstacle: Non-Zoroastrians weren't allowed to look at it.

"Oh no, you certainly cannot visit the fire," said Siyavash with a pious gasp, when I mentioned it early in our stay in Yazd.

But this was before he'd started talking to me, so after another excursion with his father I decided to ask again. Which takes us to my last afternoon in Yazd, standing at the end of a narrow street, with Siyavash placing a white cotton prayer cap on my head. In front of us was a wooden gate, with a board fixed to the brick archway above it:

ENTRANCE ONLY FOR ZOROASTRIANS

The gate was ajar; behind it, the sort of garden Alice could have visited. Pink roses were peeking out of the bushes, pomegranates hung in the groves like baubles, and the high tapering cypress trees soared over everything: a secret, walled Persian garden.* A brick wall contained them at the back, decorated with floral-patterned tiles and spilling out with steps, which carried a priest dressed in a white coat and cap—like a British milkman. He nodded to Siyavash and frowned at me, but Siyavash and the prayer cap reassured him of my credentials.

The Zoroastrian scripture, the *Avesta*, contains prayers and hymns to Ahura Mazda—the Zoroastrian God—as well as ecclesiastical

---

* The old Persian for a walled garden—*pairi daeza*—became our word for paradise, a tribute to the many beautifully tended gardens that have been created in this part of the world. Carefully shaded, irrigated by underground tunnels, often divided by rivers and fountains, Persian gardens are synonymous with tranquillity and refinement. The most famous of them all is at the Taj Mahal, built in India by the Persian-speaking Mughals.

codes, penances, ways to defeat evil spirits, and blessings, all composed over several centuries in the first millennium BCE. A copy lay on a shelf in the prayer chamber. Siyavash flicked through its pages, at the same time untying the *koshti*, a plaited cord at his waist. Moments later, the light from a row of metal bars gleamed on his face as slow, respectful steps carried him toward the silver urn protected behind them.

Here it was—the sacred cipher of the Zoroastrians. The ancient flame that burned not only when Ferdowsi was alive, but when many of the kings from his tales were breathing too. I had been anticipating the most spectacular of pyres. Instead . . . I was standing in front of a little yellow glimmer that wouldn't have been able to withstand a birthday-cake blow. After all I had read and heard about sacred Zoroastrian fires—what a letdown! I'd come here to meet the King of the Kindling, and instead I'd found an old dying crone.

But something was happening in the chamber. A wizened man in white (the priestly caretaker, known as the *herbad*) was dawdling around the fire. He picked up a metal spade, shoveled the ash aside, and lifted a spare billet onto the urn, stripped of its bark to remove impurities. It was only now—and only slowly—that the flames started to expand. They swelled and stretched, spreading their arms like an old dancer who's just remembered she still knows all the moves, tilting and swaying and belly-dancing over the crackling wood. Red embers sparkled above them like the rings on the dancer's fingers, disappearing among the puffs of smoke that flattened themselves against the ceiling.

Looking at it now, it was easy to imagine the VIPs who had stood before this fire in the past. I saw them kicking off their boots after a day on the hunt, ritually washing themselves before they prayed. I thought of all the fire-themed stories I'd read in the *Shahnameh*, and, more generally, of the importance of light in Persian culture: the light shining off the facets of mirrorwork in the mosques, the candles at *ashoura* events, the image of the sun, used as a symbol for the shahs as well as Imam Ali.

Siyavash's fingers were gripping the metal bars. His lips barely moved as he whispered his prayers, the ancient words mixing with the smoke. His eyes were fixed on that extraordinary, resilient, 1,400-year-old flame, dancing before him now as it had once danced, so many centuries ago, for the ancient kings.

~

Half a day's bus ride away, on the other side of the Zagros Mountains, in an iron-roofed house on the outskirts of Shiraz, Sina had lost the use of his legs.

"Salaaaaam, Nicholassssh!" he slurred, arms raised high and a big, broad smile splashed across his face.

"Drink!" came the order. Not from Sina—not even from his friend Farzin, who had invited us to stay—but from Farzin's whiskery, red-haired father. A glass of arak found its way into my hand and, lest anyone impugn me for a teetotaler, I drained it in one.

"Well done!" exclaimed Farzin's father. "Now—another!"

He had a history of drinking himself. Before the revolution, he'd been a teacher at a school in Shiraz.

"But after the mullahs came to power, I got drunk," he said, sitting in his pajamas on the sofa, with a tumbler of arak for a nightcap. "I went in front of the police station. I was so drunk! I shouted, 'Khomeini, I want to do you up the arse!'"

He took a sip of his arak and shrugged, as if it were just one of those things.

"Well, I never taught again," he said.

The Iranian education system's loss was our gain: There was plenty to see around Shiraz, and thanks to Farzin's father, we were easily able to get around.

The *Shahnameh* might purport to tell the story of Iran's ancient kings, but when it comes to the most famous of them all, it's strangely silent. Cyrus the Great was the "anointed one" of the Old Testament, author of the world's first declaration of human rights in the sixth century BCE and liberator of the Israelites from their Babylonian captivity. His reputation for justice was recognized even by his enemies ("no matter whom he conquered," wrote the Greek historian Xeno-phon, " . . . they found themselves longing to be guided by his rul-ings"); and he was also a supremely successful general, establishing a realm that stretched for 2 million square miles, from the Nile to the Ganges: the first transcontinental empire.

But Cyrus would soon be forgotten. By the age of Ferdowsi, his feats had been swallowed up by the earlier Aryan myths, as had his grandson Darius the Great (who built a 1,600-mile-high road that could be covered by dispatches in a week—the first large-scale postal system).* Having lost track of the shahs, Ferdowsi is only able to pick up the story with the demise of the Achaemenian dynasty. He may know nothing of Cyrus, and little of Darius too, but there was no way of shielding him from the man who would come stomping onto the Iranian plateau two centuries later. . . .

The taxi moves along the river Pulvar, on a road as straight as a line of longitude. The land around us is lush and green. Poplar trees are shimmering in the foothills and a wave of red tulips is flowering be-side a stream. After the aridity around Yazd, it's like breaking open a cardboard box full of delicious sugary pastries. If you scrubbed out the pencil shapes of the village minarets and the odd nomad's tent, you could imagine you were driving through Tuscany.

Ahead of us, under the giant hood of Mount Mercy, a limestone terrace lips out of the cove, fifty feet above the ground, covering more than a million square feet. Spiking into the air—one of Iran's most iconic and spectacular sights—are the ribbed limestone pillars of the ancient palace of Persepolis, the jewel not only in the crown of the Achaemenian dynasty, but of Iranian kingship at large (as the last shah declared to the world when he used it as the venue for his grand

---

* Because of this he was said to have "a thousand eyes and a thousand ears," oper-ating a surveillance system as impressive as the current regime's and attracting the praise of the historian Herodotus, whose description—"Neither snow nor rain nor heat nor night prevents them from completing their assigned task as soon as possible"—was adapted into the unofficial motto of the Central Post Office in New York, inscribed on its façade.

party in 1971). The pillars needle the sky like the pieces of a gigantic chessboard that's been set up for the gods.

Giant winged bull-men guard them, soaking up the early afternoon sun at the top of the entrance stairway, while griffins and lions prowl in the bas-reliefs, bulging out of the walls. All around them is order on a fantastic scale. The straight lines and right angles of the platforms and stairwells, the gates and palaces and the rock-cut tombs carved above the site, pay tribute to the formalism of Persian architecture. You see delicately fluted pillars, columned porches, and processional stairwells of a kind you'll meet again in mosques and palaces all over the country—but rarely from so early a date.

Even the living creatures carved into the walls are tightly organized. The bull-men are less savage, more regal than their famous Assyrian counterparts; the shah sticking his dagger into the belly of a lion is doing it with the poise of a dancer. And most of all, the tribute bearers on the sides of the stairwells, carrying their gifts to the supersized shah (dozens of them, from all over the empire: Greeks offering wool, Nubians with an elephant's tusk, Indians in *dhotis* bearing pans of gold) are processing in organized rows, with none of the terror that permeates similarly themed Pharaonic reliefs. The great 1930s travel writer Robert Byron criticized Persepolis for its lack of passion—but that's the point. Like the elegant but emotionally restrained miniature paintings, like the geometrical patterns on a Persian carpet or a typical Persian garden, like the courtesy of an old-fashioned Persian, Persepolis is about order, refinement, and unimpeachable manners. No wonder Sina's eyes are so bright—it's the spirit of his country expressed in stone.

"Again, come on!" he exclaims, racing up the steps onto the esplanade. "Did your heart not become happy?"

He is addressing Farzin, who flashes a smile in response. He's one of those too-cool-for-school characters you often meet among the Iranian youth—all dark glasses, jangly wristwatch, and as much emotion as the courtiers on the bas-reliefs.

Sitting on the stump of a stone griffin's foot, they're both smiling, looking around with pride—as if the old bronze-plated doors have risen out of the dust, the ivory-inlaid ceiling has slid back into place above the pillars, and Darius the Great himself (who built Persepolis in the sixth century BCE) is parading up the stairwell in front of us, its treads shallow enough to be mounted by his richly caparisoned horse.

Traveling in nineteenth-century Egypt, the French author Gustave Flaubert noticed that "a certain Thompson from Sunderland has described his name in letters six feet high on Pompey's pillar. You can read it a quarter of a mile away. You can't see the Pillar without seeing the name of Thompson, and consequently, without thinking of Thompson. This cretin has become part of the monument and perpetuates himself with it." For me at Persepolis, it's Major Harvey-Kelly, T. M. Cloyne of the Light Dragoons, and even Henry "Dr. Livingstone, I presume?" Stanley—all of whom have etched their names on the bellies of the bull-men. But I don't feel as put out as Flaubert, because these colonial types aren't alone—Persepolis has been attracting the graffiti of its guests for at least a millennium.

In one of the palaces, Prince Adud ad-Dawleh of the Buwayhids—self-styled "Shah-an-shah," who ruled most of western Iran when Ferdowsi was a boy and presented himself as a revival of the ancient kings—scribbled a notice. Barbed tips spike the ends of his letters, telling how he came here in 955 CE and "fetched someone who read the inscriptions on these ruins." It's a significant piece of graffiti—historians tend to argue that Persepolis, and most of Iran's pre-Islamic history, was forgotten by the locals until it was "discovered" for them by Western archaeologists in the nineteenth century. Adud ad-Dawleh's panel reminds us that in Ferdowsi's time—a millennium and a half after the compound was built—these ruins were still very much alive.*

Looking at Adud ad-Dawleh's inscription, I wonder whether Sina is tempted to etch a few words of his own.

---

* Although they were known as "The Throne of Jamshid," named for the king who is cut in half by snake-shouldered Zahhak in the *Shahnameh*. The same name is retained by Iranians today, underlining that it's Ferdowsi's version of history (and prehistory), rather than the drier—albeit more accurate—Western-researched version that sticks in the popular consciousness, like the names of the Zoroastrians.

"Of course not," he snaps with a flare of indignation. "We must respect this place."

But, whatever the faults of the signatures so many people have scratched into the stones, they don't amount to a hill of chickpeas compared with what Persepolis's most famous visitor did.

"Sikandar," announces a man in a parka, standing in the basalt wreckage of one of the palaces, "was a monster, a barbarian. . . . Actually," he adds, nodding at the scorched walls around us, "he was Bush."

He's talking about Alexander the Great, who turned up here in the fourth century BCE, sozzled himself on wine, and treated Persepolis like one giant party hall. He was never going to leave the place as he'd found it. Goaded by an Athenian prostitute (who was eager to avenge the Persians for their burning of the Acropolis a century and a half before), he hurled a torch into the Hall of a Hundred Columns and set it on fire. The Zoroastrian scriptures were turned to ash, marble statues were smashed, the contents of the royal vaults—which Michael Wood has described as "the greatest treasure in history"—were carted off on 7,000 pack beasts, and the land was subjected to a couple of centuries of Hellenic rule. It's the sort of behavior you'd expect a "nationalist" like Ferdowsi to berate—but, surprisingly, when he comes to this episode in the *Shahnameh*, he has few bad words to say about Alexander. Instead, he gets back at him by rewriting history. He tells us Alexander's father was in fact Iranian (the shah, no less) and the only reason he wasn't born in Iran himself was that his mother had bad breath and was sent back to Europe in disgrace.

Historically, it's a gaff and a half—although it's a cunning way of saving national face. But it does express a truth of sorts. Alexander famously fell in love with the culture he'd conquered (or, some would argue, exploited it), dressing himself in Persian-style tunics, recruiting Persian nobles to his court, adopting the hand-kissing gesture of the Persian kings, and marrying a woman from Bactria (in what is now Afghanistan) who spoke an old Iranian dialect. Several centuries later, the medieval Persians would show that their talent for alchemy wasn't confined to the laboratory. The Mongols, who started off by trashing every town they visited (in Nishapur, they even killed the cats), ended up wrapping themselves in Persian finery and sponsoring sumptuous miniature paintings on thick cream paper based on the tales of the *Shahnameh.* The Abbasid caliphs (infiltrated and overwhelmed by their Persian courtiers) and Ferdowsi's intended sponsor, the Turk-born Sultan Mahmud of Ghazni (adopting Persian as the language of his court) were similarly transmuted. It's an extraordinary phenomenon—proof of how attractive Persian culture can be to the outsider. And it's continued into the twentieth century. Donald Wilber, one of the CIA spies sent to topple Prime Minister Mossadegh in the 1950s, fell in love with Persia. When he wasn't collecting Persian carpets, he was usually to be found studying and scribbling about Persian architecture. In fact, for my own visit to Persepolis, it was Wilber's account that was my chief point of reference.

There are many more shahs, carved into the gullies around Persepolis—warrior-kings in bas-relief, with pleated cowboy trousers and sausage curls of hair half-hidden by their balloon-shaped *korymbos* crowns, impaling their enemies on the ends of their lances or trampling them under their horses' hooves. Among them was a lone female, in a loose ribboned dress and a beaded necklace, with long ringlets of hair falling over her shoulders*—the only woman in the vicinity who was allowed to air her hair. It was boiling—a lot of the female visitors were fanning themselves by flapping the sides of their headscarves. So, after clambering among the reliefs and strolling through the wheat fields between them, among nomads' tents and the bull-head capitals recycled for the Buwayhids' medieval court, we bundled into Farzin's father's taxi as lumps of dust and sweat.

For Sina and Farzin, these ruins were the country's most powerful visual symbol of national pride. It's all very well promoting mosques as the mascots of the mullahs' regime, but they can't hold a candle to Persepolis—the greatest remnant of a time when Iran ruled the world.

---

* This figure is either Queen Shapurdokhtak, the wife of King Narseh from the late third century, or Anahita, the Zoroastrian water angel.

"You know how many of these statues have been stolen from Persepolis?" asked Farzin's father as the highway tapered ahead of us. "And what does this government do about it? Nothing, of course! They *want* these things to be stolen, it is the wish of their hearts! They want these things to be in the museums of New York and London. They don't want to have these things here, because they remind us how our country was great long before the Muslims came."*

He spat out of the window, as if he'd spotted an ayatollah on the verge.

"'That castle,'" he recited, "'where Jamshid the king drank his wine / Is now where gazelles and the foxes recline.'"

He was quoting from Omar Khayyam, the eleventh-century poet and mathematician, whose *Rubaiyat* sat on coffee tables all over Victorian London. The verse is a comment on the decay and abandonment of Persepolis in Khayyam's own day, another case in which those long-ago times appear to echo the present.

For several days, Farzin kept up his image as Cool Dude No. 1. He would strum on his guitar (and took us one evening to a hilltop teahouse, where a friend of his sang along to the Eagles' "Hotel California" between inhalations on a water pipe). He introduced me to the beats of the Iranian rapper Sandi and showed me the creamy marble tomb of the fourteenth-century poet Hafez (whose *diwan* is, next to the Quran, the most likely book to be found in an Iranian home), where couples were secretly holding hands in the surrounding alcoves.

"This is where I bring all my girlfriends," he said, preening around the compound with his gelled bouffant sticking over his shades, while we lost track of Sina, last seen handing his phone number to several of the local girls. But a few nights in, Farzin's cool-dude image was shattered—when he showed me his stamp collection.

---

* This point was supported by the words of Iran's Supreme Leader himself, on a visit to this part of the country in 2008. "Those ruins are the leftovers of tyrants," declared Ayatollah Khamenei, refusing an invitation to visit Persepolis. "Iran achieved glory only after the arrival of Islam."

"This is a good one!"

You could see the excitement burning on his face as the slipcase came off. His finger rested on Reza Shah (the last king but one), with a feather sticking out of his cap and a ferocious expression (which caused ladies of his court to faint in his presence).

"What about that one!" exclaimed Sina.

He was pointing to a stamp of the last shah with Queen Farah, commemorating their wedding in 1959.

"Eh, my mother loves Queen Farah," said Sina. "She has a thousand magazines about her!"

Farzin was cautious about letting me take hold of the album—even with the plastic sheet protectors to stop me from touching the stamps—but eventually he handed it over.

I was struck by how many of the images were historical. The eleventh-century polymath Ibn Sina appeared numerous times, as did his rival Biruni, with a folded turban and a fuzzy beard. There was a postmarked set showing the winged bull-men of Persepolis, printed for the shah's 1971 celebration. And there were even stamps displaying bare-chested men in leather plus fours—*pahlavans* practicing the sport of the ancient Iranians (a sight I would see in force only a few weeks later). Most striking of all was the age of the stamps: Very few of them had been printed any later than 1979.

"Do you have any from *after* the revolution?" I asked as Farzin lifted the album back out of my hands.

"Sure, but they aren't good for my collection. Now it's only flowers and mosques. It's the ones from the shahs' time I like."

There was one surprising exception: a set of stamps printed in 1990, which were the most beautiful of them all. They were mini reproductions of miniature paintings, showing scenes from the *Shahnameh*. Here was snake-shouldered Zahhak, chained to a cave in the Alborz Mountains; there was the devious Akvan *Div*, hoisting Rostam on a rock, ready to hurl him into the sea; and here was Siyavash, riding his black horse through the flames to disprove his stepmother's slander. They were printed in tandem with an international congress, hosted by the incumbent president, Ali Akbar Rafsanjani, who had been forced into this rare public endorsement after UNESCO declared the "year of Ferdowsi." It marked a thawing in the government's attitude toward the *Shahnameh*—although the Professor and his peers considered it to have been nothing more than a token gesture.

The next afternoon we continued our journey in the Persian glory days, driving sunward between cliffs the fleshy pink of lobster meat. Shining everywhere, under the heavy glaze of the heavens, were the vivid colors of a Persian miniature—the orpiment of buttercups, the vermilion of tulips. The mountaintops turned the indigo in which they are painted in miniatures, and bushes sprouted on their foothills, as if the artist had stuck his thumb in ground malachite and dabbed it across the scene.

As we trundled toward the ancient site of Bishapur, Qashqa'i nomads appeared on the banks above a flashing silver-leaf river. The women's multilayered dresses and floral-print scarves were so bright I couldn't take my eyes off them. They were like rainbows reassembled as people. As for the men—their rich, thick brows flexed under double-eared felt hats identical to those worn by the ancient Medians on the reliefs at Persepolis as well as the magistrates of medieval Fars*—a glimpse of the past on the heads of the present.

Wriggling under their goatskin tents, the road stretched toward the fawn cliffs of the Pass of the Polo-Stick. There, orange-blossom scent drifted among the steam from the samovars as picnicking families sat cross-legged on their rugs and pulled feasts out of their hampers: rice in plastic-lidded tubs, chicken cutlets wrapped in cling-film, saucers of kidney beans and plastic bags full of *barbari* bread.

Our picnic had been supplied courtesy of Farzin's mother. We sat down to enjoy it, swapping items with a family from Esfahan, who (as Sina whispered in my ear several times) all had their city's lilting singsong accent. Behind us were the pictures that have made this such a popular spot, carved into the wrinkled cliffs above the banks about

---

* They wear, wrote Ibn Hawkal in his tenth-century geography, "caps, so that their ears are covered, the end hanging on their shoulders."

1,700 years ago. Families wandered underneath them, speculating over which king was which—"That must be Ardashir!" "Which one is Bahram?" "This must be Shapur." "How do you know?" "Because the Roman emperor is under his foot!"

They were all kings from the Sassanian dynasty—the last before the Arab invasion of the seventh century CE. Although many Iranians blame them for failing to defeat the Arabs, they were hugely successful, lasting for more than four centuries and presiding over an extraordinary range of innovations that have made life easier, more efficient, and in several cases more fun all over the world—from the architectural squinch to the banker's check, along with heraldry, windmills, polo, backgammon, and tennis.

Among the shahs in the reliefs was a swashbuckler called Shapur II. He cut a proud figure, holding his sword between his legs, with Indian prisoners and Persian soldiers below and beside him, one of them leading a horse and another one carrying a decapitated head. He isn't the most famous of the Sassanian kings, but he does star in my favorite tale from the historical second half of the *Shahnameh*. He's a classic adventurer-prince, whose escapades read like an ancient version of a James Bond story:

THE TALE OF SHAPUR II

Like many of the best kings, Shapur likes to go about in disguise. But one day he overreaches himself. He treks out all the way to the enemy kingdom of Rome (which is actually Byzantium), dressed as a silk merchant—although not dressed very well, by the sounds of it, because he is unmasked. Rather than kill him, the emperor of Rome adopts the ploy of a Bond villain—he is going to make Shapur suffer before he dies. So he has him stitched into an ass-hide, which will slowly contract and squeeze him to death. Just one little mistake: The emperor leaves a young woman as Shapur's jailer, and Shapur has the same effect on her as Bond might have done—she falls in love with him, provides hot milk to loosen the hide, and rides with him back to Iran, where he gives her the impossibly romantic name "dilafruz farrukhpai"—"lucky-footed heart-luster."

Slowly, Shapur's army is gathered together. He burns the Roman fleet, before pouncing on the Roman emperor and exacting retribution. It isn't pretty: Still enraged by the way he was treated, Shapur has the emperor's ears split, his nose bored, and a horse's bit hammered into his mouth. The Persian kings might have been fond of beauty and orderly refinement, but if you crossed them their revenge could be brutal.

The bas-reliefs of the shahs, like the billboards of the ayatollahs in Tehran, declared the power of the rulers. But the Sassanians lost that power, along with the goodwill of their subjects, thanks in large part to their reliance on their priests. The previous day, at one of the cliffs near Persepolis, I had seen a figure with a downturned mouth, carved into the rock. He was strangely familiar—the sour-lipped cleric lording over the people. But this was no ayatollah.

He was Kartir, chief Zoroastrian priest in the reign of Shapur I, who boasts (in an inscription that would have horrified Cyrus the Great) that he has caused other creeds and sects to be "smitten" and the "heretical" to be "punished with corporal punishment." Kartir is Iran's original religious fundamentalist, one of many priests who sucked the spirit out of Zoroaster's faith, turning it into a series of ecclesiastical codes and ensuring the *mobeds* a major role at the court (in a foreshadowing of Khomeini's theocracy a millennium and a half later). But they served ultimately to distance the shahs from their subjects. By the time the Arabs invaded in the seventh century, the Sassanians had lost the goodwill of the people, who no longer had the stomach to fight on their behalf.

All this is forgotten at Bishapur, where the intention of the original sculptors still holds—to celebrate the glory of the shahs. Sitting there by the banks of the Shapur, I turned to the Esfahani family's patriarch and asked why they came to this spot—it was, after all, about half a day's journey from their city.

"Is it not obvious?" His eyes were glowing like candles. "These pictures were made when we were a great country. All the world was afraid of us and our empire spread many times over what we have today. Oh yes, I know what you are thinking—the world despises us now, they think we are fanatics. But when the shahs were in power, they all looked at Iran and admired."

His family nodded their agreement, as did Farzin and Sina. Lying down on the bank, with the grass lisping between their toes, they basked in the sun and their nation's former glory.

∿

I would be leaving Sina in a few days, heading up the Zagros Mountains in search of some of Iran's most extraordinary storytellers. But there were a few more adventures to be had before we parted. . . .

Riding on the back of a hay cart, we made our way to the "Throne of Taqdis," a ring of limestone walls around a tower of scaffolding, where the Nazis sent a team of archaeologists to search for the Holy Grail. It's the only surviving building described in the *Shahnameh*—although sadly it doesn't boast the beaver-skin roof, gold and turquoise tiles, or seats decorated with rams' heads that Ferdowsi locates here. What it does have is a volcanic lake, fed by the thermal springs bubbling underneath it, where we dipped our feet beneath the burned brick ruins of an ancient fire temple.

Farther north, traveling among Kurdish villages, we hooked up with another of Sina's friends and set out in his dodgy Paykan to find the inscription of a tenth-century Kurdish chieftain on an old lichen-crusted bridge. We found the bridge (though sadly not the inscription, which had been removed to the nearby Khorramabad Museum), but the car broke down on the way back and we had to catch a lift with a noble-looking Kurd in a pickup, who had a tasseled turban and a thick twirling mustache like the man on cans of Pringles.

And something else I remember, one of those beautiful, isolated moments that occasionally happen on a journey: being woken up by the reedy whistle of a flute in the early hours of the morning in a house in Khorramabad. Sitting there in the courtyard, on the step outside the guest room, was a beautiful girl, whose eyelashes might have been likened by a medieval poet to "the blades of Kabuli daggers." As soon as she saw me, the flute popped out of her mouth and she wrapped herself up in a scarf. Here in the provinces, the codes of conduct were stricter than in North Tehran, and there was no question of talking to the daughter of the house.

5

Minstrels in the Mountains

Iran. April.

"Get up!"

I was lying on a rug-covered floor high up in the Yellow Mountain—one of the highest points of the Zagros Mountains, which run down the west of Iran like a backbone. I should have known this was a dangerous place to be—after all, I'd been warned: "Undoubtedly they rob," wrote the nineteenth-century explorer Isabella Bird about the Bakhtiari people who inhabit this area, "when and where they can, and they have a horrid habit of stripping their victims, leaving them with but one under garment, if they do not kill them." The point of a pistol was staring me in the face, and the fellow on the other end looked like he meant serious business.

"I want to kill you," he hissed.

He wasn't even going to let me have a last request. He pulled the trigger and I went down. It was the fourth time I'd died that day.

Fortunately, the pistol was made out of plastic and my assailant was four-year-old Behzad, whose grandfather happened to be my host. What a fantastic place! Sina had taken the bus back to Tehran to prepare for next term, while I traveled on alone, passing a few lazy days in the riverbank teahouses of Esfahan before riding up the mountains and stumbling into the village of Deh Cheshmeh, with my backpack and a phone number scribbled down by a friend of the Professor's.

"Mr. Nicholas," announced Behzad's grandfather, Khamandar, on my first night, "you stay for a day or a year, it is no difference!"

Deh Cheshmeh is an idyll, thick with the gurgle of its streams and the cries of the swifts wheeling over the roofs, full of hearty shouts as men with fat red cheeks hail each other through the windshields of their beat-up Paykans and carry firewood down the muddy alleys. At the back of the village, the cliffs raise a protective tower, a waterfall crashing down between hanging spears of ice. A stone victory slab is set beside the "Old Cave," recording the triumph of the Bakhtiari chieftain, Sardar-e Assad, who marched on Tehran in 1909 and caused the abdication of the shah; and on the side of a nearby street stands a carved stone lion, the traditional gravestone for a Bakhtiari warrior.

Back in Tehran, I'd heard all sorts of tales about the Bakhtiaris and their wild ways. They were said to be fond of storytelling and to have retained customs long lost everywhere else; as well as being huge aficionados of the *Shahnameh*. I was eager to meet them. But Bakhtiari country wasn't the kind of place where you could just turn up and ask for the nearest hostel. I needed a calling card—and once again, it was Ferdowsi who provided it.

Khamandar and his family lived in a rickety old brick house just off the village's main street, where the railings teetered off the third-story balcony like they weren't sure to which floor they belonged, and carpets lay scuffed and frayed on the splintering floorboards. Everywhere there was rust and dust and cracked tiles, and when you ventured outside through the abandoned ground floor, it was like you were wading through a ship that's got itself stuck on the mud-flats. But no household could ever have been as warm.

I stayed for a fortnight, and when I wasn't dancing with Khamandar's youngest, flute-playing Roozbeh, mock-wrestling with one of his brothers, or being shot at by Behzad's space gun, I spent my time with the fourth son, Shahrooz. He was a plump, round-faced music graduate, who made his living from reciting at public ceremonies like weddings and funerals and was working on a book about Bakhtiari folklore. He was wonderful company, full of information about the local customs, and like so many Iranians, he had a strong line in bawdy jokes. We would often sit together over a paraffin stove on the top floor—which was where the men of the house had their hangout (the women—Shahrooz's mother and a solitary sister—would always be found on the floor below, surrounded by the ingredients for the next meal). There, we would drink tea served by whoever was the youngest brother in the room and discuss Bakhtiari funeral traditions or the nomadic chants Shahrooz had recorded in the mountains. *The Simpsons* would be playing on the satellite TV, or sometimes something more salacious; once, when a cousin of Shahrooz's had been fiddling with the satellite dish, we spent the night watching naked Dutch mud wrestling.

"But these women must have male relatives!" exclaimed Shahrooz's cousin, seizing a moral high ground that had hardly been conspicuous when he was tuning the TV. "How can you allow them to behave in this way?"

I shrugged: Apparently I was responsible for the moral shortcomings of an entire continent.

"Shut up, you arse-baiter!" yelled Shahrooz with a laugh, launching a drumstick at his cousin and throwing a collegial arm around my shoulder. "Nicholas isn't here for this filth, are you? He's here for Ferdowsi. Now go on, there are plenty of dogs outside if you're getting excited. Me and Nicholas have got poetry to read!"

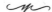

"When Ferdowsi had completed the *Shahnameh*," records the eleventh-century scribe Nizami of Samarkand, "it was transcribed by Ali Daylam and recited by Abu Dulaf . . . and Ferdowsi, taking with him Abu Dulaf, set out for Ghazni." Abu Dulaf would be the first in a long line of reciters—*Shahnameh-khwans* (or "readers of the *Shahnameh*"), as they would come to be known. No other poet was recited so widely that his reciters spawned their own title: proof of the high status of the *Shahnameh* in Iranian culture.

Even in Ferdowsi's own era, there were enough *Shahnameh-khwans* for the name to be commonly used. They are mentioned by one of the poet's rivals, the lyricist Farrukhi, and despite his initial disregard for the *Shahnameh*, Sultan Mahmud is said to have had a *Shahnameh-khwan* of his own. According to a preface in a medieval *Shahnameh* manuscript, "Sultan Mahmud was so fond of him as to always keep his company."

Over the years, the *Shahnameh-khwans* flourished. The fifteenth century found them sitting on a chair and holding an axe. In the seventeenth, the German traveler Olearius noted them standing on stepstools and carrying small canes. More Western visitors spotted them, like the Victorian diplomat Sir Lewis Pelly, who saw them on a "rude dais" in the bazaar, and in the twentieth century, Virginia Woolf's lover, the poet Vita Sackville-West, observed a dervish with a "high hat and orange nails and fierce little eyes flashing out of his hairy face" narrating epic tales in Esfahan.

But where were the *Shahnameh-khwans* now? From the moment mobile cinemas started trundling through Iran's villages in the 1930s, the nation's original entertainers had gone into decline.

"In the past the audience for our stories was huge," declared Abbas Zariri, one of the country's most celebrated twentieth-century reciters. "In those days the Western musicians and the fake heroes of foreign movies had not mesmerized the population yet, and the people naturally liked the national stories and considered them important. . . . Now our art form is approaching dissemination. I have no hopes for the future, nor do I see a way to save this art."

For several weeks, I had been on a *Shahnameh-khwan* hunt. Having encountered so many characters and stories from Ferdowsi's epic—in ancient ruins and religious festivals, in paintings, a puppet opera, and everyday proverbs—I wondered if it could be heard as it was originally intended: in public recital. The way it was heard by Sultan Mahmud when Ferdowsi brought his epic to the royal court of Ghazni all those centuries ago.

So I'd been scouring the teahouses of downtown Tehran, asking if there were likely to be any recitals. The odd fortune-teller came in—aged women with skin like walnut bark and mirror shards in their hands—and there were often paintings of scenes from the *Shahnameh* hanging on the walls. But there was no sign of the reciters themselves. I asked on Molavi Street, as the bazaaris scooped out painted chicks from cardboard boxes and sold scraps of paper, picked out by parakeets, on which were written 650-year-old verses by Hafez, which people would take as portents of their future. And when I traveled outside Tehran, every time I stopped at a teahouse I would ask again. But the response was always the same. A palm was slapped against the other and rubbed down the fingers: the Iranian's emphatic sign of completion: "Finished!"

Apparently, the *Shahnameh-khwans* were dead.

"I have 1,650 verses in my heart!"

In a butcher's shop in the small town of Farsian, where gambrels hung over our heads and soggy mounds of fat and bones were piled in buckets at our feet, Shahrooz introduced me to Rahim e-Yadullahi. The hand stretching over the counter was coarse and sticky, as you'd expect a butcher's hand to be: He'd just finished disemboweling a sheep.

"I have been reciting the *Shahnameh* from the age of seven," said Rahim.

He smoothed his baggy black trousers, cleared a spot on the counter for me to place my Dictaphone, and sat down on a stool.

"I learned it at school," he said, "along with the Quran. When I was ten I was invited to a party at 'the Old Cave,' which is where our people often go when we have celebrations. I read from the *Shahnameh* in front of many people and they liked me."

His favorite story was about the mighty hero Rostam,* who often turns up, like Clint Eastwood in an old western, to succor the good

---

* No legendary champion represents the people of the Persian-speaking world as much as Rostam. He's a lone ranger, living a solitary life in which he is fated, as he laments, to be "an outcast . . . marked out for every kind of ill." Such a lifestyle does have one advantage: Although he appears to bow to the kings, in reality he bows to

people of ancient Iran when all other hope is lost. Here, he faces a steel-clad warrior called Ashkabus, to whom "arrows were just like the wind on his tunic." It was a perfect story for someone like Rahim—a macho tussle between two daredevil warriors, a tale that needed to be expressed in a big, earthy baritone, by a reciter with a chest big enough to provide one. There were several customers in the shop, but they all fell silent as Rahim took a theatrical, air-swooshing draw of breath. Next, his tongue started rattling, like the kettle drum to which Ferdowsi compares Ashkabus's own. He prodded the air with one hand, hauling back his fist as Rostam strung his bow, rapping the other hand on his thigh to count the beat. It was a tough, macho tone, occasionally softened as the warriors take stock, then plunging into the fray at such a tempo you could almost see Rostam throwing himself into his opponent behind the counter. Drawing out the last beat of each line and hurtling through to the climax, Rahim filled up the shop with his rolling delivery, reciting more than fifty couplets without ever hesitating to remember a line, pausing only once, to wipe the saliva off his lips.

More men were gathering in the shop—some after joints of meat, but most of them drawn by Rahim's voice. As Rostam's spearlike arrow was plucked from his victim's breast, all eyes turned to the area around Rahim's feet, as if the defeated Ashkabus were lying there in front of us. A deep-pitched chorus resounded among them: They were pronouncing the *salavat*—"Peace be upon Mohammed and Mohammed's lineage"—the Shia alternative to a round of applause. Unlike the Professor and many of the intellectuals I'd met in Tehran, the Bakhtiaris found no contradiction between their Islamic identity

---

no one. When he is sent an order to fight by the shah, he decides to have a feast instead; and when the shah ticks him off, he thunders back in fury, "I am slave to none but God alone!" This isn't just pride: It's a quality that recurs throughout Iranian history. It is shared by Prime Minister Mossadegh, defying Churchill to nationalize the Anglo-Iranian Oil Company; and by the Afghan *mujahideen*, fighting off the Russians. It explains why the Persian language survived the Arab invasion and why Iranians and Afghans are so antagonistic toward foreign intervention. Because Rostam's defining quality—shared with the poem in which he is celebrated, and with the land it is celebrating—is independence.

and the pre-Islamic legends narrated by Ferdowsi. It was all mixed up, like the sheep's entrails in the bucket. They turned to each other, their faces glowing, and gasps came out along with their praise.

"The *Shahnameh* is the best poem we have," said Rahim, leaning toward me on his stool. "Some people, I know they say it is old, what is its purpose for now? But they do not understand its power."

I wondered what he meant by "power"—something in his tone suggested he wasn't talking about literary effect.

"You want an example? You want to know about the power of the *Shahnameh*?" He beamed at his audience, drawing out a murmur of anticipation. "Then let me tell you about our disputes," he said.

I thought he was going to tell me about a petty argument—perhaps, if a customer was querying the price, Rahim would shut him up with a line from the epic. But, as the *Shahnameh-khwan* continued, it became clear the "disputes" he was talking about were on a far more spectacular scale.

"Five years ago," he explained, "there was a war between two families over who owned some land in a place called Filabad. One of the families, they were related to me, so they asked me to come over to their house and recite for them. There were a hundred people there, all gathered together in the house, getting ready to fight. They needed something to inspire them, to make them ready. So I recited from 'Rostam and Sohrab'—that's the best story for getting people motivated. When I had finished reciting, you could see in their faces they were ready to take part in battle, and they went out onto the plain with sticks and fought against the other family. My recital, I can tell you, it made them ten times stronger! The other side, we scattered them like chaff!"

Rahim laughed as he remembered the occasion, as if it had only been a playground scrap. Lowering a sheep's carcass from one of the gambrels, he started cutting a joint for one of his customers.

"No one was killed," he continued, "thanks to God, and only five people had to go to hospital. When the leader of the other side came up to me afterward, you know what he said?"

He shook his head, chuckling as he carved.

"He said, 'Why did you recite the *Shahnameh*? You made those people very powerful and they hit me very hard.' And he had a scar on his head to prove it!"

Rahim's account of the battle at Filabad was proof of how alive the *Shahnameh* can be, and what a dramatic effect it can have on people's behavior—even if it wasn't being used for an especially peaceful purpose. Over the next few days, Shahrooz introduced me to many more *Shahnameh-khwans*, who all had their own stories of how the epic mattered to them. They lived in different parts of the Bakhtiari province, on farmsteads where the sweet smell of manure followed us up the rattling iron steps into their guest rooms. Their wives and daughters would rearrange their *chadors* to keep them from slipping and slink off to the kitchens to make the tea, while the shiny buttonlike eyes of their grandchildren flashed in the doorjambs. Like Rahim, many spoke of the *Shahnameh* as a motivation for action. One of them, an octogenarian called *Hajji* Murad, who had once performed for the shah, said he used to recite from the epic when he was reaping his crops.

"We would be out in the fields," he explained, "and everyone was tired. So I recited from the *Shahnameh* and at once everybody would work much faster. If it wasn't for the *Shahnameh*, we would have been out in those fields a lot longer!"

The idea that a medieval poem could act so directly on people—a Mr. Motivator of the farms—was incredible: Imagine British farmers accompanying the harvest to renditions of the *Canterbury Tales*. I'd expected to hear comparisons between the poem's stories and people's own experiences—stories similar to Reza's motivation for painting *Zahhak*. What surprised and enthralled me was the direct association between Ferdowsi's epic and the way people actually *behaved*. For the Bakhtiari, Ferdowsi's verses had the same effect as a performance-enhancing drug.

The most remarkable of the *Shahnameh-khwans* I met was Mohammed Bahdarvandi. A lean man in his fifties, with a whiskery, ferretlike face, he sat in his armchair, behind a cloud of cigarette smoke

and tea steam. Twenty years before, he explained, he had been a soldier in the long, terrible war with Iraq.

"We were on the border at Shahramshahr," he said, "about a hundred of us in the division. We had to fight a lot—if we stopped concen-
trating even for a moment they would wipe us out. I remember filling
up my rucksack with grenades and crossing the bridges the Arabs had
built, running through the marshes with our rusty old Kalashnikovs.

"When we were in the trenches, we would be leaning over the
sandbags with our Kalashes, shooting at the enemy, and you could
hear the sound of the bullets all around you. Sometimes the enemy
got close and we needed encouragement, so I knew what would work.
I recited from the *Shahnameh*. I raised my voice as loud as I could, so
everyone could hear it over the sound of the fighting, and I recited
from 'Rostam and Sohrab.' I recited from other stories too, but 'Rostam and Sohrab' was always the best one for getting people in the
mood. I would be shooting at the same time, trying to concentrate
on my Kalash and looking out for the enemy, reciting maybe twenty
or thirty couplets at once. And I have to tell you, there was a great difference. The men became so much stronger—they were inspired!"

I thought of Toghral Arsalan, prince of the Seljuk Turks in the
eleventh century, who is said to have quoted from the *Shahnameh* as
he rode out to battle. But that was centuries ago, soon after the verses
had been composed. With Mohammed, the talk was of burning tanks
and trenches filled with corpses, of barbed-wire entanglements and
minefields, of mortar dropping like rain and a mustard bomb that
put him in hospital for several months. He was speaking about a
modern, brutal, technologically sophisticated war. Yet he and his
comrades still drew inspiration from the thousand-year-old verses of
Ferdowsi.

Reciting long-ago stories is hardly strange when it comes to the
Iran-Iraq war. The *basijis*, who now have a high profile as the regime's
moral enforcers, rose to prominence for their chanting about the
seventh-century Islamic hero Imam Hossain, and the war propaganda machine insisted the men at the front were inspired by the ex-

amples of the early Shia martyrs. Journalists have recounted legions
of stories about men who were coaxed to extraordinary bravery by
these religious narratives. What Mohammed's story showed was that
there were more shades to this war than are usually assumed—the
national stories had their place alongside the religious tales, as a powerful motivation for the soldiers in the trenches.

"Because of my voice," said Mohammed, "they always asked
me to recite at the death ceremonies. I read the *Nawheh* mourning
prayer, and many times I also read from *Shahnameh*. There is so
much in Ferdowsi—things to make you angry, things to help when
you are sad. When I was reading *Shahnameh*, everyone listened. We
were fighting for Iran, so what is better to read than the book of our
history? I remember once, the Iraqis attacked and we shot some of
them and dragged the wounded back to our camp. They shouted,
'God is Great! Khomeini help us!' and we made them our prisoners.
When they heard me reciting from *Shahnameh*, they became very
scared. They didn't understand Persian, but they knew it was epic poetry and it made us strong. They didn't need to know the words to
understand that!"

Staying in Bakhtiari country was a constant adventure. One day
Shahrooz tossed a Beretta pistol into the back of his brother's old
Paykan, along with a microphone and a speaker system.

"Is that really necessary?" I asked.

"Of course!" Shahrooz threw an exasperated arm in the air. "When
the bandits attack, you want to fight them with your hands?"

In the event, the biggest obstacle was the ice: We had to stick grap-
nels to the wheels to steer ourselves through, emerging after half a day
of motorized tobogganing at a mud-brick farmstead near the town of
Bazoft. There in the yard, protected from the snow by a cotton shroud,
was a corpse. It was lying on a tripod of logs, with a cockerel perched
on the dead man's ankles. A string was tied to the bird's claws and its
wattles were vibrating as the other end was wrapped around the dead
man's feet. It jerked forward to take in its audience, its buttonlike eyes

expanding, as if it had been waiting all day for its cue and was determined not to let anyone down.

"This is an old custom," said Shahrooz. "It's from the time when
people here were Zoroastrian. They believed the cockerel would protect the dead person's soul from the devil, because a cockerel stays
awake all night."

Even though the Bakhtiari people are now Muslim, the pre-
Islamic traditions had been preserved—part of the same impulse
that made the stories of the *Shahnameh* so popular in this region.

A large group of men had gathered around the cockerel, but the
cold gradually drove them back, biting through their black-and-
white lamb's-felt coats. Only one of them remained: the dead man's
youngest son, squatting in front of the corpse. His grief lit up his
face, which was red from the slaps as he struck his cheeks. We were
called inside to eat, and as I turned back, he was still crouching by
the wooden tripod, his hair pasty with dust and his tears pouring
out between his fingers.

A Bakhtiari funeral is a spectacle, full of color and noise, in which
everyone has a part to play. We set off at dawn, about fifty of us, in
two clearly segregated columns of men and women. Among the latter, several tossed flatbreads into the air, which scattered on the grass
like cow pies.

"You know what those are for?" asked Shahrooz, jostling me
along with a hand on my arm. "They are to distract the dogs of the
devil so they don't disturb the corpse."

Had Ferdowsi himself been walking alongside us now, much of
the detail—the sheep running after the corpse as it was carried out
of the farmstead; the division of the men and women, the former en-
trusted with the corpse, while the latter did most of the keening; the
corpse itself, wrapped in a blanket and raised by three pallbearers—
would have been familiar. Only the Kalashnikov, wielded by a man at
the front of the cortege and blasted in the air like a trumpet, would
have knitted the poet's brow.

The tenth-century writer al-Hamadani describes "a house whose
master had just died ... It was filled with men ... whose shirts terror

had rent; and with women who had unloosed their hair, and were beating their breasts, cutting their necklaces and slapping their cheeks." I didn't see any necklaces, but some of the women around me were slapping their hands against their chests, and when the procession came to a halt, many of them struck their faces. Some of them were so immersed in grief they had scratched their cheeks, which were slit by dark red lines as if they'd been attacked with razor blades.

Boulders and scree forced a zig-zag down the hill to a river valley, where the dead man's brother and nephew washed the corpse in the stream. Squatting on the bank nearby, the women raised their voices for a ritual song. Their pitch was softer than before, the syllables flowing like they were keeping time to the stream; as if grief's initial stomach punch was mutating into something more mild and accepting, but no less unhappy.

Above us loomed a hillock, where embossed headstones peeked out through the gorse. Here, Shahrooz strapped his speaker to the branches of a tamarisk tree. His song was nasal—a soothing tune spinning around the hillock, drawing the mourners in for the final ritual. Reciting "God is great," they raised their hands in the air, then crammed by a freshly dug pit as the corpse was lowered and the earth piled on top. I retreated to the back, where an old woman was fitting a pile of joss sticks into the niche of a headstone. She struck a match and as a box of dates was passed around, to symbolize the end of the ceremony, the aromatic smoke gently dispersed among the slowly diminishing cries.

Events like the funeral, and my meetings with the *Shahnameh-khwans*, had made my visit to Bakhtiari country a fascinating experience. But there were other days when there was little to do. These I would often spend with Shahrooz's older brothers, Mehran and Faraz. They both had their own houses a few roads down from the family pile, where they often had me over for supper.

"I've got just the film for you tonight!" said Faraz, lying down on the carpet of his living room one evening, while his son Behzad was scrambling about with his space gun.

He switched on the video player, nodding to the overture as we settled over a bowl of okra stew. On the screen in front of us was the mighty hero Rostam, riding at the head of an army under the high peaks of ancient Iran. We were watching *The Timeless Story of Rostam and Sohrab*, a film version of the tale from the *Shahnameh*. It was made in the 1970s by the Tajikistani film director Boris Kimiyagarov, and I had told Faraz many times how much I would love to see it.

Like Shahrooz, Faraz had plenty of contact with the *Shahnameh-khwans*. Working as a teacher and theater director, he'd been involved three years earlier in organizing a province-wide *Shahnameh* festival.

"It was here in Deh Cheshmeh," he explained. "It was a big success and more than a thousand people came, but afterward a mullah complained. He said, 'We have martyrs from the war with Iraq, so it is not suitable to have festivals.' Then, the following year, we organized the festival again. But the Head of Prayer in Farsian told us not to do this. He came to stop the festival, but three thousand people had come to hear the *Shahnameh-khwans* and he was frightened they would attack him, so he ran away. When we wanted to organize the festival again last year, we were forbidden by the municipality. Some of the mullahs, they think the *Shahnameh* is all about the shahs, so they are frightened."

I had come across this conflict before—in the struggle of the Zoroastrians, for example, and the decay at Persepolis: the tussle between the mullahs and the national culture. I would encounter it several times again. Each time, it drew me closer to Ferdowsi's epic, more conscious of the *Shahnameh*'s significance to the country's blazing cultural conflict. And more angry at the way Ferdowsi—the old, broken-backed poet, wandering over the Afghan wastes—was treated by the miserly Sultan Mahmud.

I might not have been able to attend a festival, but the number of *Shahnameh-khwans* I had met certainly made up for it. After struggling to find any in Tehran, it was as if I had been given the secret code to a magic cave: There were enough *Shahnameh-khwans* here to build an army.

But there was one snag, one little drawback that made me wonder if the *Shahnameh-khwan* tradition could genuinely survive: All the *Shahnameh-khwans* I had met were over fifty. Was the trade of reciting from Ferdowsi's epic really on its last legs? On my first night in Deh Cheshmeh, Shahrooz had shown me a video of Reza Heidari, whom he considered the greatest *Shahnameh-khwan* in the region.

"Once," he said, "a mullah was preaching in the mosque when Mr. Heidari started reciting. His voice was so strong, you know what happened? The mullah fell off his pulpit!"

But Heidari had died last year, and the holes left by people like him were becoming harder to fill.

"The young generation don't have our interest," said another Heidari, Mohammed, whose house Shahrooz took me to one afternoon. "When I was a child we would sit around the oil lamp and listen to stories from the *Shahnameh*. We were interested in our ancient stories. But now the young people want to play computer games and watch TV. And in their school textbooks there isn't as much *Shahnameh* as there was before the revolution, so they don't learn about it as much."

I wanted to find a young *Shahnameh-khwan*—to find out if the *Shahnameh* still had the power to stir a new generation. I felt this was an important issue. To people like Mohammed Heidari, the conflict wasn't just between the mullahs' regime and the national culture, it was a three-way contest that included the new entertainment coming in from the West, and the latter was at least as much of a threat to the national culture. But if there was a young *Shahnameh-khwan*, somebody for whom the old stories still mattered—it would suggest that the culture championed by Ferdowsi hadn't yet run out of steam.

Whenever I asked Shahrooz, he would shrug, reminding me of what Heidari had said:

"It is the old *Shahnameh-khwans* who are interesting."

Perhaps the *Shahnameh-khwans* really were heading for extinction. I hoped this wasn't so and kept asking if there were any younger reciters, but it wasn't until my last evening with Shahrooz's family that I was offered a chink of light. Big Dad Khamandar was pouring out the curdled milk, while his daughter passed the dishes from the kitchen, when Shahrooz came bursting into the room.

"You still want to meet a young *Shahnameh-khwan*?" he asked.

"Yes, of course!"

"So tomorrow it happens!"

Another mud-brick house, with potted plants and cushions against the walls. Sitting there, cross-legged on the carpet, was sixteen-year-old Mohammed Abbas. As we stepped through the door, he leaped to his feet, pressing a hand against his chest. His eyes were big and bright, but his face was pale, as if he spent a lot of time indoors, and it lengthened as he sat down, steadying his hands on the edge of a huge brown leather-bound *Shahnameh*. He was the grandson of *Hajji* Murad, one of the *Shahnameh-khwans* we'd already met, and after talking to the *Hajji*, Shahrooz had been granted permission to meet with Mohammed.

As with the other *Shahnameh-khwans*, there was little variation in his tone. But rather than the military beat of Rahim the butcher, Mohammed's had a nasal, mystical flavor—more incantation than chant, intoned rather than announced. He sank deep into the stresses, wheeling around the verse. The pitch rose suddenly, or fell in a dying cadence, or he held onto the last vowel for an age, the muscles of his face tense and his mouth almost closed, as if the death of the hero Sohrab was a physical object in his mouth and he was trying to keep it from getting out.

"When Mohammed recited at the Old Cave," said his father, "many people cried, even the famous scholar Dr. Junaidi."

"I also became sad," said Mohammed, "because I was reciting a sad story. But," he added, with a teenager's defiant cock of the chin, "I never cry."

"Do your school friends read the *Shahnameh*?" I asked.

"I am the only one. Sometimes in class the teacher says, 'recite *Shahnameh*,' and some of my classmates cry. I like to read *Shahnameh*. I learned it from my grandfather and I want to read it in the future. I will be reading it even when I am eighty!"

He smiled as he said this, and I couldn't help but smile back. Here, as much as Reza's *Zahhak* painting, was proof of how alive Ferdowsi's epic can be. His peers might be into computer games and TV, but I felt sure that Mohammed's interest in the *Shahnameh* was genuine—he expressed it, after all, in the emotive cadences of his voice.

As he dipped once again into the recital, everyone sat back to listen, mesmerized by the magic of the thousand-year-old words—the "power" Rahim the butcher had spoken about. It galvanized the fighters at Filabad, it helped *Hajji* Murad to reap his crops, it spurred Mohammed Bahdarvandi and his fellow soldiers in the war with Iraq, and a few months later, it would inspire me too, to take the sunblistered road to Afghanistan. . . .

PART TWO

~m~

AFGHANISTAN

"You who for others' torment do not care
Cannot the name of human rightly bear."
— SA'DI, *THE ROSE GARDEN*

6

The Prisoner Poets

Herat. September.

"The war began here!"

I rub my eyes and try to concentrate. Thanks to the dogs, acting out King Kong versus Godzilla under my window at the Hotel Successful, I am in no state for an early-morning debate. But fortunately my breakfast partner isn't looking for input.

"How can the people tolerate a foreign power?" he exclaims, smearing cherry jam onto his bread.

The crumbs dribble down his beard, which is performing the function of a napkin, collecting anything that hasn't made it into his mouth.

"So the people rose against the Soviets," he continues, "and they killed the Communist agents and their families."

"Their families?"

"Of course! Then the Soviets told the army commander to punish the people, but the commander was Ismail Khan. Ha! He was no Russian donkey! He took his men to the hills, and the war began!"*

---

* The Russians, furious at the insurrection, sent in their tanks and gunships, killing around 20,000 civilians, whose corpses were buried in the hills outside Herat, near the shrine of the Sufi saint Abdullah Ansari. Ismail Khan, however, survived and continued fighting the Russians throughout their ten-year stay in Afghanistan.

Standing in the plaster-shower of my room's balcony after break-fast, I have a view right across Herat. You can tell it's been through a fight. Not just because of the roadwide craters, the walls perforated like cheese biscuits and the belch of the jackhammers, but because of the very fact you can see right across it: multi-stories don't last long in a war zone. This means I can take in the Paropamisus Mountains to the north and the *musalla** minarets—a copse of towers I passed last night on the way into the city. Still patched in parts with tiling as blue as the sky into which they have been leaning since the fifteenth century, they stand about eighty feet high. But what's surprising is that they stand at all. They are characteristic of the city: Although much of it was smashed up by the Russians, the *mujahideen*, and the Taliban, its landmarks have been blessed with surprisingly good luck.

Red woolen tassels swing off the bridles as tongas *clip-clop* past the Friday Mosque. Auto-rickshaws *tuk-tuk* past the florists' shops and burka stores, a clatter to the chime of the bicycle bells, the buzzing of drills and the squawk from the chickens sold in plastic cages on the sidewalks. Medieval Herat's most prolific export—grapes**—inspire a boom from the vendors, wheeling their produce on handcarts that squeak among the sellers of giant pumpkins and bright purple egg-plants, while on the roof terraces above them, soldiers silently tote their Kalashnikovs as they watch out for insurrection. Rising across a dried-up moat behind them, with fat round towers swelling at its corners, is the citadel. Plastic kites swoop among its ramparts, one of them trapping itself between the battlements as a small boy tugs help-lessly at his string.

---

* Literally "place of worship," referring to a religious compound built in 1417 by Queen Gowhar Shad.

** According to the eleventh-century scribe Nizami of Samarkand, the city boasted 120 varieties, which helped to make it a particularly fructiferous place—especially in the autumn, when eglantine, basil, and yellow rocket were in bloom. In the tenth century, Prince Nasr of Bukhara was so enchanted by Herat that he considered it superior even to the Garden of Eden.

This is the hub of old Herat. When Ferdowsi came by a thousand years ago, en route to the court of Sultan Mahmud at Ghazni, it's here he would have stayed. Although the citadel has been rebuilt, it is in the same location as in the poet's era, when Herat boasted "a castle with ditches . . . in the center of the town," according to the tenth-century geographer Ibn Hawkal, "fortified with very strong walls." Nearby is the Friday Mosque—another building that's been rebuilt but is still in the same spot. I sit down on a cool marble ledge in its central courtyard and start jotting in my notebook.

Men wearing turbans long enough to stitch a shroud are carrying their shoes as they march up the courtyard and prostrate themselves in a hall to the left of the main prayer niche. The tiles around them conjure a Persian garden—flowers, tendrils and fronds twisting up to the lancelike ligatures of the holy lettering, while geometric patterns swathe the minarets in the ceramic counterpart of a Persian carpet. It's making me dizzy, so I jump off the ledge and set out to do some fieldwork.

When Ferdowsi "alighted in Herat," according to the scribe Nizami of Samarkand, he stayed "at the shop of (the poet) Azraqi's father, Ismail the Bookseller." He would have spent much of his time among the literati, and I'm hoping to do the same. Although Afghanistan's political capital has shifted over the centuries, Herat has always been its cultural heart, beating with the lines of its poets and pumping out the new techniques to the rest of the country.

There was a city here long before Alexander the Great turned up. He had it rebuilt, as "Alexandria of the Aryans," and when Sultan Mahmud was taking charge of the region more than a millennium later, it was the capital of Khorasan, a playboy's playground where Mahmud's son had naughty pictures painted on the walls of his palace. But it was in the fifteenth and sixteenth centuries, under the Timurids—the dynasty started by the "world-shaker," Tamerlane or "Timur the Lame"—that Herat reached its political and cultural peak.

It's hard to decide what or who was responsible for the city's vitality at this time. Several fingers point toward Tamerlane's daughter-in-law, Gowhar Shad, the "Happy Jewel," who organized the construction of a college and mosque near the *musalla* minarets and whose influence in public matters suggests women were treated with a lot less contempt than they would be five hundred years later under the Taliban. Not only were mosques and minarets being raised: The court historian Mirkhwand was constructing an enormously influential "History of the World," while the miniaturist painter Kamaluddin Behzad was running a world-famous academy. A master of light and dark, he soaked his paintings in the rich colors with which Persian culture is associated (as well as the spiritual imagery of Sufi mysticism). And when he wasn't conjuring princesses in silver-leaf pools or ancient shahs in fields of malachite, he would mix with the cultural high society of the day—poets like Abdur-Rahman Jami and Alishir Navoi. Herat was so full of scribblers at this time that the latter objected, "You can't stretch a leg without poking a poet in the arse."

Wandering through the cracked, dusty streets of Herat today, it's hard to imagine the vibrant city of Behzad and Navoi, and even harder to imagine such a richness of culture ever being revived. In 1507, a tribe of Uzbeks came raiding from the north; just three years later, the Persian shah Ismail Safavi weighed in, drinking a victory toast from the Uzbek chieftain's skull. Herat would never be at the center of things again—at least, not until the anti-Soviet uprising and Ismail Khan's insurrection in 1979—the event described by my napkin-bearded breakfast partner. But even though recent years can hardly compete with the shining light of the Happy Jewel, I've heard that the Russian tanks and cluster bombs haven't entirely snuffed this culture out. So I stroll past a row of bookshops behind the Hotel Successful, looking to find out what is left of it.

"We were open even under the Taliban!"

Ustad (or "Master") Rajey, the gray-bearded chairman of Herat's official "Literary Society," is sitting on a back-buttoned sofa with a glass of green tea. The society, he says, has been around since 1932, when Afghanistan was run by a king.* None of the tempests of the country's turbulent late twentieth-century history have managed to finish it off—not the fall of the last king, Zahir Shah, in a coup, nor the Russian invasion, nor the civil war and the rise of the Taliban,** although it wasn't at its most active under the latter.

---

* That king was Nader Shah, who was assassinated during a military parade about a year later. He was succeeded by his son, Zahir Shah, who became one of the country's longest-serving monarchs, but also one of its most ineffectual. A studious nineteen-year-old with a passion for miniature paintings, he hardly welcomed the role that had been thrust upon him. He'd been walking with his father when the assassin's shots rang out, and his trepidation may have been increased by the fact that, of the three previous kings, two had been forced to flee and the other murdered in his sleep. One of these, Amanullah, decided that Afghanistan needed westernizing. Advising his tribal chiefs to shave their beards and wear top hats and tails, he embarked on a series of reforms—including coeducational schools, a minimum age for marriage, and, most notoriously of all, a demand for women to shed the veil. To most Afghan men, a man whose wife let her hair out in public clearly didn't deserve their obedience, so within a couple of years, Amanullah was fleeing the country in his beloved Rolls-Royce.

Zahir Shah was more cautious, but like Amanullah he had a fondness for the ways of the West. Slowly, he introduced some of its better innovations, like free speech, the right to form political parties and women's suffrage. But economic reform was slow and a three-year drought at the turn of the '70s put him in a vulnerable position, which was exploited in 1973 by his cousin Daoud, who in traditional Afghan style arranged a coup and seized the royal palace, where he would be assassinated by his own air force five years later, as the Communist party and the Russians took control.

** Who emerged originally as a check to the immorality of some of the *mujahideen* (the guerrillas who had ousted the Russians and, in the early 1990s, started fighting against each other over who would rule the country). In 1994, a *mujahideen* leader paraded a small boy on his tank as his "bride" and squabbled over the boy's possession with another *mujahideen* chief. Disgusted by this behavior, a half-blind cleric called Mullah Omar led a gang of his students on a raid of the *mujahideen* leader's HQ, hanging him from the gun of his own tank.

This, at least, is the legend. The students (or *taliban*) grew from strength to strength, providing order where there had previously been chaos, and at first they were welcomed, especially among Pashtun communities that shared the Taliban's ethnicity. But gradually their policies (such as banning kite-flying, stuffed toys and laughter) and especially their punishments (such as cutting off women's fingers and hanging people from lampposts) lost them the initial goodwill. In non-Pashtun, Persian-speaking Herat, they were always unpopular, as several conversations would reveal.

"Women weren't allowed," he explains, "and you couldn't write about politics. Or," he adds, scratching his beard with a sigh, "print photos. Or write about foreign languages."

Those who did tended to find themselves on the wrong end of a Taliban whip. But one subject you could write about was the *Shahnameh*, and Master Rajey has published many articles about it.

"Ferdowsi didn't just write about the history of Iran," he says. "It is the history of Afghanistan too, of the Aryan people and our Aryan culture. In fact, many of the most famous stories take place here, not in Iran. The people of Afghanistan love *Shahnameh*. In the winter, people sit in the villages and the *Shahnameh-khwans* recite the stories."

This talk about "Aryans" has recurred throughout my journey. "Iran" comes from the same root as "Aryan" and refers to the Aryan roots of the ancient Iranian people—migrants from the Eurasian steppes who emerged on the Iranian plains around 4,000 years ago.* The Persian-speaking Afghans, who dominate the west and north of Afghanistan, share this root—and therefore the stories told in the *Shahnameh*. In one of the epic's most romantic stories, the princess of Kabul lets down a tower's length of hair so her lover can climb up to meet her—a parallel with Rapunzel, whose story was unearthed by the Brothers Grimm from Germany's stock of ancient Aryan tales. Another story, the tale of Rostam and Sohrab (which I saw at the puppet opera in Tehran), shares a remarkable amount of detail with the Irish legend of Cú Chulainn, who also tricks his unknown son and kills him. It's no coincidence that the names of Ireland (or Eire) and Iran come from the same root. Long before Hitler made Aryanism unpalatable, it suggested a shared ancestry spanning the Indo-European world.

For me, here in Herat, what this talk of Aryanism emphasizes most of all is the close ethnic relationship between Iranians and Afghans. Both of Afghanistan's dominant tribal groups—the Pashtuns and the

---

* One of the earliest recorded references to the Aryans is carved into a cross-shaped, rock-cut tomb from the fifth century BCE that I visited a few months earlier in Iran, near the old royal palace of Persepolis. There, King Darius the Great describes himself as "an Aryan, of Aryan lineage."

Persian-speaking Tajiks—trace their origins to the Aryans (hence the national airline is called Ariana), although this didn't stop them from falling out in the brutal civil war that scorched the country throughout the 1990s. Pashtun commanders burned the homes of Persian-speaking civilians, whose only crime was not being Pashtun, while the allies of the revered Persian-speaking commander, Ahmed Shah Massoud, raped Pashtun women in reply. To many people in Herat, what made the Taliban especially obnoxious was not their repressive laws (as several of the city's literati pointed out, the Persian-speaking leaders such as Ismail Khan were only a little less severe) but the fact they were Pashtun; and they made themselves especially unpopular by banning the speaking of Persian in public.

The link between Iran and Afghanistan is emphasized again when I step off a dusty alley, inside the metal gate of an elegant courtyard house. Sitting in a room at the top, spinning on a swivel chair in front of his computer, is a man with slicked-back hair and a leather jacket—like a rocker from the '50s. He is Saeed Haqiqi, a correspondent for the BBC Persian Service, and also one of Herat's most prominent poets.

"Two hundred years ago," he says, "the region of Khorasan was both Iran and Afghanistan. And we have people in Afghanistan who are living on this side of the border, but their relatives are on the other side. Our culture is the same."

It would certainly have been the same for Ferdowsi. For him, there would be no crossing between Iran and Afghanistan. Herat would be part of the same province as his own city, Tus, administered by the same governor—Amir Nasr, the brother of Sultan Mahmud. But it isn't just geography that's linked—so is time. As I talk to Haqiqi, I realize that whether we are talking about Ferdowsi's era or now, the writers would still have difficulties to face.

"The Taliban were such monsters," exclaims Haqiqi, with a small tilt of his head. "They destroyed our library. In fact, the only books that were saved were the ones we moved before they could get to them. And if you wrote what you thought, you were in big trouble. There was one writer I knew who wrote about his ideas and he was given thirty lashes with a whip."

I wonder what the eleventh-century religious scholar Baghawi of Herat would think of this. "The ink of the learned is holier than the blood of the martyr," he wrote, citing this as a saying of the Prophet Mohammed himself. Like the teachings of Jesus, misapplied by Crusaders and Conquistadors, Mohammed's words have been twisted and abused by the very people who claim to be his closest followers. The ink of the learned is rarely deemed holy enough to spare their blood from being spilled.

I think of Ferdowsi and the writers who suffered in his era. Men like the lyricist Farrukhi, who was for a long time one of Sultan Mahmud's favorites, but ended his life in poverty; the polymath Ibn Sina, who was chased around the region for several years because news of Mahmud's tempestuous attitude toward scholars had reached him before the sultan's army; the scholar Biruni, who once spent six months in confinement for outsmarting the sultan.* I think of the stories of Sultan Mahmud's soldiers making bonfires of "heretical" books—which were matched a millennium later by the Taliban—and of the way by which writers in this area have always worked their way around censorship.

"We use images like night and storms," explains Haqiqi, "even now, although the situation is more open, because we have got into the habit of using symbols. So the poets who were using symbols in the Taliban time, now they have a chance to say it openly, but they can't, because they are accustomed to writing in symbols."

---

* He aroused Sultan Mahmud's ire when he correctly predicted how he would exit his summer house. The sultan thought he had Biruni outwitted by smashing a hole through a wall and making his exit that way. But Biruni knew the sultan pretty well by this time, so he had written that outcome down on a piece of paper. As a result, the sultan did what any self-respecting megalomaniac might have done in his place—he had Biruni hurled off the rooftop, where he was saved by a conveniently placed mosquito net. When it turned out Biruni had predicted this too (he'd written in his almanac, "Today they will cast me down from a high place, but I shall reach the earth in safety, and arise sound in body"), Mahmud was so enraged he had Biruni incarcerated. It was six months before he finally relented and set the scholar free, presenting him with a gold-caparisoned horse, a slave and a handmaid, along with gifts of money, a royal robe, and a satin turban—proof of how helter-skelter life at Mahmud's court could be.

When I turned up in his office, Haqiqi looked the archetype of Afghan cool. But now his chin is sinking between his hands as he explains how peculiarly his perspective has been skewered.

"When the Taliban were in power," he says, "I wrote two poems a day. But now I am lucky if I write one poem a month. You understand? The cause of my anger has gone."

"You mean—?"

"The Taliban were really bad," he says. "But I had so much to write—and I'm a poet!"

How insane—and yet how much sense it makes—for a writer to long for the good old days when, okay, maybe people were being whipped in the streets and strung up on lampposts, but at least he was getting regular visits from his muse.

Talking to Haqiqi makes me think about the Professor back in Tehran and all the troubles he's suffered. I remember a friend of his, a magazine editor called Ardashir, who was imprisoned in the early days of the Iranian revolution for membership in the Communist Party (although in fact he wasn't a member—his name was in the address book of someone who was).

"Sometimes the guards would tie me to a bed," he said, "and they whipped me with cable wires. Other times they just boxed me with their fists. I thought they would kill me, and then they would print my picture in the papers next day, saying, 'this was an enemy of the Revolution.' When I heard the gunshots at night, I thought it would be me next. But," he said, lifting his hands as if to thank God, "I survived."

Stories like this are a reminder of how widely cultural oppression has cast its shadow in the recent history of the Persian-speaking world. But they take me back in time too: They add another shade to my image of Ferdowsi—of the ragged old man carrying his life's work to Sultan Mahmud. I think of the Professor's words that afternoon, several months ago, at the university in Tehran: "Bright-thinkers in this country, we always had difficulties. Look at Ferdowsi!" And that's what I do—I look at Ferdowsi, and I see him at the front of a line stretching all the way to the writers I'm meeting now. It seems there is a little bit of Ferdowsi in these writers; and there's a little bit of them in my image of Ferdowsi.

If any of these writers captures the spirit of the tenth-century poet, it's Jalali. Officially, he is a flower seller. Short and squat, with a blue waistcoat over his *shalwar qameez*, he has a bald, shiny head like an enameled egg, tufted around the sides with scrags of hair. There is something of the gnome about him as he waddles into his shop and hauls himself onto a stool. Strings of marigolds dangle off the shelves above him, while button daisies and begonias are lying in cellophane wrapping, alongside a bunch of plastic ferns, and the familiar smell of the florist's—earthy as well as fragrant—wafts around us.

"I write about the suffering of the people," he announces, leaning close as he adds, "so of course in the Taliban time I had plenty of material! I had to distribute my poems in secret—after all, I didn't want them to kill me. But they still took me to jail six times, once for seven months."

"Why?" I ask.

"I wrote a poem about the Taliban—I said they are onions. Because their turbans look like onions and they are as brainless as vegetables. But they couldn't prove it was me, so they only jailed me."

He shakes his head as the memories express themselves in his frown.

"No radio, no paper . . . Oh! Can you imagine what this is like for a writer? And all we ever got to eat was bread, bread, bread!"

His poems have the earthy, irreverent texture of the medieval satirists. One compares the Taliban's moral police to "long-tailed donkeys." Another mocks Mullah Omar (the Taliban leader), when he paraded the Prophet Mohammed's sacred cloak in Kandahar, describing him as dung dressed in an ass hide.

"I wrote whenever I could," says Jalali, "as long as there was kerosene I would write throughout the night. And I hid my poems in a secret place in my house."

"But how did people read your poems?" I ask.

"Sometimes they didn't need to. The children would hear my verses and chant them behind the backs of the Taliban, and then they would run away before they were caught."

It wasn't only the Taliban he criticized. He speaks of Ismail Khan and the other *mujahideen* leaders with equal contempt, because after the Soviets withdrew they went on pilgrimage to Mecca and announced the fighting was over.

"But then," he fumes, "they came back and the fighting started all over again! So I criticized them, because that is a writer's duty, isn't it? Throughout history, most poets were on the side of the leader. If you look at the kings and their courts, they were always full of poets, *terrible* poets—dishing out praise and groveling on their knees, just so the rulers would fill up their mouths with gold. But not all of them! You know about Sadi Salman? No? Well, let me tell you about him— he *wasn't* on the side of the leader. He was for the people! And because of this he was in jail for twenty years in the time of the Ghaznavids."*

A customer has come in, asking for a funeral wreath. Jalali drops off his stool, taking me by the arm to the door, peering out onto the street to check the wrong people aren't listening. I can hear the autorickshaws *tuk-tuk*ing past, and the cawing of the pigeon-doves in a plane tree over the road.

"You know how many poets there were in Herat under the Taliban?" he says. "Maybe thirty. But I was the one in jail, because I was the one who spoke for the people. It's the same with Ferdowsi. He was for the people, not for the leaders, and this is why he had such a big problem with Sultan Mahmud."

He rubs his palms together, filling the air with a long, resigned sigh and the earthy scent of his hands.

"If you are for the people," he adds, "you will always suffer."

---

* He spent so much time in jail that he perfected the "Habsiya," a genre of poetry specifically about jail. "Ever since I was born," he wrote, "O wonder! I am a captive . . . How long, O heaven, will you continue every hour hammering on my brain? Why, I am not an anvil!"

Over several days in Herat, I meet up with many more writers, who all have their own tales of oppression under the Taliban. Few of them share Saeed Haqiqi's ambivalence—most are happy to see the back of a regime that was so hostile to creative thinking, although wary of what the current regime has to offer. Among them is a stout, gray-bearded university lecturer, Dr. Mohammed Rahyab, who meets me on the university campus and tells me about the cunning ways in which he circumnavigated the Taliban's restrictions.

"Poetry is in our blood," he exclaims, sitting down behind a wooden desk in his classroom, "so how could the Taliban stop us? A line of verse can bring an end to a family feud, or it can stop a fight. You know what they wanted me to do? They wanted me to teach only Islamic jurisprudence and the Quran. But they were ignorant fools—how would they know what I was teaching? I grew a very long beard and never criticized them in public, and I taught exactly the same subjects as before: stylistics, literary criticism, foreign writers like Shakespeare and Nabokov."

I think of the medieval poet Sa'di, who wrote, "If you cannot cut the hand of the king, then it is best to kiss it." Dr. Rahyab has been practicing the old Persian knack for dividing the public and the private. This is emphasized, most of all, by the solution he found for one of his biggest dilemmas: the Taliban's ban on teaching female students.

"I wasn't having it at all!" he exclaims. "Why should girls not be allowed to learn? I told them to come to my house, and if anyone asked what they were doing they said they were going to tailoring lessons. They carried needles and thread in case anyone checked, and when the officials looked in, my wife would pretend she was teaching them to sew."

One of these students is a young woman in her twenties, called Nadia Anjoman. She greets Dr. Rahyab on the creaking veranda outside his faculty, smiling shyly under eyelashes thick with mascara.

"I wanted to shout when the Taliban were in power!" she fumes. Her lips are brightly rouged, but as she talks, they stretch across her face, expressing her anger. "The poems I wrote in those days," she says, "they were like shouting. I didn't really know how to write so well, because how could I learn? Sometimes I would gather with other girls to discuss our poems, but even this was difficult because it was hard to leave our houses. The Taliban wanted us to be like cows in a shed. They didn't want us to play any part in society, not even to do the shopping. But you know, it isn't just the Taliban who don't like poetry. Sometimes . . . "

She stops, flicking back a strand of hair that's fallen from her scarf, and turns to a sheaf of papers in her hands. She starts sifting through them, as if she's forgotten about our conversation, and it is only when Dr. Rahyab has led us into one of the classrooms that she speaks again.

Among the papers in the sheaf are some of her handwritten poems. She is compiling a collection of them for a volume, called "The Crimson Flower." She puts them down on a wooden desk, shaking her head as she holds on to them, her eyebrows drawing an arched, suspicious expression across her face.

"Where could we even publish them?" she says. "For men in this time it was difficult, sure, but for a girl it was a hundred times worse."

She is frowning, but for a moment her face relaxes, her cheeks lifting ever so slightly, and she loosens her hold on the poems.

"We did," she says, "have one advantage—because the Taliban didn't try to encounter women, so it was easy to go behind their backs. We would go to our teacher's home and take lessons there, but always in secret. In those times, everything I wrote was about my rage. It's only now that I am writing artistic poems."

I look at one of the verses, trying to work out its meaning, which I'm unable to fathom until later in my hotel room:

"*Don't search for the meaning of joy in me, all the joy in my heart has died. / If you are looking for stars in my eyes, it is a story that doesn't exist.*"

For the moment, all I understand is the sadness underpinning Nadia's words. I imagine her, sitting alone in a tiny room, with a pencil and a sheet of paper, pouring herself—pouring all the expression that's forbidden on the streets—into those pages.

"Good luck," I say.

She smiles, stretching out a hand—a unique occurrence for me from a woman in Afghanistan—and lightly touching the ends of my fingers. I have jotted down some of her other verses in my notebook and I'm hoping I will be able to work out what they mean, but the journey distracts me. A whole year will pass before I look again at Nadia's words—inspired to do so by a terrible piece of news.

"*I am caged in this corner / Full of melancholy and sorrow . . . / My wings are closed and I cannot fly . . . / I am an Afghan woman and so must wail.*"

The report is imprecise. Apparently Nadia's family disapproved of her verse, and after her book came out they were ashamed. It is her husband who is arrested. He says she poisoned herself, but that doesn't explain the bruises on her body. If her family permitted an autopsy perhaps the truth would be established, but they don't. So Nadia is buried, just twenty-six years into her life, with so much left unlived and unwritten, and all that is left of her are those sad, claustrophobic verses.

> *What should I do with a trapped wing,*
> *Which does not let me fly?*
> *I have been silent too long,*
> *But I never forget the melody,*
> *Since every moment I whisper*
> *The songs from my heart,*
> *Reminding myself of*
> *The day I will break this cage,*
> *Fly from this solitude*
> *And sing like a melancholic.*

Nadia Anjoman RIP.

7

M

Tea with a Warlord

Herat. September.

Of all the poets with whom Ferdowsi could have rubbed shoulders in Herat, by far the most significant wouldn't have been tall enough to tug the poet's beard. His name was Abdullah Ansari and he was the four-year-old son of a shopkeeper. Although the lack of children in the *Shahnameh* suggests Ferdowsi wouldn't have been especially alert to his potential, it would have been clear he was a child of exceptional promise—only a couple of years later, he had succeeded in learning the whole of the Quran by heart. Encouraged by his father, who didn't envisage a future for him stacking shelves at the family store, he tramped around Khorasan visiting the great Sufi mystics of his age. Inspired by these experiences, he composed the first mystical verses to be written in Persian*—dramatic, visual poems that captured the public imagination:

> *I see breasts scorched by the burning separation from you;*
> *I see eyes weeping in love's agony.*
> *Dancing down the lane of blame and censure,*
> *Your lovers cry out, "Poverty is my source of pride!"*

---

* The dominance of Persian poets in Sufi literature is a testament to the language's genius for poetry as well as its suitability for mysticism. Apart from Ibn Arabi, there are no Sufi poets in Arabic who reach the depth or lyrical beauty of the great Persian

"A Sufi," Ansari wrote, "is something that neither harms the soles of the feet nor leaves a trail of dust behind." The tracks to their origin are certainly hard to trace. Some scholars connect them to neo-Platonism or ancient India. Ferdowsi agrees with the latter, linking them in the *Shahnameh* to the ascetics who hung around with Alexander the Great. But it is with Islam they are intimately associated, as the mystical expression of that faith. Although, since mysticism and orthodoxy have never been great friends, they have often found themselves in conflict with more literal-minded theologians.

Ansari was accused of anthropomorphism and banned from teaching by an assembly of sheikhs—the Taliban of their day. He was also exiled and spent a short period in prison. But he was back in favor toward the end of his life—invested with a robe of honor by the caliph and the title "sheikh of Islam." He retired to Herat and there, in a convent built by one of his own teachers, he died. And it's there, as I am about to discover, that his memory lives on.

The smell of resin is pinching my nose, wafting out of the umbrella pines soaring over the taxi. A plain of powdery white sand spreads underneath us, like we're sliding into a giant sugar bowl. About three kilometers away is Mount Gazurgah, hunched over a pastry-colored tomb complex as if it's made out of hard blocks of toffee.

Marble headstones fill the court, framed in a horseshoe of brickwork with a hundred-foot *iwan* rising out of its groin. I clamber around the graves, toward a tree on which stones have been tied and nails driven into the branches, the latter ritual carried out as a tradi-

---

Sufis: poets like Rumi (who numbers Madonna in his modern-day fanbase), Hafez (the most revered of all poets in Iran), and my personal favorite among the Sufis, Farid ud-Din Attar (whose *Conference of the Birds* sprinkles tales of nonconformity into an overarching narrative about the flight of the world's birds in search of their one true king). The great Perso-phile Edward Browne suggested there may be another reason for the popularity of Sufism among the Persians: that it was "a reaction of the Aryan mind against the Semitic religion imposed on it." The same point is made by the Indian scholar Mohammed Habib, to whom "The development of mysticism in Islam was mainly the work of Persian thinkers." If this theory holds, then Persian Sufism shares with the *Shahnameh* an impulse to steer away from the Sunni Arab hegemony.

tional remedy for toothache. I can hear a tremendous grunt—a deep "aghhh!" Behind the tree is a group of dervishes, all dressed in dusty brown *shalwar qameez*. They are holding hands in a circle, and one of them is singing in counterpoint to the grunts. The "agh!" slows and stretches, an "l" forming between two vowels, and eventually clarifies as the word they are repeating: "Allah."

I've come across Sufis before, a few years earlier in Turkey—the Whirling Dervishes, who wore cone-shaped camel-hair hats and pirouetted in a sophisticated and dizzying dance. But these Afghan Sufis are much earthier (if one can describe a process designed to heighten your spiritual senses as earthy). There is no discernible art to what they are doing, instead an extreme concentration—a detachment from everything around them. This is Sufism at its most raw.

At the foot of the *iwan*, decorative tendrils climb toward the stalactite drum of a carved headstone. The dry, silvery branches of an ilex tree reach out over it, to the worshippers who perch on the ledges of the graves, raising their hands, prayer beads, and voices, and bowing to the tomb of Ansari.

One of them is reciting from a beat-up copy of Ansari's most popular work, *The Intimate Conversations*,* but his words are drowned by the grunt thickening beside him. It is coming from an old man with an enormous gray beard, who is rocking between a pair of headstones. His cheeks are smudged with tears as he repeats "Allah, Allah, Allah," the words shooting so fast he barely has time to breathe. His torso is swinging so hard that he's in danger of being knocked out by his own beard.

What is going through his mind? There is no opportunity to ask: he has cocooned himself in the world of meditation and for him at least it is soundproof. But as he swings to the name of God, I think of a contemporary of Ansari's, Abu Sa'id, who described how his "breast was opened" by hearing that same word in a Sufi convent. "Whenever

---

* A collection of thoughts addressed to God, in which Ansari rejects the traditional boons of paradise, like the luxurious mansions and the black-eyed virgins, just as the dervishes around his tomb were rejecting the world as they called out God's name—a practice evoked in *The Intimate Conversations*, in which every stanza opens with the cry "O God."

drowsiness of inattention arising from the weakness of human nature came over me," he related, "a soldier with a fiery spear—the most terrible and alarming figure that can possibly be imagined—appeared in front of the niche and shouted at me, saying, 'Abu Sa'id, say Allah!' The dread of that apparition used to keep me burning and traveling for whole days and nights, so that I did not again fall asleep or become inattentive; and at last every atom of me began to cry aloud, 'Allah! Allah! Allah!'"

All around me, men are reciting it: "Allah! Allah! Allaghh! Alaghh! Aaghh! Agh! Agh!" If Ferdowsi had visited this convent a thousand years ago—and with his range of interests it's tempting to imagine he could have done—this is the same sight and sound he would have encountered. I sit down on a headstone, switching on my Dictaphone to record the recitals and jotting in my notebook. But it's hard to write, because several men are crowding behind me, apparently as intrigued by my scrawl of Roman script as I am by the clustered dots and coils of Persian and Arabic on the headstones.

"You came here," one of them asks, "to pray to Ansari?"

"Well . . . "

"You have a problem with the law?"

"Why would? . . . "

"You are going on a difficult journey?"

"Well . . . Yes! Yes, that's it."

He is called Abdul Aziz. Around the same age as me, in his late twenties, he has more beard than me but less hair on top. Smiling with soft, watery eyes, he takes me by the hand and leads me into a small mud-brick hut near the entrance to the compound, where we cross our legs on the earthy floor and drink black tea sweetened with lumps of fudge. From the other side of the room, the fruity smell of a water pipe is seeping into our nostrils.

"Really," he says, "you are praying to Ansari? This is wonderful! I also pray to him when I have a problem. Many people here do, but I never met a foreigner who did this."

I am about to confess: "Well, I wasn't exactly . . . "

But Abdul Aziz is not to be deterred. "You saw a man with no hair?" he says. "Under the *iwan* by Ansari's tomb? He is a thief. You understand? This place is closed; you cannot be arrested if you are with Ansari."

He places his tea glass on the ground and takes my hand, smiling gently as he tells me how this thousand-year-ago poet has affected his own life:

"Ansari did a miracle for me."

I'm pretty blasé about miracles by now. In Iran, I was told about paraplegics who were given back the use of their legs through the personal intercession of Imam Ali, while the Professor often laughed about the War Propaganda Office's claims that tulips had miraculously sprouted from soil irrigated by the blood of "martyrs" in the Iran-Iraq war. Abdul Aziz's is a less ambitious, smaller scale sort of miracle—and all the more convincing for it.

"Last year," he says, "I had a car accident. I was working for a construction company and I did not have a good experience with their vehicles. One day I turned onto the road too fast and I hit someone, he didn't die but he went to hospital and he still has a problem with his legs. Well, I was very nervous about this. The man who I hit, his father wanted to put me in jail. So I came here, I came to the tomb of Ansari. It wasn't like today, it was late at night, so there were only the men who are always here. I knew the police could not take me if I was with Ansari, but this was not the reason I was here. You see, I wanted to ask Ansari for advice. So I sat down beside his tomb and I prayed for his help. And do you know what happened when I got home? It was a miracle! Because when I got home, I found out that my father had spoken to this man—the man who wanted to put me in jail— and he had agreed to drop the charges."

Abdul Aziz shakes his head in disbelief, as if it has only just happened and he is still recovering from the shock.

"How could this fortune not shine on me," he says, "if it is not for the blessing of Ansari?"

"You mean," I say, "Ansari actually *saved* you?"

An eleventh-century Sufi poet—credited with keeping a man out of jail. Even if I'm skeptical about the poet's involvement, I can't doubt Abdul Aziz's belief in it. It is this—his unshakeable faith in the Sufi poet's intercession—that represents such a striking connection with the past. And how typical of Persian culture to produce a poet—a man remembered not for any great political acts but for the verses he wrote—who is also regarded as a saint. If Abdul Aziz was alone, I might put his story down as an intriguing oddity. But what is striking, as he guides me around the compound, is how many others echo his experience.

"Oh yes," says a robust-looking man on the other side of the hut, laying down his pipe and offering it to us with the nozzle facing away, in accordance with accepted water-pipe etiquette. "I too have benefited through the blessed Ansari. I am a builder, so I have to climb a lot of high walls. Well, two years ago, I fell off a wall and lost consciousness. My family was at the hospital talking to the doctors, and they were sure I was going to die. My sons came here to light some sticks and pray to Ansari, because they knew this was the only chance. And now look at me! I am in good health and I have seen the birth of three grandchildren."

There is more. Outside one of the tombs, we meet a man who works for the Catholic Relief Services—a job he insists he wouldn't have secured "if Ansari did not make this happen." And there is a middle-aged man in a suit, quietly reading *The Intimate Conversations*, who tells us his house was set on fire by the Taliban.

"It was at night," he explains. "None of us could have survived. But the day before, my wife prayed here to Ansari, and because of this we lived."

"I think you don't believe these people," says Abdul Aziz, squeezing alongside me in the bus back to the city.

The women are at the front and the men at the back—dozens of us, squashed so tightly together we can feel each other's hipbones.

"But tell me," says Abdul Aziz, "you saw some bullet holes in Ansari's tomb place?"

"Well, no . . ."

"You see? This place is protected. We have had so much fighting in the last few years and all the places in Herat were destroyed, but not this place. God was protecting it."*

I'm fascinated by people's willingness to attribute their good luck to Ansari—there's something deeply self-effacing about it. Whereas in the West we are inclined to claim credit for ourselves, many of the people I've met are eager to put it all down to a man from the past.

But it isn't only Ansari who helped people—during the Taliban era, the Sufis were helping themselves—as I learn the next day when Abdul Aziz takes me to a *caravanserai* in the city center—an old merchants' rest house converted into a school. One of the teachers, who has been instructing Abdul Aziz in English, is also a Sufi poet.

"The Taliban didn't like us at all," he says.

His name is Hamid. Tall and bearded, he has a moon-shaped face, beaming out as he pours black tea in the staff room.

"One day when they were in power," he continues, "they broke up our assembly at the Friday Mosque. But after this, hundreds of Sufis came together at the mosque and we said if the Taliban act against us we will withstand them. The Taliban knew they could not defeat us, so they backed down and didn't give us any trouble again. You see—in Herat the Sufis are very powerful."

I think of Ali Hujwiri, who wrote the first Persian treatise on Sufism in the eleventh century. "The sun of love and the fortune of the Sufi path," he declared, "is in the ascendant in Khorasan." Judging from what I have seen and heard in Herat, it still is.

My encounter with Abdul Aziz turns out to be one of those chances on which a visit to a new city often depends. Over the next few days, he takes me on a tour of Herat's most famous mausolea. We stand under the shade of an ancient pistachio tree, listening to an old "white-beard" reciting stories of kings and beggars by the marble slab

---

* This isn't strictly true: The pavilion over Ansari's tomb was damaged on November 20, 2001, when a U.S. food drop landed on top of it.

where the fifteenth-century poet Abdur-Rahman Jami lies. It's said the city's ruler of the time, Sultan Hussain, spent hours shedding tears of grief over the grave—a hint of the close relationship between artists and the authorities of the time, which recent history has been so far from emulating.

In another corner of the city, we chat with a French diplomat under a dome the color of the sky, which crowns the resting place of Jami's sponsor Gowhar Shad—the Happy Jewel, whose patronage was such a spur to the city's fifteenth-century artists. And one afternoon we end up on our backs at the "Rolling Tomb," where men spin across the pebbles in imitation of Baba Qaltan, a medieval Sufi who, on setting out to visit Jami, decided to roll rather than walk. You place your head on a gravestone, close your eyes, and recite a prayer about the oneness of God; if you roll a good distance, it's deemed to be proof that your prayers will be well-received. Unfortunately, my own effort is both stilted and short, prompting one of the onlookers to announce, "This is because he is an unbeliever"—which isn't especially reassuring in light of my coming journey.

In between the tombs, we stroll around the bazaar, under wooden domes and high vaults where grit and plaster pour onto the tracks, loosened by a wheelbarrow of beans or a donkey cart carrying a sack of peanuts. The smell of hot freshly baked bread oozes out of the bakeries, where teenage boys are using long wooden paddles to scoop the flats of dough from the underground ovens, distracted from their work by the sight of a brightly dressed girl whose exceptional deportment is being tested by the water jug on her head.

There's noise all around us—a *chapan* seller is calling out the prices for his rainbow-colored gowns; the metalworkers are hammering at their aluminum sheets; there are cobblers with horseshoes and a cheerful swordsmith, his gold tooth gleaming, chiseling a gazelle-horn scabbard over a mound of chippings the same ashen color as his beard. In between advice about the steel (when it's clean it smells like an onion, he explains, and "if it's good, it becomes soft like wax and the dirt skims off it just like a dry onion"), he recites from the *Shah-*

nameh: "Not lion nor dragon nor *div* can evade/ The terrible edge of my well-sharpened blade." The verse, he tells me, reminds him of the importance of swordmaking "for our people for thousands of years."

One evening, when I've just woken from a nap after my excursions with Abdul Aziz, he turns up at the Hotel Successful in a cauliflower of dust.

"Again, come on!" he shouts, leaning forward on the hemp saddlebag of his Honda motorcycle. "My father invites you for dinner."

Behind a high adobe wall is the first Afghan house I've visited. We step inside a metal gate, passing a satellite dish impaled in the concrete of the courtyard.

"We couldn't put the dish on our roof," says Abdul Aziz, "because the Taliban would have seen it."

Ahead of us, a frayed brown rug stretches across the concrete floor of a large unfurnished room. There's a pile of mattresses in a corner, presumably for guests to sleep on, and a picture of the *Ka'aba* of Mecca is hanging on the wall, under a clock.

"God is kind," says Abdul Aziz's thin, scraggly bearded father, as he offers me his hand.

God, I will soon be told, is also wise, powerful, and clement—the reason not only for my being here but also for the meal we are about to be served. His instruments in this instance are Abdul Aziz's mother and sisters, who are hard at work in the kitchen. When I ask if I can meet them, it's suggested that I eat more of the rice, which is slithered with carrot and dripped in sheep's fat, served on a single platter into which we all dig. Having been prepared by their hands, it is the closest I will come to an encounter with the women themselves.

The meal is conducted mostly in silence—every time I'm about to open my mouth to speak, Abdul Aziz's father gestures for me to eat more. But with the dish wiped almost clean, he starts pouring out his questions.

"You know our poetry?" he asks.

I tell him I'm especially interested in the *Shahnameh*, which prompts a warm smile.

"Agar juz bikam-e man ayaad javaab," he recites, "man u gurz u maidan u Afrasiyaab." *And should this reply with my wish not accord, / Then Afrasiyab's field, the mace and the sword.*

"This is Rostam," he announces, one hand swiping the air, as if the warrior has just entered the room and needs to be introduced. "It is when he is fighting against the Turanians. Would you not agree he is the greatest of the heroes in *Shahnameh*?"

I wonder if he's a scholar; but when he tells me he runs a shop (one of a row of metal shipping containers on the road to the *musalla* minarets), it's no surprise. This is another example of how the *Shahnameh* resonates among ordinary Persian speakers. Listening to him, I'm sure the scholars I've met are right—that the same literary Persian culture survives on both sides of the border.

There is a creak behind me. I turn to see two thin black-clad arms stretching through the door. A tray is held between them, which is taken by Abdul Aziz and set on the rug. The tea is lemon-scented, served in tapering tulip-shaped glasses with silver rims. Beside it is a bowl of fresh fruit—grapes of several different colors, a couple of burst pomegranates, their seeds glistening like rubies in a cave, and a pair of blush apples, which Abdul Aziz peels with a knife, forming spirals out of the paper-white flesh and the shiny green rind.

"Ismail Khan was good for us," says his father—we have moved on to politics now. "He fought against the Taliban; they were our enemy."

"Because of their repressions?" I ask.

"Because they are Pashtun."

He strokes his beard, greasing it with the sheep's fat dripping off his fingers.

"We are not Pashtun, so why must they rule us? [President Hamid] Karzai is the same. You know our poetry, so you understand. We are a cultured people, but what did the Pashtuns ever create? What poetry did they write?"

Given what he thinks of the Pashtuns, I'm not surprised when he advises me to change my travel plans. He spits a grape seed into his hand and lets out a grunt as he shifts his belly over his crossed legs.

"You must not go south of Herat," he says. "If you want to see Kabul you must take an airplane. But you must not go south, because you will meet the Pashtuns. And you do not need me to tell you how foolish that would be."

I play it Persian: nodding to what he has said, agreeing that he has given me excellent advice (to do anything else would be to cause offense—especially in front of his son) and making up my mind to go ahead with my plans anyway.

"Wisdom is a gift from God," he declares.

He's smiling, even though I'm sure I can see in his eyes that he knows what I'm thinking: The code of Persian etiquette has designated a role for both of us, and we're acting to the script.

He pushes the fruit bowl toward me, gesturing with an expansive palm. "Have a pomegranate. According to our great scientist Ibn Sina, it is good for the digestion."

The next day, Abdul Aziz turns up at the Hotel Successful once again.

"My father was very interested to meet you," he says. "He invites you to come for supper any time you wish."

"Thank you!" I reply. But I know this is the politeness code I've come across so many times in recent months. One meal is enough—the worst kind of guest is the one who keeps turning up.

This morning we have a particular mission, and having a local like Abdul Aziz is going to be an enormous help. He escorts me a few minutes from the city center, to a broad metal gate set between marble-tiled columns. Stocks rattle as a group of sentinels raise their Kalashnikovs.

"No journalists!" one of them shouts.

"I'm not a journalist," I reply. "I'm a—well, I'm writing a book about history. The history of Herat. And if I can't include—er—Governor Khan—well, it won't look very good. I mean, people might think he's not very important."

The soldier takes a moment to flex his brow, then he leads us inside the gate, where we stand in front of enough Toyota Land Cruisers to set up a showroom.

"Stay here!" he barks, before disappearing into a rose garden.

Just to meet Ismail Khan would be exciting enough. Not only is he the most famous man in Herat—he's an icon of modern Afghanistan, his biography an illustration of how topsy-turvy political life here can be. As a major in the Afghan army in 1979, he refused to fire on the local rebels when they massacred the Soviet advisers and their families—instead he took his men to the hills. A ten-year war between Khan and the Russians had begun.*

Within three years of its conclusion, after the Russian withdrawal in 1989, Khan declared himself "amir of Western Afghanistan." But he was weakened when Herat was bombed by General Dostum, a rival *mujahid*, and a later Taliban assault forced him back into the hills. Dostum continued to be a thorn in Khan's side: A year on, his deputy lured him into a Taliban trap. He was chained to a pipe in Kandahar, and for three years he lived on a single piece of bread a day. Even when a sympathetic guard helped him escape, he was still haunted by bad luck: His getaway car hit an anti-tank mine and his legs were broken. But he kept going, thanks to a rescue mission by his own loyalists, and was smuggled into the safe haven of Iran.

He didn't take back Herat until 2001, assisted by the US bombing campaign. As governor, he rebuilt schools, roads, and parks, establishing the city as the safest and most prosperous in the whole country, and held public meetings where his subjects could petition him for favors, like the best of the ancient shahs. But Khan is no longer in charge. Accused of treating the province as his personal fiefdom, of arbitrary arrests, illegal detentions, and a moral code not much more lenient than the Taliban's** (and—more crucially for President Karzai's

---

* The Soviets had no inkling of the trouble Khan was going to cause them. Andrushkin, the Soviet general, dispatched a message of warning, insisting that Khan's fate would be the same as the guerrilla Ibrahim Beg, who had resisted the Russians at the beginning of the century before his eventual demise. "You Russians still remember Ibrahim Beg after seventy years," wrote Khan in defiant response. "I want you to remember me for two hundred!"

** For example, men caught drinking alcohol had their heads shaved, and women who had been found alone with an unrelated man (even if that man was a teacher, or a fellow passenger in a taxi) could be taken to the hospital and "inspected" to confirm their virginity.

central government—of failing to hand over tax and customs revenues, along with refusing to grant the U.S. an air base), he has lost his job amid mayhem on the streets. UN offices were set on fire and demonstrators chanted "Death to Karzai" (although conversations in Herat show Khan has plenty of opponents too, hoping his removal will bring them greater freedom). But even though he's lost his handle on power, I imagine he has kept some of the trappings—and I'm eager to glimpse what is left of his court.

"Come!"

The soldier whisks us into the rose garden. Grape branches tunnel over our heads, while pink tiles slide under our feet and more pink appears in the stuccoed columns on either side of us. This I certainly didn't expect: an Afghan warlord's lair, looking like it's been done up by Dame Barbara Cartland.

Men with waistcoats over their *shalwar qameez* are sitting on benches between the columns. A line of them gives way to a stocky man dressed entirely in white: skullcap, sleeveless shirt, trousers, beard, and even his prayer beads—as if he's the guardian of a tacky TV version of heaven. Only the arch of Khan's eyebrows betrays a more devious side. Others are keen to talk to him, so we're nudged farther along to mingle with the *mujahideen*. We sit down at the end of a bench, next to a glum-looking man who shows us the stitches on his calf.

"Gunshot wounds," he says nonchalantly. "Fighting against the Soviets."

I ask him about his experiences with Khan: the "how do you know the host" question you ask at a party when you can't think of anything else.

"We were in Kandahar together," he says, his lips rising for a nostalgic smile, as if he's about to set off on a fond trip down memory lane. "In a Taliban jail," he adds, "chained to the pipes."

More *mujahideen* sit around us, with turbans, long beards, and the obligatory Kalashnikovs, cross-legged on the carpet since there is no more space on the benches. Glasses of tea are proffered on a silver tray, and as they are being drained, a man stands up to recite a speech in praise of Khan. He has a deep, bombastic voice, which he hurls at his audience like he's trying to knock us off the benches. Although he is speaking in Persian, I find his words difficult to understand, so I turn to Abdul Aziz for help.

"He says," explains Abdul Aziz in a matter-of-fact whisper, "the problem for Afghanistan is foreigners. He says they try to exploit us and Islam is the only true religion."

"Oh." I smile weakly at the men on the bench opposite, but they only give me stony looks in reply.

When the man has finished his speech, he takes Khan's right hand in his, and presses it to his lips, which prompts a click of Abdul Aziz's teeth.

"Tskk!" he hisses. "What this man is doing is wrong. In Islam, you should only kiss the hand of your mother, your father, or your teacher."

Had I wanted to kiss Khan's hand myself, when I am summoned to sit beside him, the look of it would have turned me off. It's hairless and alarmingly pink, as if its outer skin has peeled away.

"We fought against the Russians," he says, gesturing with that hand to include most of the gathering, "because we were against Communism. We were Afghans, and Muslims, and we wanted freedom."

"But why," I ask, thinking of my conversation with the poet Jalali, "didn't you stop fighting when you had your freedom?"

"Because as soon as the Russians collapsed, Pakistan interfered. They didn't accept for Afghanistan to be a strong military country. And we *were* strong, because we had weapons from the Russians, so Pakistan was afraid we would hurt it."

He is referring to the Taliban, who were created under Pakistani auspices and are seen by many Afghans, especially the non-Pashtuns, as representative not of their own country but of their meddling neighbor.

"It is very hard to live under the power of ignorant people," says Khan, "especially for us here in Herat, because this is the most cultured province in our country. They hanged our people on the lampposts, they took away our education so now we have many young men who are illiterate, but the people of Herat are resourceful. Whether they were distributing pamphlets or secret poems, they never allowed the Taliban to control us."

It's a surreal conversation. One moment he's fulminating against the Pakistani secret service. The next we are debating the gender of pronouns in application to countries (can you call Afghanistan a "she"?). I bring up Ferdowsi, hoping he'll quote from one of the poet's battle stories, but he gives a brief smile before enumerating what he's achieved for the culture of Herat.

"We have done a lot," he says. "In the war many streets and homes were damaged, but we rebuilt the schools and now we have ten faculties and our own books."

When I mention the rumors he was funded by Iran, he responds with an arch of brow and a flash of eye.

"There are a million Afghan refugees in Iran, and we share a long border. Of course we should have good relations. But we are different— our culture is different. We are Afghanistan!"

So much for the cultural unity suggested by the writers I've met: With politicians, it's all about the differences.

There is one more thing I want from Khan—advice for my forthcoming journey. A battle-hardened war hero like him—he should be able to give me all sorts of useful information. Maybe it will be the magic detail that could end up saving my life. But he is still in politician mode and is reticent about dishing out advice.

"There are still many Taliban making difficulties," he says. "There is peace in some provinces. But not in all of them."

This has already been confirmed by one of his *mujahideen*. Tea glass chiming against his rifle's stock, he inquires where I am planning to go next.

"Ghazni!"

The word is passed along the row like a live grenade.

"But that's in Pashtun country," he says. "You must wear Afghan clothes or they will shoot you."

"Don't listen to him," says another *mujahid*, shaking his head. "He's just trying to scare you. They will only kidnap you and ask for some money."

For my plans to be considered dangerous by men who fought the Russians, and bear the wounds to prove it, is a little disconcerting. But as I wander around Herat in search of advice for the journey to Ghazni, these turn out to be some of the most positive appraisals I receive.

"If you go to the places you are talking about," says one of the teachers at Abdul Aziz's school, "then they will kill you. If the evil ones see you or hear about you, they will kill you."

I am sitting in the staff room with several of the teachers. Having just taken a class, I'm hoping for their goodwill—but I'm struggling to receive any encouragement for my journey.

"What if I find someone to go with me?" I ask.

"And where," comes the response, "will you find anyone crazy enough to do that?"

"You know," says Hamid, the Sufi poet I chatted with a few days ago, "the Taliban are offering a free motorbike to anyone who helps them kill a foreigner?"

"A free motorbike!" declares another of the teachers, called Javed, his bright eyes flashing. "I could do with a motorbike. Maybe I should give them a call!"

He bursts into the sort of roar you might expect from an especially amused lion.

"I'm a war child," he adds, to explain his carefree attitude. "I'm from Kabul. People here in Herat, they had it easy. I saw people burned alive, I saw nails hammered into people's fingertips. I used to go on the rooftop and watch the Scud B's shooting into the city. My father got so angry, he'd shout at me, 'Get down from there!' I never did! I wasn't scared."

"Your point being?" I snap. I'm having something of a humor bypass at this point.

"Do you believe in destiny?" says Javed. "We Muslims—we believe in destiny. If it's your turn to die, then if you aren't shot by the Taliban, you will be hit by a car."

That sounds like Ferdowsi. Fate, he tells us, is like a polo stick: "We, bandied each way / By profit and loss, are the same as the ball." Maybe this is the time to pull to the side and stop, to follow the advice I've been given and call it a day. But I know I won't. Something has been tugging me toward Ghazni for several months now—ever since the Professor narrated the story of Ferdowsi's visit to the court of the miserly Sultan Mahmud. Even if there *is* a bullet with my name on it, waiting in a bandolier somewhere out in Helmand, I've come too far to turn back.* So I decide to do something pragmatic: I send off an e-mail and the next day a note turns up on my door at the Hotel Successful:

Nick, Where are you? Call me—Fereydoun

I have contacted the *Sunday Times* correspondent, Christina Lamb, who's put me in touch with her old fixer. He comes along to dinner the next day, in the hotel restaurant, and over oily chunks of lamb kebab I tell him about my plans.

"Really, you are interested in *Shahnameh*?" he says. "This is wonderful. I met many Westerners, but no one is ever interested in Ferdowsi."

It's going well, and we seem to be establishing a rapport: Surely I have found myself a guide! Surely, one more time, Ferdowsi has turned out to be the key.

"I want to help you," says Fereydoun, wiping his mouth with a napkin, which he drops onto his emptied plate, "because you are a guest in my country. You are a friend of my friend and you are writing about Ferdowsi, who is from my country."

But then comes a blow.

"I am training to be a doctor," he says, "so I've stopped working as a fixer. I'd love to come with you—but I can't."

I can feel a lead weight navigating its slow plunge through my innards. Will I have to go it alone? The thought of traveling unassisted through the Taliban heartland is doing strange things to my stomach.

---

* The Sufis would, I think, agree with this attitude. In one of their stories, a young Sufi disciple spots Death in a teahouse in Baghdad and overhears him talking about the calls he is about to make. Panicking, the disciple flees to faraway Samarkand to be sure of escaping a visit. Later, Death meets the disciple's guru and asks about the disciple, but the guru doesn't know where he's gotten to. "Yes, it's strange," says Death, consulting his list. "It says here I've got to pick him up next week, in Samarkand of all places!"

I trudge beside Fereydoun back to his jeep. He turns the ignition, reaches for the handbrake, and as I'm lifting a hand to wave him off, he leans out of the window:

"You know, there is someone who . . . Wait for tomorrow, but I can't promise . . . "

What does he mean? What is he talking about? Someone who *what*? I'll have to wait until six in the morning. . . .

A rap on my door. Behind it is a man in *shalwar qameez*, like most Afghans. But there's something different about this one. Maybe it's the polished black brogues on his feet, or the signet ring flashing on his right hand, or the shiny-buttoned blazer he's wearing over his knee-length shirt.

"I come before you," he announces in a high rolling voice like a circus ringmaster, "by the hand of Ferrrrreydoun."

Hassan-Gul hardly looks like the ideal guide for the Afghan badlands. His blazer and the wax on his mustache suggest a dandy, which isn't helped by his habit, as we sit over breakfast, of dabbing the crumbs off his blazer with a spotted handkerchief. I've met plenty of Iranians who were obsessed with their appearance, but the people I've encountered in Herat seemed to be a hardier bunch— more Afghan hounds than Persian cats.

Or so I thought. I certainly never expected to meet an Afghan with a spotted hanky. And the fact that the second part of his name, "gul," means "flower," doesn't bode well in a country run by the gun. Is he really the right man to guide me into "Taliban country"? To cross the terrifying wastes of Helmand and set out for the final stretch to Ghazni? A single word confirms that he is:

"Pashto."

"You speak it?" I ask.

"Thanks to God, Mr. Nicholas, my tongue is in languages like a bird in flight!"

As I will discover—and as his dress sense implies—Hassan-Gul isn't impartial to the odd poetic flourish.

"I have many friends in that part of the country," he says. "When we reach Farah, I want us to place ourselves at the house of my friend Nasrullah."

"So you speak Pashto and Dari?"*

He wipes another crumb off his mustache and neatly folds up the handkerchief, before fitting it in the top pocket of his blazer. "If I did not," he says, "then how could you place your feet in your destination?"

We spend breakfast discussing the itinerary and haggling over his fee. Since he is training to be a doctor and has an exam to write in two weeks' time, he insists on leaving the next morning.

"We must think about your appearance," he adds, leaning forward to scrutinize my face. Fortunately, I've spent long enough in this part of the world for my usual pasty complexion to attract a little color, and my nose is large enough to pass as an Afghan's. But, Hassan-Gul concludes, there is still plenty of work to do.

"It is possible for you to look like us," he decides at last, "but you must wear our clothes. And of course you must put your glasses away."

"My glasses?"

"Yes—you didn't notice, Mr. Nicholas? Afghan people never wear glasses."

I take them off and he responds with an encouraging tilt of his head.

"This is much better, is it not?" he says, adding, "and it is good that your hair is dark. And you have a beard, so this is also good. Although I must tell you, Mr. Nicholas, it is not very thick."

"But *you* haven't got a beard at all."

"That is correct, but it is *you* who people will be suspicious about—especially when they hear you speaking. . . . In fact, it is better if you don't speak at all."

"What? Pretend I'm a mute?"

---

* The Afghan dialect of Persian. It has roughly the same relationship to the Persian spoken in Iran that Scottish English has to the Queen's English.

"A . . . ? Oh yes, Mr. Nicholas, a mute! Yes, this is an excellent idea, this is exactly what you must do. Otherwise they will know you are a foreigner—and I must tell you, that would not be good."

He looks me up and down once more, like a new suit he's thinking of trying on, then gives a satisfied nod.

"Your heart is trembling?"

"Nnnno!"

"But if you are afraid, then why are you doing this journey?"

"I'm not afraid!"

He leans forward, patting my wrist with what must be the most manicured male hand in Herat.

"I promise you, Mr. Nicholas, if you do what I say you will be safe."

To travel incognito . . . there's something strangely attractive about that—and authentic too. I think of Sarah Hobson, who wandered around Iran in the early '70s dressed as a man, or Robert Byron, a few years before World War II, daubing his face with burnt cork to visit a shrine in Mashhad. Or even the BBC correspondent John Simpson, scuttling into Afghanistan in a burka on the eve of the American invasion. In a land so full of secrets, Westerners have often turned to secrecy themselves to make their way through it.

Early next morning, the call to prayer has still to be sung when I tie the cord of my trousers and pull on a shirt as long as a nightgown. I wind a turban around my head, strap on a pair of plastic sandals, and wrap my backpack in a bedsheet to look like a local's bundle. A glance in the mirror in the unlit corridor shows the silhouette, at least, of an Afghan, ready for the journey to the troubled south.

In the taxi to the transport terminal, the driver is chatting away to Hassan-Gul.

"Your friend is quiet," he says.

His sharp eyes glance at me in the rearview mirror.

"He is my cousin," replies Hassan-Gul. "He has not spoken since he was a small boy, when the Russians burned down his father's house."

He turns to me: "Is that not the truth, Abbas?"

I nod.

PART THREE

IRAN AND CENTRAL ASIA

"My sister, guard your veil;
My brother, guard your eyes."
— SLOGAN ON A BANNER IN TEHRAN

8

Tahmineh's Secret
Tehran. February.

The place was collapsing in on itself. Plaster poured down the mud-brick walls, which were patched with scaffolding and canvas sheets, while lime scale was dribbling down the pipes. Somewhere along here, a few doors down from where Reza the ponytailed artist lived, was a house that had been eaten away from the outside. Its facade had been stripped away, revealing the internal workings—pipes, beams, wires—like a body that's been flayed of its skin but still keeps going. There was a courtyard at the back, where a group of men had zipped up their jackets to keep out the cold. It was the morning of *ashoura*, the anniversary of the martyrdom of Imam Hossain. The men's eyes were alight with anticipation as newspaper was spread on the ground underneath them—they all knew what was about to happen; so did Reza, who was standing beside me.

"This is not something you can see in the north of our city," he said.

My image of Persian refinement was about to burst wide open. From the moment I saw a tall, curly haired man stepping onto the courtyard, gripping a twelve-inch knife in his hands, I sensed I was in a very different place from the Iran I was used to.

"Oh, Imam Hossain!" exclaimed one of the men.

His voice was urgent, as if he were calling out to someone he'd lost. Others joined in: "Imam Hossain!" they cried. "Imam Hossain!" Soon I was the only one who wasn't chanting; even Reza was calling out the holy name—the name of the Prophet Mohammed's martyred grandson.

Two of the men had white cloths around their necks. They knelt down on the newspaper, while the man with the knife stood behind them, catching the rising sun on the tip of the blade. His lips were quivering as he intoned a prayer; the rivet handle shook. There was a flash of light, then the knife rested an inch above the men's heads. As soon as they stepped away, now hooded in the cloths around their necks, their places were taken by others. It was the same each time— they would step forward, kneel, then disappear inside their bandages. There was only one significant change: The newspapers on the ground were turning red.

"Oh, Imam Hossain!" they cried. "Oh, Imam Hossain!"

Another volunteer took his turn, but this time he seized the knife for himself. He wiped the sweat off his brow before shaking the knife in front of his chest. His eyes were enormous, as if he had fitted matchsticks inside them. As the blade trembled in his hands, an older man dropped to his knees and broke into tears, while there were tears also dripping down the face of his son. A cry of "Imam Hossain!", the light thud of steel as he sliced into his head, his tears turning red as they mixed with the blood pouring down his face.

"Oh, Imam Hossain!" he screamed. "Oh, Imam Hossain!"

He stretched out the name like a bandage to keep his wound from hurting. The knife quivered as his blood dribbled onto the green scarf around his neck, turning it an episcopal purple. He was helped into a chair by the scullery, where Reza leaned over him with a cloth soaked in ethanol.

"What do you think?"

Reza was leading me into the living room, where one of the qama-zanis, or "dagger-strikers" as they are known, invited us to sit on the rug, with a pile of dates between us.

"Well, it's quite . . . bloody," I whispered.

I expected Reza to agree—he had, after all, been helping to bandage the dagger-strikers' wounds. But instead his eyes narrowed and the skin bunched above his nose.

"It is passion," he exclaimed. "Are you not able to understand this?"

I felt bad. I thought of images I'd seen of Mexicans and Filipinos whipping themselves during Holy Week—was it so different from Christian practices?

"You know why we do this?" asked the man who had offered me the dates.

When he struck himself on the courtyard, he had been screaming "Imam Hossain," his face taut with a savage fervor; the kind of intensity, I imagined, that burned among the battle troops in the war against Iraq. But now he was reaching out his arms, with the plate balanced on his palms, as if we were in a high-society drawing room.

"We do it," he said, "for Imam Hossain."

Trickles of blood were spilling down his face, which didn't exactly boost my appetite. But I was keen not to cause any more offense, so I picked up a date and popped it into my mouth.

"Imam Hossain wasn't a mullah," he continued, "he was like us. He was against the mullahs, actually—he was against oppression. When Imam Hossain's head was cut off, his sister Zeinab hit her head against a date tree and her blood poured out like a fountain. So now we do this act as a symbol of Zeinab's pain and our love for Imam Hossain."

"If we have any wishes," added another, "we do dagger-striking and our wishes are answered."

I turned toward this man. He had the same uniform of blood all over his face, while the crown of his head was lumpy with scabs. He heaved himself across the rug, until he was so close that a drop of his blood splashed, like a raindrop, on my knee.

"I will tell you something," he said, "and then you will believe. It is about my wife. She was a good woman, the best of women, but one day we discovered she was ill. God is merciful! She had a problem with her heart, it was too difficult for her to breathe, so we took her to hospital and the doctors did everything they could. Not just one operation, not two, but three! Three times, you understand? Three times they operated, but still they could not make her better. You know what they said to me? They said, 'We are sorry, there is nothing else we can do.' The doctors said this! The doctors, with their certificates and their training! They said there was nothing they could do!"

He tapped his head, which was still bleeding—judging by the wet red stains on his fingers.

"That same night," he said, "I took out my knife and beat it against my head. The wound was so deep the blood poured out until sunrise."

Even the unsmeared parts of his face were turning red now, as if he were challenging me to doubt his conviction.

"And you know what? It was worth every drop! Because my wife became better, of course. The next day there was an improvement and a week later she was able to leave the hospital, and now she has excellent health. All because of the blessing of Imam Hossain!"

He looked up, nodding, as if the imam were watching over us, and several of the men recited the *salavat*: "Peace be upon Mohammed and Mohammed's lineage."

When I first met Reza I saw him as a typical rebel—the ponytailed artist who painted stories from the *Shahnameh* in protest against the government. It was only during the *ashoura* festival that I started to understand how different he was from other "nationalists" like the Professor. I had assumed he shared the Professor's obsession with "Persianness," but I was starting to realize that, to Reza, Islam was just as important a part of his Iranian identity. This was why he'd painted *Zahhak* in the first place—because he felt the mullahs had betrayed the true Islamic principles on which the revolution was founded. The Professor knew exactly where he stood in Iran's cultural battle, but for Reza it was more complicated, because he was standing in the middle. No wonder he'd told me he was "divided from society."

"You know what the shah's wife bathed in?" he said during one of our evening chats. "Milk! Is this someone whose heart is open to the ordinary people? And *Savak* tortured anyone who didn't support the shah, especially the Communists. But now look—these fat mullahs, with their mistresses in the Gulf and their shiny new cars. It's the same all over again, we might as well ask the son of the shah to come back!"

Reza didn't slice his head at the dagger-striking ceremony (he mentioned his drinking, insisting he didn't have sufficient "nafs," or spirituality—dagger-striking was a privilege only for the most pious). But he did take part in another of the *ashoura* rituals, as I saw later that day when we squeezed through the streets to the city center.

Men were handing out dishes of mutton and jugs of watered-down yogurt around us, while actors in tinfoil armor were camel-riding between the chains of the crowd. Passing by several hundred prostrating bodies, Reza led me through a wooden door decorated in gold writing and hexagons of glass. At the back of the prayer hall, raised on a dais seemingly formed from the hands of the worshippers reaching out toward him, was a *rawi*—a reciter. He had a tangled beard like a river god and on his head was wound an enormous example of what the Professor would have called an "onion"—with which he shared the ability to induce tears.

The story the *rawi* was telling—hurling it against the walls in a deep, rumbling bass, then soaring up into the vault in a trembling alto—was the death of Abu'l Fazl, Imam Hossain's brother, at Kerbala. It's the middle of the caliph's siege against Hossain. Abu'l Fazl has been sent to fetch water, but he refuses to drink even a drop before he has slaked the thirst of the children. He will never have the chance to complete his mission: as he's filling up a leather gourd, his body is ripped apart by the arrows of the caliph's soldiers and he falls dead against the riverbank.

I turned on my Dictaphone, the reels spinning like my head in that dank, sweaty chamber. There was an old man underneath me, who was cradling his forehead in the outstretched fingers of a hand. In front of him was a mullah in a turban as woolly as his beard, and to his side a teenager in a New York Yankees baseball cap. They were all shaking. Tears streamed down their faces and greased their beards so that their hands slid down their cheeks.

Then a sound like thunder: The teenager had struck his face. Another thumped his forehead against the palm of his hand, while the old man underneath me assailed his cheeks as if he were trying to knock out his teeth. The sound of thumping echoed around the hall. The reciter's cries ricocheted against pillars that were being used by some of the worshippers as an alternative to their hands. Here was the old Iranian way of showing your grief—a ritual that is enacted by grief-stricken characters in the *Shahnameh* (for example, by Kawa the blacksmith, bewailing the killing of his seventeen sons by snake-shouldered Zahhak); a ritual that is still central to the Iranian mourning culture.

Panting beside me, a man had grabbed the shoulder in front of him, moaning over his neighbor's neck. Now he pulled himself up and started unbuttoning his shirt. It was, to be fair, very hot, but he didn't just undo a couple of buttons: This man was taking it all off. And he wasn't alone. Shirts and vests were unbuttoned, unzipped and unpeeled. Everyone around me was wriggling out of their tops, rushing toward the reciter. Surrounded by this nakedness, I felt naked. I turned to Reza—but he was taking off his shirt too.

"Wait here," he whispered.

He stuffed his shirt in my hands and disappeared into the crowd. Arms were flailing and hair swinging, a stew of sticky skin spreading around the prayer hall, shirts dropping in its wake. I felt dizzy and clung to the pillar to keep myself upright. The stench of body odor and smelly socks was punching through my nostrils, the smacking of hands and heads was thundering in my ears, and the air was too heavy to swallow. I pressed against the pillar, convinced that I was going to faint at any moment. But I could feel a tingle all over me, as the reciter's words swam through the crowd and a tremulous wail echoed from behind the bookshelves dividing us from the women.

Why had Reza, who compared the mullahs to a mythical tyrant in his art, stripped off his shirt and thrown himself in front of a cleric? He didn't explain it, but perhaps it was for the same reason the crowds in the streets, and here in the mosque, had burned with such passion. Imam Hossain had a pull on people's hearts that I never encountered at any other time in Iran.*

The Professor would have been horrified. When I vaguely mentioned "such rituals" to him a few days later, he let out a dismissive snort: "These people are sheep! It is the same for them as if they are taking drugs." But Reza was closer to the pulse of Iran's religious sensibility. Brought up in the Shia cooking pot of the bazaar district, with many religious members in his family and an uncle who painted pro-mullah murals, he was unable to detach himself when the fervor of *ashoura* reached out to touch him.

Holding on to the pillar, I peered into the crowd. All around me, men were plunged into an act of imaginative gymnastics—hurling themselves into the past so that, as Reza put it later, "in my heart I was *there*." Boosted they might have been by the hallucinogenic of religion (and the *rawi*'s rousing recital) but they were showing that the distant past really can come to life—in this case, with enough intensity to make grown men weep.

Watching Reza rip off his shirt and dance in front of the *rawi* made me realize the Professor and his family occupied only one side of the culture. It was as if there was a river cutting through the city and Reza was on the other bank. But Tehran isn't split neatly in half by a river, and no one really knows where the different sides divide. So every once in a while they slide into each other, washing temporarily over the divisions.

---

* Although Reza didn't articulate it, many Iranians have, stressing the link between Imam Hossain's story and the traditions preserved by Ferdowsi. "Why do Iranians ignore all the other imams?" wrote the founder of Iranian blogging, Hossain Derakhshan. "Why don't we perform festivals filled with passion plays, color and music to commemorate them? Because they were all conservative; pragmatic but two-faced— all those things that are despised by our culture. Yet the characters surrounding Hossain could have come straight out of the *Shahnameh*."

TEHRAN. APRIL.

"Oh, Farhad! Oh, Farhad!"

Tahmineh was kneeling on the floor, wearing a sequined gown over bright red pantaloons, her head wrapped in yellow silk and gold thread, a pickaxe gripped between her hands. Lying beside her was a man in a long black robe with eyes turned pandalike by kohl. Given that he hadn't moved since knocking himself out with the same pickaxe a few moments earlier, there was only one logical conclusion: He was dead.

Wailing beside him, Tahmineh flung out her arms—then, like the mourners at the *ashoura* ceremonies, she slapped her forehead. The splintered shriek emanating out of her was so impressive you could hear it bouncing against the walls, echoing like a cry in a cave.

"It is true," whispered the Professor sorrowfully.

Sitting in the vinyl seat beside me, he was dabbing his eyes with his wife's handkerchief. As I looked at him, then at Khanom—her small brown lips pursed in a mother's proud smile—I realized they were watching two completely different people. To Khanom, the girl on the stage was her daughter, but to the Professor, she was Princess Shirin—wife of the Sassanian shah Khosrow Parviz and heroine of Persian literature's most famous love triangle.

The tale of Khosrow, Shirin, and the sculptor Farhad is the *Romeo and Juliet* of Persian literature, its storyline familiar in every corner of the Persian-speaking world. Khosrow is the shah, who falls for the beautiful Shirin at first sight. But a sculptor called Farhad is also in love with her. So the shah sets him a challenge: He can have Shirin's hand in marriage—*if* he manages to cleave a road through the enormous Mount Bisotun. No one at the royal court gives Farhad an onion's skin of a chance, even though he has the muscles of a bull and the strength of two elephants. But his strength isn't the only factor in his favor: Driven by a combination of his love and the assistance of nature (moles tunneling through the rock and birds breaking the stones with their beaks), he comes perilously close to completing the task. Khosrow is astonished, but his wits haven't deserted him. He sends a message to Farhad, informing him that Shirin has died of a fever. The sculptor can't believe the shah would lie, so he climbs to the top of the mountain and throws himself off (or, in the more stage-friendly version, he smites himself with his pickaxe). When she finds out what has happened, Shirin is devastated. She builds a dome over his grave and turns her heart away from Khosrow, refusing to forgive him until she is sure of his remorse.

The play was one of three shorts being performed in the theater of a medical college in west Tehran. A cloth-covered trestle table was set up in the tiled lobby, with plates of pastries and plastic cups of orange juice under a medallion of the region's most famous doctor—the eleventh-century physician Ibn Sina. A queue had already formed, but as we followed the Professor and Khanom to join it, Sina pulled me back. He had spotted a familiar face in the crowd.

Standing by a stout concrete pillar was Reza, his ponytail swinging behind him as he waved, his long, angular face as melancholy as ever. Greetings were exchanged, then Sina sprung away to pick up a few cups of juice, while Reza and I stayed by the pillar, keeping out of the Professor's line of sight.

"Did you enjoy it?" asked Reza.

"Oh, sure, it's a great story," I said.

"In the West, the romance tales always have a happy conclusion, don't they? But here our love stories are sad."

"Well, not *all* our stories are happy," I said. "I mean, *Romeo and Juliet* isn't exactly a bundle of laughs."

"So you weren't surprised by the ending?"

"No, not really," I said. But it wasn't any similarity with tales from my own part of the world; there was a more practical reason why I had known how the story would end.

"You know it's Sina's sister playing Shirin?" I said.

"Oh yes, of course!" Reza shook his head and slapped it with his palm, not so much in mourning as to say what a dunce he was. "So maybe you heard her practicing her lines?"

"Heard her? Reza, for the last two weeks I haven't heard anything else!"

I remembered Khanom muttering in the taxi to the theater: "I feel like I could say her lines myself." And she wasn't the only one. Because Tahmineh had been practicing those lines, loud and clear, at every available opportunity. You knew the shower was occupied because you could hear Shirin singing her love for Farhad under the sound of the spray. When you asked Tahmineh to pass the cherry jam at the breakfast table, she would deliver it along with a couple of lines in praise of the bull-muscled engineer. And even when you were watching the news, the latest bomb scene in Baghdad would be accompanied by Shirin's lament for her dead lover.

The role of Shirin was Tahmineh's first part since I'd been staying at the Professor's. That it was a story from medieval Persian poetry seemed to be providential—although hardly unlikely, since it's the era of the most popular stories. I'd been fascinated by the theater since I was a child, and spent a considerable portion of my student days skulking around cramped, dimly lit studio theaters—so I was eager for a back-stage glimpse of the Iranian stage. All I needed was an intro—and when Tahmineh left her script behind one afternoon, my chance had come.

"Let your hand not be injured!" I declared to Khanom in my best Persian burr. "For me this duty is pleasing!"

The rehearsal building wasn't far. All it required was the most basic kind of trip you can take in Tehran—an hour and a half, three shared taxis, and a couple of near crashes—before I was shouting into the intercom at the gate of a three-story block.

"Salaam! Please may I speak to Madame Tahmineh?"

Static crackled, mingling with what sounded suspiciously like a giggle:

"That is me!"

Inside on the top floor, the actors were sitting on square wooden classroom tables. The men were in jeans and T-shirts, but the actresses were all wearing their headscarves and hadn't taken off their trench coats. One of them kept flapping her scarf to cool herself down, and you could see the beads of sweat on her forehead.

"You saved my life!" whispered Tahmineh as I handed over the script.

There was another actress sitting beside her, whose makeup gave logic to her name—Mahtab or "Moonlight." She pressed a hand to her chest to greet me, while a short man brushed between the women, carrying a blackfaced marionette like a golliwog on strings.

"I greet you with a kiss!" he declared, lifting the strings so the marionette's nose was touching mine. It was part of his act as "black-player," a comic role in traditional Iranian theater.

"Oh, don't mind Valli," said Tahmineh, laughing as she whispered to me. "Don't let him stand too close to you!"

The director was itching to rehearse, so I sat on one of the tables while the actors positioned themselves in the center of the room. Most of Tahmineh's lines were from the twelfth-century verses of the poet Nizami (who adapted the story from an earlier, much shorter account in the *Shahnameh*). She enunciated them in a fast but stagey rattle, and when she wasn't speaking, she wrapped herself in a haughty intensity, like a vamp in a 1920s silent movie. One moment flicking back her head, her nostrils flaring with pride, the next her eyes were darting about and her face flushed. The director was delighted. At the end of the scene, his announcement of "God's blessing" appeared to be directed principally at his leading lady.

Iranians have always loved a show. In Ferdowsi's day, the marketplaces buzzed with mimics and minstrels, as well as shadow plays and full-on sketch shows, like the *Play of Abu'l Qasim of Baghdad*, in which a scurrilous scrounger, "more stinking than the smell of the tanners," dresses up in a cleric's gown and chastises a party of revelers with self-righteous quotes from the Quran. Oddly enough, one of Tehran's biggest box office hits of the past couple of years had been a film called *The Lizard*, in which the hero is also a reprobate disguised as a cleric. But whereas the medieval version flirts with a singing girl, farts in her presence, makes jokes about the plumpness of slave girls, and descends into a drunken stupor, the "Lizard" ends up seeing the error of his ways and finds God: proof that writers in this region could get away with a lot more in the past.

Anyone who doubts the Iranian aptitude for acting only needs to take a taxi in Tehran. You ask for the fare and the driver declares, "Let your hand not be injured!" You ask again and he proclaims you to be his guest, declares himself "your sacrifice," and implores God to pour down blessings upon you. But when you ask for the third time, he doesn't just demand the fare—he wants double. You've been stung by *taarof*, or "offer"—the Persian politeness code.

"But sir, did we not agree? You must pay twice as much as this!" he will exclaim, his brow creased with the sort of expression you'd expect if he was six years old and you had just strangled his pet hamster. It certainly pays to have elastic features here—which is why taxi drivers tend to display the most expressive faces in town.

Up a flight of stairs and through a swinging glass door, cigarette smoke drifted up our noses. Moonlight, taking a packet out of her handbag, inserted a Pleasure Light into the Cupid's bow of her lips and puffed out streams of smoke as she put on her best pout.

The talk was mostly about the play, and it was a couple of notches above my ability, so I found myself watching the other tables instead. A boy was entertaining his friends with a joke, but judging by the looks he was stealing across the aisle, the joke was really for the benefit of a girl at the brushed metal table beside him, who was holding a hand to her mouth like a geisha while pretending to listen to her friends. At the table in front of us, another boy dropped a piece of paper before striding on. A young woman in a white beret, who was sitting opposite an older, serious-looking man, picked it up and unfolded it. The man leaned forward to see what it was, but she scrunched it up like waste, before dropping it casually into her pocket.

"You know what this boy is doing?" whispered Moonlight, leaning toward me.

"Oh yes!"

I'd spent enough nights on the town with Sina to know why boys had a tendency to drop pieces of paper whenever they were in the vicinity of attractive young ladies. No doubt, later this evening, there would be a phone call exchange.

The performance that stuck most in my mind was Tahmineh's. Directing everyone's attention to whatever she considered amusing, she had taken the role of the table's emcee.

"Look at those *chadoris!*"* she exclaimed with a sneer, pointing through the window at the conservative women outside in their black nylon robes. "It's a good idea! If they get lost they can sleep in the park—they already have a tent!"

She didn't let present company off the hook either. Moonlight was upbraided for her makeup ("When she goes to bed at night, she covers herself in cheese," said Tahmineh with a laugh. "Well, at least I don't look like a chocolate," Moonlight retorted—a reference to Tahmineh's unusually dark skin—according to her friends, she was the only girl they knew who had ever used a tanning bed), while I was the inevitable subject of ridicule when Tahmineh noticed I was wearing an odd pair of socks.

"All his other socks have holes in them," she said, laughing. "I don't know how it happens—I think there are special mice who come from all over the city just so they can eat through Nicholas's socks."

As the milkshakes and snacks were handed around, I was grateful for the distraction. The conversation took a new turn, and to the slurps of their drinks the girls shared stories about their encounters with the Morality Police.

"Oh, don't speak about those *basijis!*" said Moonlight, laying down her fork on a plate of sliced melon. "They are always telling me not to wear a colored headscarf or heeled shoes."

Tahmineh talked about a recent experience, when she had been walking past a grocer's just down the road from the house, with her

---

* *Chadori* is used as the collective name for women who wear the most severe and unrevealing clothes. Tahmineh was a *manteaui*—someone wearing the knee-length coat and loose scarf. The difference between the two styles tends to be the difference between conservative and liberal women (although the distinction is by no means exclusive).

hair under a baker-boy hat. A *basiji* had stopped her and told her to put on "the correct headscarf," but she didn't have one with her.

"I thought he is going to hit me," she said. "But the grocer came out and said, 'Go to your grave! This girl is my niece and she is a good Muslim.' And the *basiji* went away."

Here was an example of Iranian "role-playing"—the importance of acting on the street (with the grocer "acting" as Tahmineh's guardian, easing her passage between Iran's public and private worlds). It also cast a spotlight on the public pressure for women to play the role of the silent virgin.

The situation hasn't always been like this. "The Persian women since 1907," claimed the American lawyer Morgan Shuster, "had become almost at a bound the most progressive, not to say radical, in the world." Shuster was brought to Iran to reform the treasury in 1911, in the wake of the Constitutional Revolution, when many women took part in demonstrations against the excesses of the Qajar shahs—such as Mrs. Jahangir, who threw herself in the way of the shah's carriage. But it wasn't until 1962 that women were granted suffrage, and although this survived the revolution, many of their other rights didn't. Ayatollah Khomeini pressed his finger on the rewind button and kept it there. Forced to cover up, denied rights to divorce or retain custody of their children, allowed to inherit only half as much property as their brothers, forbidden from riding a bicycle, and afraid of their faces being slashed by *chador*-clad women in government SUVs, women aren't all that much better off than in Ferdowsi's day, when they were "prisoners in the hands of men."*

"My heart's wish," announced Tahmineh, lifting a paper napkin to wipe the milkshake off her mouth, "is to play in *F.A.N.Z.*"

I'd watched this play in a box at Vahdat Hall—one of Tehran's biggest theaters. It starred the country's most famous actor, Parvez

---

* According to the theological scholar al-Ghazzali. One of Ferdowsi's closest friends, the poet Asadi of Tus, expressed the medieval and the modern mullahs' fear of women when he wrote, "Outside of women is green and lush as a tree, / But inside they have venom."

Parastoui (who also took the lead in the film *The Lizard*), as an English soccer fan who dedicates his life to Manchester United but won't allow his daughter (the part Tahmineh was after) to play soccer herself. No one in the audience was under any illusions: It wasn't about England.

"But here," said Moonlight, "we can't even go to the soccer stadium."

"Yes we can!" Tahmineh threw back her head with a chuckle, before adding, "Only, you have to disguise yourself as a man."

Acting once again.

Watching Tahmineh in the coffee shop, I was struck by how normal she was. She wanted to go to parties and concerts, she exchanged tips with her friends about makeup, debated with Moonlight about which colors were in fashion this year, argued with Sina about the likely plot twists in the popular soap opera *Narges*, and had a poster of Madonna on her bedroom wall. It was only because she was in Iran that she was marked as a rebel—if she'd been born almost anywhere else in the world, doing the things most women take for granted, she would have been as conventional as they come.

Circumstances might be easier for men in general—but not when it came to Valli, Tahmineh's fellow actor and operator of the "black-player" marionette. In a country where body language can be as confusing as the verbal sort (hence Sina would innocently take my hand when he was leading me over the road, and kisses of men's cheeks were a common ritual on the threshold of a house), it wasn't easy to identify Valli as gay. Had the girls not pointed it out, I might not even have been aware of it.

"You should talk to Valli," said Tahmineh, that afternoon at the café.

Valli had been chatting to someone at another table—"maybe that's his new boyfriend," whispered Moonlight, giggling into her milkshake—but eventually he came over and sat down with us. The girls weren't especially warm with him, which drew Valli naturally toward me, as the other outsider in our group.

"I went on a date with him once," he said, nodding to the guy at the other table. "It was one of my better dates."

He smiled—the broad smile of someone who was acting up—and, to avoid the girls' ridicule, he continued in English, which he'd learned to make life easier in "the community."

"If you understand English," he said, "you can talk and the sons of bitches won't hear. It's not just English—we have a special code we use on the chat sites so the *basijis* won't catch us." He let off another of his actor's smiles. "When you've been hit for the hundredth time with the wires, you make sure you know the code."

On a visit to New York in 2007, President Ahmedinejad insisted, "In Iran, we don't have homosexuals like in your country." So perhaps I was mistaken about Valli. Perhaps, when a middle-aged man who was giving me a lift up Valiasr Street one evening reached his arm over the gearstick, I was mistaken about his intention too. "I know a special place," he said, "maybe we can go there and have some pleasure." Perhaps he was just talking about sharing a water pipe. Perhaps the pair of old queens Sina and I encountered a few times at the local sauna were nothing of the kind. Sina told me he knew someone who'd agreed to share a changing cubicle with one of them, "because he needed to buy some books for his studies."

I met Valli a couple of other times. Once, I stumbled into him as I was coming out of the language institute and he gave me a lift on his motorbike. Another time we met outside the City Theatre and went to a teahouse together.

"Sometimes I think I should get a sex change," he said.

He was wearing a loose lumberjack and a leather cap, and there were blotches under his eyes. I wondered if he'd spent the night in a cell—it would explain his strange clothes and the bitterness in his voice—but I didn't know him well enough to ask.

"That's what other guys did," he said. "A friend of mine, he wanted to be with his boyfriend so much he went to Mirjalali."

"Who's he?" I asked.

"The surgeon."

Valli picked up his tea—he drank it with firm, fast gulps, throwing it down his throat. "Anyone can do it—all they need to do is sell one of their kidneys. Then Mirjalali will take out your intestine and turn it into a cunt!"

"Is it legal?" I asked.

"Of course. Ayatollah Khomeini said sex changes are allowed.* You see? They want you to be one thing or the other. People like me, they *encourage* us to have sex changes—anything but same-sex playing. They even help you to pay if you can't afford it."

There was another man in the teahouse, sitting in a corner, under a painting of Imam Hossain at Kerbala. He was reading a book—the *Diwan* of Hafez, written in the fourteenth century, of which there was a pile on a dusty shelf in the corner.

"We used to know each other," whispered Valli, as the man came over to greet us.

He had small gray eyes, which darted around the teahouse furtively, settling for a few moments on me.

"He is asking," said Valli, "if you need a lift anywhere."

I looked at the man, who had cast his eyes to the floor, as if he were following the path of an invisible mouse, and then at Valli's lifted brow.

"I think it's a good day for walking," I replied, "but . . . thank you."

The man shrugged, treading back to his table, but occasionally exchanging comments with Valli, which were too idiomatic for me to understand.

"If we get caught," Valli explained, turning to me again, "they can kill us. It's not like the Taliban, but it's not good, is it? This is why we have to be secretive. You heard about Mahmud and Ayaz?"

"*Sultan* Mahmud?"

The sultan had many slaves at his court in Ghazni, but one was favored above all the others—a Turk called Ayaz. Mystic medieval poets

---

* In 1983, Khomeini issued a fatwa authorizing "sex reassignment surgery" after a transsexual called Maryam Molkara was beaten up by the Supreme Leader's security guards in an attempt to gain an audience with him. Molkara explained her situation to Khomeini and soon afterward sex-change operations were legalized.

wrote about their relationship as the archetype of "innocent" love, although many scholars have suggested that it went a lot further.*

"No, no, no!" exclaimed Valli, laughing. "But that is appropriate. I'm talking about Mahmud Asgari and Ayaz Marhani. They were arrested for having sex with another boy—they are all teenagers; now they are going to be hanged. But it is interesting you think of Sultan Mahmud. How many men do you think he slept with?"

"Well, I don't know. It's not something the history books are specific about."

"But it was a lot, huh? This is the Persian culture. Same-sex playing has always happened here, so when the president says it doesn't exist, I think he must be blind. The mullahs say it's against the Quran— well, maybe they are right, but it's not so strange in our history, is it?** If a great sultan was allowed to sleep with boys, then why can't I?"

Later, when I was saying goodbye, the other man came over and whispered to Valli. I walked away toward Ferdowsi Square, but as I reached the corner I turned back to see the two men strolling in the other direction, hands clasped together—one gesture that wouldn't give them away.

෴

---

* A typical example occurs in the twelfth-century *Conference of the Birds* by Farid ud-Din Attar. Mahmud, distraught when his slave falls ill, declares: "Ayaz, what could this Evil Eye not do / If it destroys such loveliness as you."

** The poetry of Ferdowsi's age is rife with homosexual references, which are often surprisingly direct, such as the words of the Sahib Ibn Abbad, one of the leading politicians of the age, who exhorted a favorite to "spend the night with a beardless youth, a wide-buttocked lad, a loved one, / For wine and copulation, after indulgence with him—these are the really good things of life." Like the *bachhe bazi* or "child-playing" that is still common in Pashtun society, these medieval texts often veer on pederasty: hence the "beardless youth" who, in Abu Dulaf al-Khazriji's *Ode of the Banu Sasan*, is given "a stewpot whose contents will send him into a drugged stupor," after which "the penises of the beggar leaders go into him, without him being aware of it." However, other medieval poets have a more romantic approach to same-sex relationships—such as Hafez, who wrote of a lover who "with looks disheveled, flushed in a sweat of drunkenness, / His shirt torn open, a song on his lips and wine cup in his hand . . . at midnight last night he came and sat on my pillow."

Moonlight often visited the house. She had her own car, a shiny silver Peugeot 206, in which she would drive Tahmineh to the cinema or to see their friends. It was on one of these visits, when Tahmineh was taking an eternity to get ready, that I found myself being asked about her secret.

"Nicholas," said Moonlight, beckoning me to the kitchen table with her index finger. A copy of French *Vogue*, brought over from Dubai by Khanom's sister, was covering half her face like a veil, with the pages held between her nail extensions.

"In your country," she said, "boys and girls, they go out all the time?"

"Yes."

The magazine lowered and she leaned across the table.

"But you know," she said, "that in our country it is difficult?"

"Slightly!" I said.

She moved closer. "So many of us, we behave in secret ways. But you know, it is not always necessary. Between friends, for example . . ."

She was leaning so far across the table that I could see her collarbone.

"And you know," she continued, "I think Tahmineh, she behaves in secret ways."

As she drew back into her chair, it dawned on me what she was up to: I was being sourced.

"So do you know anything about her . . ." She paused, whispering the next word as if it were a top-secret code and I'd better not repeat it: "boyfriend?"

One evening at supper: While the Professor was raging against the closure of another reformist magazine, Tahmineh turned away from the talk and the only noises she made were the beeps on the buttons of her mobile phone.

"His identity is still a secret?" whispered her mother, to which Tahmineh replied with a click of her tongue.

Before, I wouldn't have known what they were talking about. But people were starting to speak more slowly and a lot more clearly. . . . At least, that's what it felt like: My Persian classes were starting to work!

Tahmineh was aware of the mystery, although she wasn't giving an inch. I imagined she was enjoying all the fuss. But one morning after breakfast, I realized something more uncomfortable was going on.

"What are you reading?" asked Tahmineh.

She had brought a plate of sliced melon and a glass of tea into Sina's room, where I was seated at the desk, trying to read a passage from the Professor's green-jacketed copy of the *Shahnameh*. The language was a toil and even with the help of my dictionary, I could make sense of only one couplet in every three or four—but the thrill of working out even half a line made it worthwhile.

"It's very hard!" I said. "Maybe I should try something easier—like Harry Potter!"

"What is the story?" asked Tahmineh.

It was about a warrior called Bizhan, who falls in love with a princess after hunting down wild boar in a meadow.

"Do you know it?" I asked. "I'm at the bit when Bizhan's cutting the heads off the boars. I've got this line—it says he wants to carry their tusks before the shah."

"Ehhh, baba loves this story. Give it!"

Sitting down on the bed, she let out a short laugh as the book rested on her lap.

"How heavy is this!"

She licked a finger to turn the page and read so fast her pupils barely appeared to be moving.

THE TALE OF BIZHAN AND MANIZEH
(PART ONE)

It is the princess, Manizeh, who sets the story in motion. Inflamed with desire for Bizhan, who cuts a dashing figure in his brocade gown and jeweled belt, she invites him to join her for a picnic. Loosening the girdle from his waist, she washes his feet in rose water, fills him up with wine and meat, and in case he is thinking of deserting her, she gives him a honey-flavored drug and has him carried back to her chambers, hidden under a curtain. But this is where the trouble begins: Manizeh is the daughter of Afrasiyab, the evil king of Turan, and when he finds out she's been at it with an Iranian knight, there is serious dudgeon.

"A man may be crowned but is truly ill-starred," read Tahmineh, "Who has in his household a daughter to guard."

These words are spoken by Afrasiyab, who flings his daughter out of his palace, bareheaded in a single wrap, while Bizhan is chained from head to foot and thrown into a pit blocked by a boulder so heavy it has to be transported by elephants. . . .

This was as far as Tahmineh read. She closed the book slowly, a palm on the top cover, her face stiff. Her bottom lip disappeared under her top teeth and she looked down at the picture of Ferdowsi on the cover as if she were seeing something else under all the swirling black and green lines. This was the *Shahnameh* at its most immediate, cutting away the centuries of distance and speaking to personal experience. I wanted to ask what she was thinking, what she was seeing as she stared through the cover. But it was enough just to catch her eye, alight like a flame at its fullest. As she pulled herself away from the book, I sensed the lid had lifted just a little over her secret. She presented the book like a gift, with her politest expression and both palms outstretched. Before I could think of anything to say, the door had closed behind her.

For the next couple of weeks, Tahmineh's relatives made no progress in the hunt to uncover her secret. Several times, I heard Sina's cousins asking if he knew anything, but he would always give them a short reply. Occasionally we went on a runaround to the bazaar district. The CD player would spin and Reza would fill up our tumblers with gin, while the elderly man from downstairs would knock on the door when the noise was too loud and gently ask us to keep it down.

"No, no, no," he would say to Reza's apology. "It is not a problem for *me*. But you must be careful of the *basijis*."

I remember Sina and Reza having a play-fight one night as we were leaving. Sina pulled at Reza's earlobes and Reza thrust his arm around Sina's waist, then threw him to the floor. But before he could step away, Sina had grabbed his foot and soon they were rolling over each other on the carpet, engulfed in laughter. They hugged each other with such affection that I'm sure Sina couldn't have had any suspicion. It was the last time I would see them together: Within a week the secret was out.

"Reza," announced Sina, "is a *koos-ghol*!"—a "cunt-ogre."

Over the next few days, I understood the revelation of Tahmineh's "misalliance" less in terms of words than in the atmosphere, since the tense whispers or full-throttle slanging matches were delivered too fast or idiomatically for me to translate. It was as if the wind had come billowing through the mosquito-net door and although it hadn't knocked anything over, havoc had been unleashed. The Professor would sit at the kitchen table, building a pyramid out of the ash from his Bahmans, while Khanom knocked on Tahmineh's door and tried to coax her out.

"This is *big* trouble," said Sina. "Baba doesn't like Reza's family, he is really angry. By the way, I don't want you to say anything to anyone."

He pressed a finger to his lips and I promised to keep mine sealed. Then he led me through the gate and hailed Mustafa.

"Come on," he said, "we're going for a hubbly-bubbly!"

Reza was nowhere to be seen. For the next two weeks, whenever I went out with Sina, our route would studiously avoid the bazaar district, and if I mentioned him, Sina would turn cagey. "Reza is not necessary!" he once snapped. "*I* am your friend," adding a phrase that I can only translate as "his mother has a donkey's cunt."

The Professor was the hardest hit by the revelation: If he had been a cartoon character there would have been a rain cloud over his head. There wasn't the same energy at our evening vodka sessions, and when I mentioned a romantic tale from Ferdowsi, I sensed a flash of pique behind his owl-like eyes.

As their guest, my loyalty should have been with the family. But there was something uncomfortable about all this male anger. Everyone withdrew into themselves and whispered among themselves. I would come back from class to see Khanom and the Professor talking furtively in the kitchen. But as soon as I approached them, the air would fill with a stubborn, formal silence, or, even more frustrating, they would talk very quickly. I had thought I was getting to know the whole family, but a new screen had shot up and I was on the wrong side. When they spoke, I sensed there was a subtext—and my Persian wasn't proficient enough to work out the sub.

"Reza?"

One afternoon, a few days after the secret had come out, I found him standing outside the language institute where I had my classes.

"You will come and see me?" he asked.

"I . . . I should . . ."

"You dropped me? I am not your friend anymore?"

He'd never exactly been Mr. Ecstatic, but Reza's face was now so long it was threatening to drip into his chest.

"No, of course not," I insisted, "but I . . ."

"So you will come and see me?"

"Um . . ."

My first thought was that I should be loyal to my host. If the Professor didn't like Reza and I was staying under his roof . . . My second thought was that I would really like to find out what was going on. . . . I had a quick internal tussle and the outcome expressed itself in my next sentence:

"So," I said, stepping closer to Reza, "when shall I come over?"

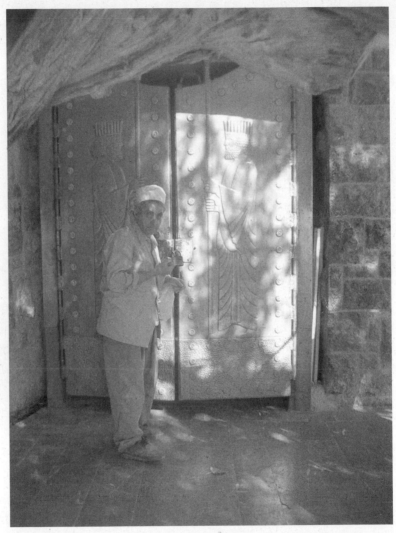

The Zoroastrian guardian of the Chak-Chak (or "Drip Drip") shrine near Yazd, where a daughter of Iran's last pre-Islamic king was said to be swallowed by the rocks.

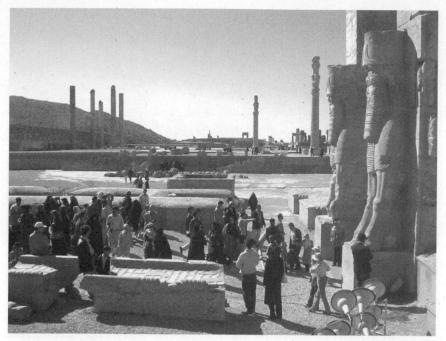

The Gate of All Nations at Persepolis, the palace complex built in the 6th century BCE by Darius the Great.

The Roman emperor Valerian and Philip the Arab submit to King Shapur I in a bas-relief in southern Iran. It is said that Shapur further humiliated Valerian by using him as a footstool.

A *zurkhaneh* or "strength-house" in Tehran, where the ancient Iranian sports are still practiced.

Traditional fortune-telling in Esfahan: a parakeet picks out a verse by the medieval poet Hafez, which will be taken as providential.

Men taking part in the *qama-zadan* or "dagger-striking" ritual, in honour of Imam Hossain, the Prophet's martyred grandson.

After the ritual, extensive bandaging is required.

Rahim e Yadullahi, a *Shahnameh-khwan* or "reader of the *Book of Kings*," with fans in his butcher shop in the Bakhtiari region of Iran, shortly after reciting one of his favorite tales.

Mohammed Abbas, the youngest of the *Shahnameh-khwans*, with his father.

A funeral procession in the Bakhtiari region.

Villagers in Pazh, where the poet Ferdowsi grew up. Several of the villagers claim to be his descendants.

A portrait of the
poet Ferdowsi in the
Tus Museum in eastern Iran.

The poet's mausoleum in Tus.

Women outside the mosque of Tehran University.

Qashqa'i tribeswomen in the Fars region of southern Iran.

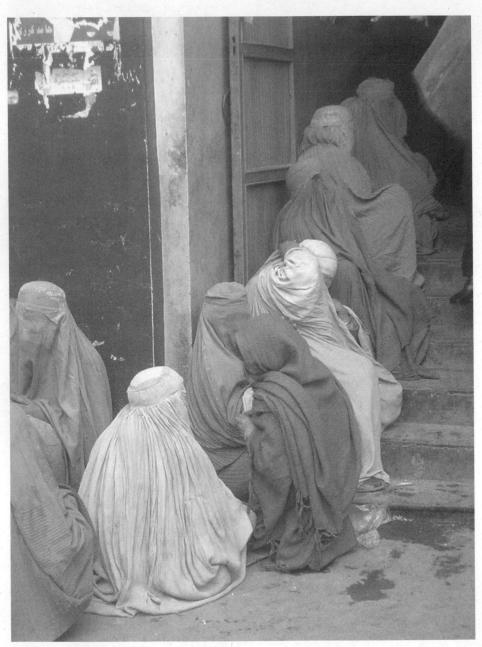

Women outside a mosque in Afghanistan.

The author with friends in Sistan, the southeastern region of Iran near the border with Afghanistan. Many of the people in this region claim to be *pahlavans*, descended from the epic hero Rostam.

. . . and in Afghanistan, having grown a beard for the journey.

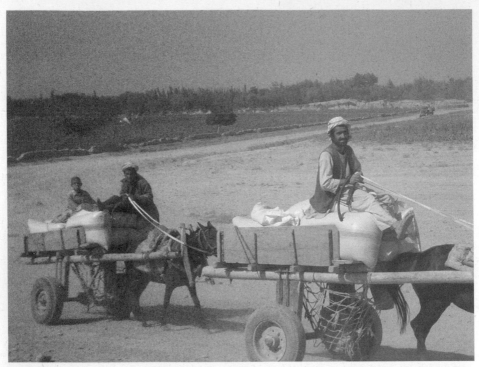

Traditional transport in northern Afghanistan.

The opium ritual.

Men wearing traditional *telpek* hats in Turkmenistan. These "high fur caps" were noted in the 10th century by the scribe Maqdisi and are made from the fells of month-and-a-half-old lambs.

A minstrel in the sugar market of Khojand, in Tajikistan. He is performing on a *dotar* and singing words written in the 10th century by the poet Rudaki.

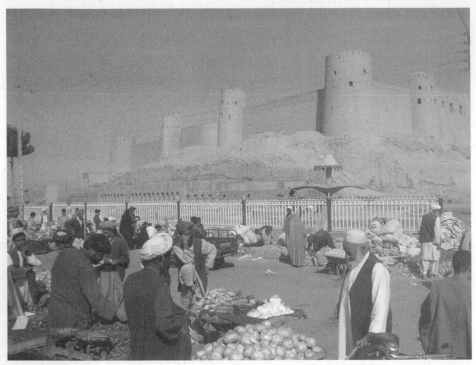

A market outside the citadel of Herat in Afghanistan.

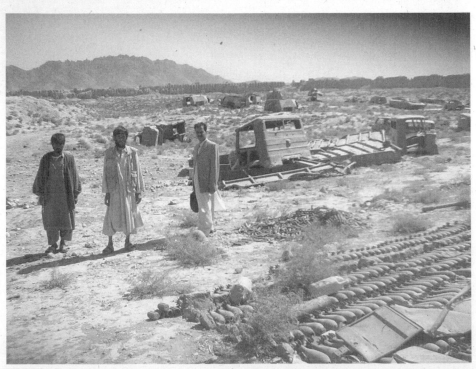

Wrecked military vehicles and weapons in the fort of Farah in southern Afghanistan.

The court of Sultan Mahmud, painted by Master Hadi Tajvidi in 1936. The long-bearded man in the chair to the left is Ferdowsi.

The ruins of a palace in Lashkar Gah, in the Helmand region of Afghanistan. In the 11th century, this was where the Ghaznavid sultans came for their summer retreat.

The tomb of Sultan Mahmud in Ghazni.

And the Sultan's modern-day counterpart—the governor of Ghazni today.

A mural of Ferdowsi outside a school in Tehran, with words from the *Shahnameh* written beside the poet.

9

The Man in the Moon
Tehran. April/May.

Traveling on the Metro emphasized the difference between the north and south of the city. Without seeing it change around you, it's like you've stepped into a wormhole, emerging in a different world—more crowded and less polished than the one you've left. Mowlavi Station was clearly in the south: The streets weren't particularly narrow, but the clutter closed them up. Handcarts tilted between the pickup trucks, with rolled-up carpets swinging like tank guns, and a man in Afghan *shalwar qameez* had to bend back as he was abluting himself in a streetside canal, to avoid being poked in the eye by a construction rod.

Keeping watch over this mayhem was Ayatollah Khomeini, peering down from the facade of a mosque as if to remind you that all this was transient. A similarly pious, otherworldly aura drifted across the hall to which Reza had given me directions.

There, seated on a marble pulpit, with an otter-skin drum between his thighs, was a man in a damp blue vest called Akbar. He was reciting prayers to Imam Ali, while the men underneath him—standing in a meter-deep octagonal pit, most of them in vests and many with loincloths around their waists—were chanting the names of the twelve imams. Whenever someone new arrived, Akbar slammed a bell under a mirrorwork arch. If the new arrival was especially venerable, he rapped on the drum as well. All around me, I could hear the religious verses and holy names, hanging in the air like talismans of Islam.

"Thanks for coming," said Reza, who was in the process of wrapping his own loincloth. His bare chest was already soaked in sweat, which glistened in the glare from a skylight. "What do you think?" he asked.

"Well . . . it's not like the gyms back home."

He smiled. "We call it a *zurkhaneh.*" A "strength house." "You know it's the oldest sport in Iran? We've been doing it since the time of Cyrus the Great."

Reza picked up a mulberry-wood block, setting it on the floor of the pit and performing push-ups on top of it. As I was watching him, an old man in an astrakhan hat lowered himself onto a bench near me, facing the pit. He invited me to sit next to him, introducing himself as "Sede Ismail," and calling to a boy to bring us tea. He poured his glass onto a saucer to cool it, placing it against his mouth and tipping the contents down his throat, all the time lifting his eyes to watch the men in the pit.

Hanging on the wall behind us was a series of framed black-and-white photographs. Bare-chested men stood proudly in leather plus fours, swinging large wooden dumbbells or packed together in matching shirts, like a rugby team. Among these figures was Takhti, the national hero, who won gold for freestyle wrestling at the 1956 Olympic Games but was poisoned in his prime because he insulted the shah's brother.*

"We call these men *pahlavans,*" explained Sede Ismail. "But Takhti was the greatest, so we called him 'Pahlavan of the World'" (which is the same title given to the hero Rostam in the *Shahnameh*).

We continued looking at the photographs, but a drumbeat was resounding. All eyes turned to Akbar, who was about to start a new recital:

> *Alighting, they tied both their steeds to a boulder,*
> *Advancing in casque and the garb of a soldier;*

---

* He was found dead in a hotel room in 1968. The government proclaimed his death a suicide, but popular belief blamed it on Savak, the shah's secret police.

Though troubled at heart, each as fierce as a pard,
They wrestled and parried till sweaty and scarred . . .

Sweat was dripping off Akbar's brow as he recited, while the men in the pit did their push-ups on the mulberry-wood blocks. They were bathed in the sunbeams pouring through the skylight, their bodies yo-yoing to the rhythm of the verse. I was riveted, not because of the speed with which they were performing, nor the stagelike synchronicity (which became even more pronounced when one of them juggled with a pair of dumbbells, spinning around the pit like a whirling dervish), but because the words were from the *Shahnameh*.

"It is poetry," said Akbar, when I asked him why he recited these verses, "and Ferdowsi makes us feel strong. He writes about sports and battles, so he is good for the strength house."

The verses, taken from the tale of "Rostam and Sohrab," weren't the only details to recall the pre-Islamic era. According to Akbar's brother, Mohammed, the dumbbells "are symbols of the ancient warrior's mace." The mulberry-wood blocks on which the men had been performing their push-ups represent "the soldiers' shields." When you lift them up you're echoing the practice by which the soldiers would form bridges across the enemy trenches in ancient battles. An iron shaft, looped with copper discs, was "a bow, like the one Rostam used," while the men's leather plus fours symbolized the leather apron of the ancient hero Kawa, who raised it as a flag in the fight against snake-shouldered Zahhak. The drum represents the drums beaten in battle, and the bell is struck to signal the end of play, just as bells proclaimed the end of the ancient battles. Here was the old Iranian military system—preserved down the ages, like a prehistoric insect in amber.

"Ferdowsi is our culture," said Akbar, when I asked about the different sources of his recitals. "And so is the Quran."*

---

* This dual culture is summed up by a popular story about Imam Ali and Rostam. One day they meet in a strength house and take part in a friendly wrestling match. There is nothing to divide them, so the match looks like it will end in a draw, but in the closing stages, Imam Ali calls out to God for help and wins the match. The point of the story is that they are exactly equal in Iranian culture—only God tips the balance in the imam's favor.

Living with the Professor, I had fallen into the assumption that the *Shahnameh* belonged to an exclusively nationalistic, secular "Persian" culture, distinct from the world of the mullahs. What I was starting to realize—what Reza and his neighborhood represented—was that you could be "Persian" and "Islamic" at once—in touch both with the country's ancient culture and with its current religious identity.

In some ways, though, the older members of the strength house were very similar to the Professor. Sede Ismail had been coming here since the 1950s and he shared my host's concern for the decline of recent years.

"We had so many people here in the shah's time," he said wistfully, "because everyone was rich then. But now it is only the ones who have a good income and can afford the time."

Back in the old days, the *pahlavans* were the most powerful men in the bazaar. Many of them acted as "thick-necks," operating protection rackets but also looking after families within their communities. But now they are the old guard, as detached from events as Khomeini on the mosque facade outside, no longer able to take a leading role in how their streets are run.

"This country is rotting," exclaimed another elderly *pahlavan*, in a twill jacket, who had sat down beside Sede Ismail. Clicking his teeth, he sighed at the photographs of his predecessors. "When we were young," he continued, "the air was clean. Now it's polluted. Everyone used to help each other. Now there are too many opium addicts and same-sex players. The economy is ruined, all the good things are being destroyed."

He peered despondently into his tea saucer, then looked up at me, as if I should be able to answer his next question.

"The strength house is the soil of Iran," he said. "If we lose these things then please tell me—what will be left?"

The strength house was one of several places where I came across the *Shahnameh* in an unlikely setting. Unlikely, at least, for a medieval poem—but not for *this* medieval poem. As the *Shahnameh-khwans* had told me, it could inspire farmers, feuding villagers, and soldiers;

as Tahmineh's reading of "Bizhan and Manizeh" suggested, it connected with the feelings of a person in love; as the opera of "Rostam
and Sohrab" highlighted, it evoked and celebrated the Persian culture
that it had been so instrumental in sustaining; and as Reza's *Zahhak*
painting showed, it commented on political circumstances today.
Chaucer, eat your heart out.

The Professor, more than anyone else, had introduced me to the
Shahnameh—and I was extremely grateful for that. But it was Reza
who had shown me the light it shines on today, and the strength house
had added another layer to my appreciation of Ferdowsi's poem,
demonstrating how it coexists with a strong Islamic sensibility. On a
broader level, this illustrated how the two most significant elements
of modern Iranian identity—religion and the national culture—don't
have to be kept apart, like squabbling in-laws at a wedding, but occasionally can be called upon to behave themselves and sit peacefully together at the head table.

"I think you know what my heart wishes to ask," said Reza.

I had a hunch. We were in his kitchen, sitting at the table where I'd
drunk a gallon or six of "London" gin over the past few months. Given
all that he had shown me in this time, I clearly owed him a favor. But
even more than that—I was curious to know more about his relationship with Tahmineh. At the Professor's, the only information came in
hints: the molehill of ash from his cigarettes or the slam of Tahmineh's
door. Now, sitting in Reza's kitchen, he answered everything I asked
him, volunteered more, and turned the story from a rumor into a full-
blown romance.

Tahmineh had often accompanied her brother to Reza's gallery
shows. Once, when she needed a poster for a student play, Reza had
offered to help:

"So I gave her my number. I didn't think she would call me, but
she did and I was very happy. So where was the best place for us to
meet? Well, here of course, in my flat."

The play had come and gone, but the meetings had continued.
They usually took place after dark, to avoid her being seen by the
furniture restorer across the street.

"We think he's an information man for the *basijis*," explained Reza.

When they met in the day it was at the National Park, where they would look at the peacocks, or in the coffee shops around Tajrish Square, the most youth-friendly area of the city. Although the law didn't approve of fraternizing between the sexes, it usually turned a blind eye to couples taking a promenade, and they had even managed to go to the cinema together. There in the back row—something I never expected to hear about in Iran—they had kissed.

On the occasions when he managed to smuggle her into his block, she had taught him about the old prerevolutionary films. Reza, in return, showed her how to sculpt a head from plaster and had even written poetry for her—although he refused to show it to me.

"Drop it!" he said. "I know what you want. You want it to be the same as Ferdowsi, you want me to say her voice is like a nightingale and these things! But it isn't like that. It doesn't even rhyme, it is free."

Since Tahmineh's phone had been confiscated, Reza was having trouble communicating with her, especially as she was grounded and allowed out only for classes and rehearsals. I looked at the piece of paper on which he was scribbling. It was easy to see why he had me down as an ideal emissary. Not only was I living at the Professor's— so I could pass on his notes without any trouble—but I could read Persian only in tidy print and certainly not the spaghetti scrawl that Reza was producing. It might contain instructions for a secret meeting; it might be an erotic billet-doux. But whatever it was, it was as impenetrable to me as a medieval spy's letter in invisible oak gall ink.

"Reza," I protested, "I'm a guest."

His eyes narrowed as he pressed the paper into my hand.

"I didn't think you were a coward," he said.

There was a pair of dumbbells, of exactly the kind they used in the strength house, in a corner of the living room at the Professor's. I wanted to talk about my visit—to ask the Professor what he thought about the connections between the sportsmen's equipment and the

Shahnameh. But each time I was about to mention it, my more practical side kicked in.

Tahmineh said nothing when I gave her the note. Her eyes were glued to the Jam-e Jam pop station and whenever I stole a glance, she kept whatever she was feeling under wraps. At least, until the Professor picked up the remote control and turned to the Geography Channel. She might not want to let on about her romantic state of mind, but there would be no discretion when it came to the TV.

"Tahmineh-dear!"

In the struggle for power, it was inevitably the father whose words proved the stronger, physically acting on Tahmineh so her shoulders sank and her head dropped, and soon she wasn't there at all. There was a slam of her bedroom door, followed by the staccato beat of sobbing, which gave way in turn to the songs of Googosh.

An hour later, I was writing at the desk in Sina's room when the door crashed open. Enter Tahmineh with a tray—a glass of tea and a plate of sliced melon. It was just like a few weeks ago, when she'd read me the story of "Bizhan and Manizeh." She set it down on a pile of hardbacks and offered a toothy smile. I thought she was thanking me for Reza's message, but when the door had closed I saw that the contents of the tray weren't just for my refreshment. Underneath the plate, written on a sheet of notepaper and sealed with tape, was a new message. Printed on top, in ink clear enough for me to read, was a single word: "Reza."

THE TALE OF BIZHAN AND MANIZEH
(PART TWO)

In the first part of the story, Manizeh is a giddy party girl, a "jasmine-bosomed beauty" who sprinkles the air with rose water. But in the second part, she fulfills a different feminine role: the constant beloved. Reduced to begging at people's doors, she collects what scraps people throw at her and pours them into a tiny hole above the pit in which Bizhan has been imprisoned. Things are looking bleak for the lovers, but help is at hand.

Rostam has been alerted to Bizhan's whereabouts by the surveil-lance camera of legendary Iran—a magic cup "that mirroreth the world." He sends a roasted bird wrapped in bread, inside which he has hidden his signet ring, and when Bizhan receives it he knows he will soon be saved. Manizeh stokes a bonfire to light Rostam's way, and when he arrives he picks up the boulder on top of the pit, then hurls it all the way to China. He hauls Bizhan out with his lasso, snapping his chains and passing him to Manizeh, who clings with joy to her emaci-ated lover. Before long, they are happily married and will never have to worry about a father's wrath again.

Killers say that once you've committed your first murder, the next one is easy. So it is with delivering romantic messages between the daughter of your host and his enemy's nephew. After my initial reservations, I was starting to enjoy it: Having watched all these people acting around me, I finally had a role of my own.

In a passage from the tale of Khosrow and Shirin (the story in which Tahmineh had been acting), a court painter is dispatched by the prince to the land of his beloved. There, in a meadow where Shirin often picnics, he hangs a painting of his master on a tree branch, in the hope that she will fall in love with him. Delivering Reza's messages to Tahmineh, I felt like I'd landed the part of the painter. Every few days I would turn up with a new secret message for Tahmineh, and once I was even asked to carry a present.

"It's not . . . well . . . " I suggested, "it's not exactly the most roman-tic gift I've ever seen."

But Reza was operating on another wavelength. "She'll under-stand," he said.

It was a Saddam Hussein rubber mask.

Perhaps I should have said no and refused to play postman. Per-haps I should have been more loyal to my host. But if Persianness is about anything, it's about love and secrets and people going behind the backs of higher authorities—although I doubted this would hold any sway with the Professor if I were caught.

As the summer heat intensified—squeezing out the sweat until you were like a juice carton that's been pierced by all the kebab skewers in the kitchen drawer—I continued delivering Reza's messages, wondering if they would ever run out.

ᴍ

TEHRAN. A FEW WEEKS LATER.

"Do you think," said Tahmineh one evening, "there is a man in the moon?"

We were standing on the balcony, gazing up at the stars. They glimmered like fireflies in smoke, shining through the violet haze of the smog.

"I did when I was younger," I said.

"When I was small, people told us Khomeini was in the moon. If you lit a fire under a glass and looked at the moon you could see his face."

She picked my lighter off the balcony rail and lit it under her glass. The moon was only a few nights off the full, but it was hard to twist its surface into the face I saw on the billboards every day.

"Well, I can't see him," I said. "Can you?"

"Of course not!"

She pressed her hands on the rail, swaying as she breathed in the air. She wasn't smiling—she was looking up at the sky as if she was searching for something; as if she was half expecting some galactic space-hopper to turn up and carry her away. It was a long while since I had seen her smile.

There had been no messages from Reza for a fortnight. I had feared that one of them would be intercepted by the Professor or Khanom, that I would be hurled out of the house in disgrace and my relationship with the Professor's family would be wrecked, but of course this hadn't happened. Instead, Reza had lost interest and started talking about a girl he knew from his sculpture classes.

Even when Tahmineh and I were alone in the living room, out of everyone else's earshot, she didn't mention him anymore. A few days earlier, we had been watching a prerevolutionary film starring her favorite actress, Googosh—one of those joyously uplifting stories about a young woman who watches her lover die, terribly slowly, of an incurable disease. Tahmineh had spent most of the film looking at the palm of her hand, occasionally moving her index finger to scoop a tear off her cheek.

"Will you miss us when you're away?" she asked.

I was heading off soon to travel east, into the mysterious neighboring region of Central Asia. Given the atmosphere in the house, I was looking forward to it.

"Of course," I exclaimed. "My heart will become tight."

She laughed at my use of the expression. "So many places you will see, and I saw nothing."

"I bet you will one day."

There were no teeth in her smile. She pressed down on my shoulder and squeezed.

"Say hello to the world," she whispered. She turned on her bare heel, treading softly on the chipped tiles as she stepped back inside the mosquito-net door.

10

Poets, Polymaths, and Pleasure-Daughters
Iran/Central Asia. June.

Planning a trip to Central Asia was one thing—getting in was another.

Sheep scuttled out of the farmsteads, sticks beating against their backs. Bony rock poked through the flesh of the hills underneath them and broke out above us in menacing formations, while gray clouds were hovering like zeppelins, threatening to empty their contents over the bus. This was the Galway of Iran. The brawler of landscapes. The sort that could give Fars a black eye.

The Turkmen officer was housed in a wooden hut with only a tiny gas heater to warm himself up. He looked like he'd been sentenced to man this post forever—and like his face had been growing longer ever since he'd started.

"Border closed," he said.

"Closed?"

"Terrorism."

"What?"

"Closed. Terrorism. Border closed."

"I don't underst—"

"Terrorism!" He stood up and snarled, "Tashkent! Border closed!"

"Tashkent? The bombs? But that's in Uzbekistan."

Slowly it was unraveled. There had been a series of bomb blasts and shootings in Tashkent and Bukhara a few days earlier, in which nearly fifty people had been killed, and the Uzbeks had closed their border with Turkmenistan. It shouldn't last long, but until it was resolved I wouldn't be allowed in. My entry date was specified on my visa, which was only a five-day transit. Which meant that, unless I could wangle my way into Turkmenistan in the next two days, it would be useless.

There was just one loophole. I knew of another border, at Sarakhs, about three hours' drive east. I crossed my fingers and hitched a ride with an apple truck.

There's nothing like a good scenic diversion to raise the spirits. Grass furred the hills around Sarakhs and rolled across the meadows down to the brooks, more plentifully than anywhere else I'd seen in Iran. Turkoman nomads were flitting among their felt tents, pegged above the banks in a village of cloth, with clouds of shaggy-coated sheep billowing beneath them. In this sort of setting, how could I not feel optimistic?

"Sir," said the customs official in the passengers' hall, "they do not permit the transit travelers to pass."

Was Central Asia intent on keeping me out? I clutched my passport, sitting down in the waiting hall, sinking into the gloomy realization that my foray to the East just wasn't going to happen, when fate decided to offer a nudge. Two brightly dressed women were struggling with an enormous rolled-up carpet. Their minivan was parked on the road outside the customs hut and their papers had already been stamped. I helped them to heave the carpet into their minivan, along with a couple more and a dozen cardboard boxes filled with small porcelain tea bowls, and consequently found myself hidden behind the merchandise. When I stumbled into the light, it was flashing off the gold lapel pins of the Turkmen security guards, all bearing the plump image of Turkmenbashy—"father of the Turkmen," one of the most eccentric dictators of recent times.* Fortunately, the guards were sufficiently confused by all the teaware in the minivan to wave me through.

---

* Among numerous innovations, Turkmenbashy renamed the months after members of his family, built gold statues of himself throughout the country (including

"Well yippadeedooda!"

I was so pleased to have crossed the border that I was perilously close to breaking into song. My driver, however, didn't exactly look like he would welcome such an occurrence. He pulled me back down to earth with an expression of unremitting misery.

"Turkmenistan rubbish!" he muttered.

We were driving across a desert devoid of anything. A desert in the most literal sense of the word: the Karakum, or "Black Sands"— a giant oven where nothing grows except for the odd silvery sauxal bush and a few scarlet threads of camel thorn.

"I'm sure it's not *that* bad," I said.

I wouldn't be staying long enough to find out. My visa required me to pass through as quickly as possible, so I would be taking the old Soviet railroad toward Uzbekistan and the city I was itching to visit: Bukhara.

I tried to tell the driver what had spurred me here—the great Samanid empire of the tenth century, the biggest power in the Eastern Islamic world when Ferdowsi was a boy—a kingdom that traded with China and Tibet and had so much fruit it was fed to animals as fodder. But the bridge between his Turkmen and my Persian was too flimsy to cross, and as I peered out at the bare landscape around us, it was hard to find anything with which to refute him. Throughout my travels in Iran, I had always been surrounded by mountains; but now it was as if the horizon had lost its defense. It was as naked as the strangely un-scarfed heads of the women I would see in the Central Asian cities.

All that had become familiar in recent months—mountains and melon juice, shared taxis and Shiism—was being swept aside for the new: *marshrutnoe* minivans, soda drinks sold out of big glass tubes like scientists' alembics, and a Turkic language that left me pining for Persian. Even the names of the countries I was traveling through— Turkmenistan, Uzbekistan, Tajikistan—spelled out uncertainty and

---

a twelve-meter effigy in the capital, revolving throughout the day to face the sun), and composed a national epic, the *Ruhnameh*, or *Book of the Soul*, with a day of the week set aside for the population to read it and questions set on it for anyone who wanted to pass their driving test.

strangeness. No wonder Rudyard Kipling called this region "the back of Beyond."

Before I traveled to Iran, like many people I had thought of the Central Asian countries as Russian satellites. After all, they were gobbled up by the tsar in the mid-nineteenth century and they remained under Moscow's thumb until the breakup of the Soviet Union in 1991, while their current borders were the work of Stalin in the 1920s. But the Professor had told me about another side to the "stans"—the Persian side. He often talked of friends in Dushanbe (the capital of Tajikistan), hard at work on books about the *Shahnameh* or Zoroastrianism, and of trips he'd made to the city of Bukhara, to research the old Persian heritage.

"You will see if you go," he said. "The Tajik government is proud of our Persian culture, not like our onion-heads!"

Slowly the Soviet covering was lifted and I began to see what was underneath. A few generations ago, there were Persian-speaking khans, oriental despots in the traditional manner, who hatted themselves in lambswool and begemmed their gowns with precious stones from the Badakhshan Mountains. The British officers Charles Stoddart and Arthur Conolly made their acquaintance in the 1840s, when Central Asia was being tugged between the Russians and the British as part of the "Great Game." For their troubles, they ended up in a bug pit in Bukhara, from which they were finally lifted only to have their heads chopped off. The suspicion of foreigners is still at large—as I discovered on the train across the Black Sands Desert. Having been refused a ticket by an anxious station clerk, ordered to sit on my own by a couple of soldiers, and finally (when a sympathetic party of Russian judo players spirited me onto the train and stowed me in their cabin) ordered to pay a bribe by the ticket inspector, I was at my wits' end. I was starting to sympathize with the nineteenth-century mullahs who preached against this new form of transport, calling it "the devil's cart."

The amount I'd been asked to pay was $2,000—just the sort of sum, in the ticket inspector's opinion, that a foreigner should have on hand, but not the sort of sum I was likely to part with, even if I could. In the end, it took the negotiating skills of a pair of prostitutes from Tajikistan (the only Persian speakers I could find on the train—and therefore the only people who could act as my go-betweens) to haggle the ticket inspector down. I ended up handing him a crisp ten-dollar note.

Stoddart and Conolly witnessed a dying world: A generation later, Central Asia had fallen to the tsar. To the region's traditions of hospitality, veils, turquoise-tiled mosques, and some of the best headwear in the world, the Russians would add collectivism, vodka, and—as I would soon discover—prostitutes in fishnet tights, along with the railroad on which I was traveling and an improved education system. Whether the old Persian ways had survived, though—whether the culture that flourished under the Samanid empire had been smothered by the centuries—I was hoping to find out. . . .

✑

"If a person stand on the fortress of Bukhara and cast his eyes around," wrote the tenth-century geographer Ibn Hawkal, "he shall not see anything but beautiful green and luxuriant verdure on every side of the country: so that he would imagine the green of the earth and the azure of the heavens were united." He would be shocked if he saw Bukhara now. From the top of the fort, I had a magic carpet's view of flat-roofed houses and water tanks, turtle-shell domes and burnt-brick towers squiggled with storks' nests. At dusk the walls turn golden brown, so it looks like the whole city has been baked in some giant cook's fantasy oven, with the odd splash of aquamarine icing where a dome or a *pishtaq* mosque-screen rises. But however far you peer, it's hard to find the greenery celebrated by Ibn Hawkal. And that's not because the old hundred-mile city wall has been flattened. It's down to a policy introduced by the Soviets, which is threatening to destroy the whole of Central Asia.

Monoculture. What the mullahs have tried—but failed—to do to Persian culture, the Soviets succeeded in doing with Central Asian horticulture: They stripped it down to a single component. Fields and orchards, once bright with the different colors of rice or wheat, paprika, tomatoes, onions, or olives, now turned the white of cotton.

The waters of the region's great rivers, the Oxus and the Jaxartes, were diverted into canals and irrigation ditches. Bled for the cotton, the rivers shriveled, while the Aral Sea shrank to the size of a pond (and the population around its banks is stricken by typhoid, intestinal infections, lung diseases caused by industrial pollutants, hepatitis . . . the list goes on). At the same time, the salt rose, encrusting the land and making it infertile. If this continues, Central Asia will run out of water altogether and the whole region will be uninhabitable.

Ibn Hawkal offers a glimpse of the region at its peak—but as you look out from the rooftop of Bukhara's citadel, it's hard to imagine it will ever be like that again.

It wasn't only its fertile soil that made Bukhara bloom. The tenth-century historian Tha'alibi called it "the Focus of Splendor, the Shrine of Empire, the Meeting-Place of the most unique intellects of the Age." Its royal library enchanted the physician-philosopher Ibn Sina, who claimed he had "never seen such a collection of books either before or since"; while its book bazaar was unequaled, filled with pages pulped from the branches of the local mulberry trees, according to an old Chinese recipe; and its princes divided their time between the polo field and the songs of the latest lute players. But not everyone was impressed. "Bukhara," announced Abu Bakr the Secretary, "is the anus of the world, and we have rushed headlong into it! Would that it would fart us forth at this minute, for we have stayed there too long!" It was overcrowded and filthy, its streets full of garbage and its buildings prone to fires. It's still pretty filthy, and its walls hang together like conspirators. Pipes clank overhead and plaster sprinkles the children who kick tins against the walls, while you have to duck when an iron-bossed door flings open and a housewife—holding up a bucket as lethally as a medieval archer with a quiver of poplar-head arrows—sprays the day's slops into the alley. The city looks like what it is—a backwater that once ruled the roost. There's a world-weary atmosphere seeping between the stones, as if to say, "We know how it works. You get all dressed up, everyone loves you, then one day they can't even remember your name." Bukhara is the ultimate has-been.

One of the reasons for the city's decline turned up here in the thirteenth century. Central Asia's vandal supreme—Genghis Khan (hurtling across the steppe in revenge for the shaving of his messengers' beards by the ruler of nearby Khwarezm)—tore the place apart and put thousands of its citizens to the sword. Only one building from the Samanid era survived his purge, saved because it had been buried under a graveyard (and it was only rediscovered in the nineteenth century, by a Russian scholar with a pitchfork).

An artist was sketching this monument as I came by, holding out his brush like a wand to conjure the old Samanid era to life. Gripped by pillars on either side, with salt-cellar domes peeking around the cupola on top, it was the size of a garden shed and the color of an oatmeal cookie. A spray of geometric shapes splashed across its surface, the baked-brick texture weaving a latticework, making it look like a giant wicker basket and underlining the Samanids' replacement of wood by brick as the principal material of construction.

Inside was equally manic. Diamonds and wheels were spinning in the spandrels and racing up the squinches to parade around the cornice. Light was seeping around them, pouring through squares and crosses and coupling with the shadows to conjure a play of penumbra over the tomb. It was like being in some kind of expressionist light-box, where the activity of the shadows was almost as adventurous as the extraordinary sculpturework.

The building is widely known as the mausoleum of Prince Ismail, the most revered of the Samanid amirs, who was welcomed to Bukhara in 874 CE with a scattering of coins over his head. But according to a barely legible inscription on a lintel in the doorway, the tomb is actually the resting place of Nasr, Ismail's grandson, who ruled the Samanid empire in the mid-tenth century.* Which gives another layer of meaning to this remarkable building—because it was in Nasr's reign that Bukhara rose to its eminence as the cultural center of the Islamic world. His patronage of many of the region's best poets

---

* The lintel was studied by the Russian scholar V. I. Belyaev, who attributed it to Nasr, as did W. L. Treadwell in the *Political History of the Samanid State.*

turned Bukhara into the Parnassus of its day. A new literary culture was established, snowballing around the Eastern Islamic world—a phenomenon that scholars call the "New Persian Renaissance." It was arguably the most significant cultural flowering the Persian-speaking world would ever witness—culminating in the composition of the Persian language's most important single work: the *Shahnameh*.

What is extraordinary about this beautiful mausoleum is how vividly it expresses Nasr's cultural philosophy. He was especially keen on his Zoroastrian heritage, which is reflected by many of the motifs. The box shape of four arcaded walls is cribbed from Zoroastrian fire temples, while a triangle outside the doorway suggests the Zoroastrian motto of "good works, deeds, thoughts," and the wheels framing the spandrels are the Zoroastrian symbol for eternal life. In hints and codes, the pre-Islamic culture whispers over the mausoleum like a half-revealed secret, just as it did at the court of Nasr. His poets wrote elegies in praise of Zoroastrian festivals like *Nowruz* and addressed him by the old royal Persian name of "Khusraw." When he was toppled in a coup, this brief cultural fireball started to fizzle out, but its embers would make their way across the Black Sands Desert to inspire Ferdowsi.

While I was looking around the mausoleum, a group of women in striped pantaloons and colored shawls was squatting near the tomb. Sitting at their center, like a mother hen among her brood, was an ancient-looking lady, with wiry silver coils peeking out of her headscarf. She was mumbling a prayer, but the clack of a skewer-like heel on the floor made her turn around.

The newcomer was wearing a knee-length skirt and her arms were bare under a denim camisole. She looked like some starlet beamed over from the French Riviera. Her face was pinched with an anxious expression as she made a triple circuit of the tomb, before placing her hands in a hole at the end and murmuring a prayer. When she finished, the old woman gave her a handful of pomegranate seeds and floated her hands over her face (the *amin* ritual that Central Asians perform on religious occasions and whenever they eat—I would come across the same ritual in Afghanistan). A smile flickered across the lady's lips, but, like a bird looking for the right branch, it vanished before it could settle.

I was intrigued by the hole, so when the group had dispersed I asked the old woman what it signified. She looked at me, one brow tilted and the other one straight, as if they were weighing up my credentials, and finally the words came out of her small, parched lips in the disembodied tone of a sibyl:

"When a woman wishes to have a child, we believe she must place her hands inside the tomb. If earth falls on them, it is a sign that her wish, God willing, will be fulfilled."

"And did that lady? . . ."

"Tchkk!" A spark flashed in the old woman's eyes. "I can see you are a nosy young man! The answer to that question does not belong to you."

Nowadays, Uzbekistan's dominant language is Uzbek, which is related to Turkish. But this isn't the case in Bukhara. Here, the population has retained the Persian language, as well as the culture that goes with it. They are Tajiks—a Persian-speaking ethnic group who dominate the neighboring country of Tajikistan. Along with the Iranians and the Dari-speaking population of Afghanistan, they are one of the three pieces of the Persian jigsaw.

Among them was a copper-chaser called Sadriddin. I met him across the street from the mud-brick guest house where I was staying, in a converted *caravanserai* where he was displaying his work— ghoulish men hobbling across the dishes, lovers sipping wine under plane trees, and the ancient Persian shahs riding out on the hunt, surrounded by intricate borders of geometric strapwork and elaborate gadrooning. He was holding his knife over his work as we talked, brown eyes blazing on his face, which was as clearly cut as if he'd etched it himself out of one of his plates.

"There is no one like me," he whispered in a tone of tremendous secrecy. "I have a gift from God!"

He shook his knife at the stone ceiling of his workshop, the blade's edge catching a spark from the dusty light outside.

"Most of the artists have a master," he said, "but I studied with no one. Why should I? I did not need to!"

Sadriddin's straightforward confidence was disarming—I warmed to him at once. He seemed to be intrigued by my Persian, so he was happy to meet again, and over the next few days we made a habit of hooking up by the Labi Hauz—where men in padded *chapan* coats were clicking their backgammon counters on carpeted bedsteads around a water tank. We would stretch out our legs on the bedsteads, dipping Russian dumplings in sour cream or eating Persian-style kebabs, with a bottle of Shohrud wine between us.

"Ibn Sina recommends wine in his *Qanun*," said Sadriddin, "so why should we disagree?"

He was referring to the eleventh-century physician and philosopher,* who wrote: "When wine is taken in moderation, it gives rise to a large amount of breath, whose character is balanced, and whose luminosity is strong and brilliant."

"He also says mulberries are good for the stomach," I added, plucking a couple off the branches over our heads and passing one across, to a laugh from Sadriddin.

Chatter like this was par for the course, but occasionally the talk would take a darker tone. Like most Tajiks in Bukhara, Sadriddin had an identity crisis, which he was keen to tell me about.

---

* I had come across Ibn Sina several times on my journey—medieval Persia's greatest physician, who impressed Europe enough for the Italian poet Dante to "honor" him with a place in the first circle of hell, as one of the "virtuous heathens." In the city of Hamadan, I stepped inside his rocket-shaped mausoleum. Visitors filled up the tomb chamber and kneeled beside Ibn Sina's tomb-slab to utter a prayer, while herbs from his medical prescriptions were arranged in glass cases on the walls around them. "You know what these people are doing?" said a schoolteacher called Mehdi, sitting down beside me in the park beside the mausoleum. "They are going inside to have a look at Ibn Sina's *Qanun*. Maybe they know someone who is ill so they are looking for a cure." "But shouldn't they go to a doctor?" I asked. "Ha! Don't you know how much that costs? Let me tell you something. Last winter, my son had a problem with his stomach and the doctors could not make him better. So I looked in the *Qanun* and Ibn Sina told me to take cumin and a special flower and mix it with butter, and when I gave this to my son he became better." As far as I could understand, his son was suffering from enteritis, for which Ibn Sina recommends "three drachms each of the nasturtium and cumin ground together, sieved and thoroughly mixed with cow-butter."

"My passport says I am Uzbek," he explained one evening over a bottle. "But I am not Uzbek—I am Tajik. This is the same for most people in Bukhara."

"Would you prefer to live in Tajikistan?" I asked.

"No! Tajikistan is a disaster, the economy there is really bad and there is no security. But I am not a Turk, that's for sure! The government here hates the Tajiks—they force us all to speak Uzbek and they say the Tajik symbols are not really Tajiks. For example, you know about Ibn Sina, of course. Well, the Uzbek government—they are saying he was a Turk. You see? They want to take away our culture.* And they make it difficult for people in Tajikistan to visit us, or for us to visit them. You know they plant mines around the border? There are thousands of them. So to be a Tajik in Uzbekistan is hard. Tajikistan is a disaster, Uzbekistan is not our country. So where do we go?"

This connection to figures from the medieval Persian past was a way for Tajiks to keep their sense of identity. Apart from Bukhara, there were few ancient sites they could claim as examples of their people's former glory—and certainly nothing on the scale of Persepolis. So they linked themselves to the personalities instead, turning figures like Ibn Sina, the scholar Biruni, and the minstrel Rudaki (who was the superstar of Prince Nasr's mid-tenth-century court) into totems of Tajikness. This obsession with figures from the Persian-speaking past would strike me even more forcefully when I made it to Tajikistan itself, but it was present in all sorts of little ways even in

---

* I came across this politicization of medieval history myself, in Tashkent (the capital of Uzbekistan), when I met some of the scholars at the prestigious Oriental Institute. Dr. Vakhma Alimova, apparently a medieval expert, informed me that Ibn Sina was of Turkic origin—like the Uzbeks themselves. Given that his mother's name was Sitareh (Persian for "star"), he wrote several books in Persian (even though Arabic was the language of books at the time) and most of the population of the Samanid empire were Persian-speaking, this was a ridiculous claim. One of her colleagues, Dr. Mirsadiq Izkhakov, insisted Ibn Sina's contemporary, Biruni, was also a Turk. They were rewriting the ethnic history of the region to bolster the Turkic agenda of President Karimov's nationalist government.

Bukhara. It would be reinforced, in fact (in what at first glance was the most unlikely of settings), when Sadriddin took me to meet his "girlfriend."

The idea of meeting an Uzbek-Tajik's girlfriend intrigued me—Central Asia wasn't exactly brimming with couples out for a romantic promenade—so I was curious to see how the ritual of courtship was acted out. Was it as secretive, I wondered, as the separated lovers I'd left behind in Tehran?

Inside a concrete block on the outskirts of Bukhara, a noxious combination of gas and rotten food followed us up the banister. A man was fixing a lock on a door, behind which was a cozy, domestic scene—fresh fabrics and a hint of peppermint—while Alpine landscapes hung on the walls and between a pair of sofas was a walnut table where the tea bowls were already set. It was the kind of place you'd expect to be introduced to somebody's aunt.

"So," said the only lady who could fit this role (she wore a shimmering silver dress and a mouthful of gold teeth), "which of my girls do you want?"

"Ahhh!" Now I got it.

The guest room was being used, so Sadriddin's "girlfriend"—a matchstick in a tiny black skirt and nothing under her vest—pinned a sheet to the walls in a corner of the room. The sheet only vaguely covered their modesty—once they had undressed, the corner of the room became a cross between a blue movie and a shadow play. I felt embarrassed—especially when I caught the aunt figure's hawklike eyes. A couple of girls were coming in and out of the guest room, both in their underwear, and one of them in a pair of fishnet tights. The latter spent a few minutes on the sofa opposite me, smoking a cigarette with an expression of utter boredom, before leaping off the sofa and springing back into the guest room.

"The Soviets gave us *this*," declared the aunt figure, pointing a sharp red fingernail at the guest room door.

"Gave you what?" I asked, slightly confused. "Fishnets?"

"No, you fool! *This*. Oh, I know," she added, flashing her gold teeth as she laughed, "we had pleasure-daughters before—but they were only for the khans. This is what the Communists taught us— if a man has two thousand *sum* (about five dollars at this point in time), he can have a pleasure-daughter too."

There was another girl, cross-legged on the floor with a glass of Coke, whose expression—studious and a little severe—didn't go at all with her black boob-tube and shiny red microskirt. She looked up at me, without smiling, and turned back to a book she was reading: a short story collection by the Tajik author Sadriddin Ayni.

"Is it good?" I asked.

She lifted her shoulders noncommittally and turned back to the book.

I wanted to ask her more, but Aunt was eyeing me from the other side of the table.

"You want her?"

"No."

"So why are you talking to her?"

I felt awkward. I wasn't sure whether I should wait for Sadriddin or make my excuses and leave, and feeling somewhat fidgety I turned to a backgammon board on the table, moving the counters absently while I was working out what to do. But Aunt was more decisive: She leaned across the table, setting the counters in place, and challenged me to a game.

"I am a good player," she declared.

She was right: In five minutes I was beaten.

"Now you have to give me something," she said.

It was like a slap in the face. She was going to take all my money! She was going to call on the man fixing the lock (surely it didn't take *that* long to mend a door—he must be here for something else), and if I didn't cough up she'd get him to beat me up. But it wasn't my money, apparently, that she was after.

"Take off your shirt," she instructed.

The girl with the book was nodding. "This is correct," she said— like it was enshrined in the national constitution.

I don't think it was the wine I'd drunk at dinner—I don't think it was even the fact I was outnumbered. I did consider maintaining my position as the lone prude in the room, but the words "to hell with it" were whizzing through my head and before I knew what I was doing I had unbuttoned my shirt, handed it over to Aunt, and was squaring my naked shoulders over the re-set board. Barechested backgammon in a brothel—don't knock it till you've tried it.

The fear of having to discard anything else concentrated my mind, as all those games with Tahmineh started to bear fruit. Thanks to a few lucky turns of the dice, I marched my counters along the rows, blocked five of them ahead of the twenty-fourth, and secured my home area. Soon I had two of Aunt's counters imprisoned in my corner, with no way out.

"So why do you come to Bukhara?" she asked.

Hmmm—a cheap delay tactic if ever I heard one!

I mentioned my interest in Persian culture and the *Shahnameh*, but I felt silly doing so; poetry seemed out of place in a brothel (although, in retrospect, that was stupid—prostitutes and poets have always gotten on rather well.)*

"Rukhana knows many poets," said Aunt, smiling at the girl with the book.

So it appeared. Rukhana looked up and, in a soft, weary voice, started reciting. Her voice was so flat and her expression so blank that I didn't pick it up at first, but a few lines in I realized it was a poem I knew, a poem written more than a thousand years ago.

According to the story, Prince Nasr was neglecting his court, holidaying in Herat and enjoying himself so much that his courtiers were in despair. To their rescue came Rudaki, Nasr's favorite poet. He set off with his harp and sang the verses Rukhana was now reciting, which so inflamed the prince with love for Bukhara that he was on his horse and riding back home before he even had time to put on his boots:

---

* Especially in medieval Muslim lands, where the ninth-century polymath Jahiz describes "singing-girls" who knew 10,000 verses by heart, but remarks, "their origins in pimping-houses throw them into the arms of fornicators."

> *The Ju-yi Muliyan we call to mind,*
> *We long for those dear friends long left behind.*
> *The sands of Oxus, toilsome though they be,*
> *Beneath my feet were soft as silk to me.*
> *The moon's the prince, Bukhara is the sky,*
> *O sky, the moon shall light thee by and by.* *

It's hard to imagine an English equivalent: a Soho call girl quoting from *Beowulf*? Momentarily startled, I tried to focus on the game. Aunt conceded defeat well before it was certain, swiping the counters and folding her arms over her chest. I waited, wondering if I would get my shirt back. But she turned to Rukhana, who crossed her arms behind her neck and slipped out of her top.

"Rukhana is my body," exclaimed Aunt, her gold teeth flashing as she laughed.

Rukhana wasn't laughing. She sat motionless, like an artist's model. She was well formed, and I had a feeling that her state of undress was an act of gamesmanship by Aunt, or part of a ploy that would end up with the magical disappearance of my wallet. As the next game began, I tried not to look at her, to concentrate on the board, to make sure I didn't lose any more of my clothes. . . . But before I could make my first move, there was an interruption. I noticed it before it happened:

---

* I knew the poem because a musical version of it, recorded in the 1950s by the Iranian duo Banyan and Manizeh, was often played on a tape at the Professor's house in Tehran. A few weeks later, in the Tajik city of Khojand, I would hear it again. This time it was in a very different setting: a sugar market. Among stalls selling rock crystal, boiled sweets, and bags of sugar cubes, an old man was seated on a metal cart. His jacket was tied around his waist with a sash and was in as threadbare a state as his trousers, while a pair of pointy-toed shoes dangled off his feet. Underneath him, a cap lay in the mouth of a large leather bag, filling up with the banknotes of the passersby. But he didn't appear to notice: He was too carried away with his song, his head tilted back and his eyes like gems. The rounded end of a *dotar* rested in the crook of one arm, while the fingers of his other arm plucked its strings as if he were picking the petals of a flower. He had been a minstrel, he told me, for sixteen years and had traveled widely in Tajikistan, performing not only Rudaki but many of the other Persian greats. "I sang in many villages during the fighting," he said, "and my songs gave comfort to many people in this time."

I was trying to keep Rukhana out of my line of sight, and my eyes had latched onto the sheet at the back of the room.

The pin holding it up was wobbling, as if it couldn't contain its excitement over the activity it was concealing. It fell in a dive, but the sheet's descent was more graceful: a gentle flutter, as it draped itself over Sadriddin's girl, so that for a moment she turned into a pantomime ghost. Then, as she pulled herself up, the sheet slipped down. She reflexively crossed her hands over the most notable details of her nakedness and raced across the room, barging through the door to the guest room and provoking a furious growl from behind it.

"So, Nicholas," said Sadriddin, yanking up his trousers as he swaggered toward the table, "did you win?"

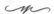

It's September 1991. All over the Soviet Union, the old system is falling apart. In Dushanbe, the capital of Tajikistan, crowds are gathering on Prospekt Lenina, the main thoroughfare. They make their way toward the government headquarters: farmers, factory workers, the disenchanted. They throw a lasso around the giant statue of Lenin and, with the help of a crane, drag it to the ground. And what do they set up in its place? A poet. A man made of bronze, with a long wild beard and a flame in his hands.

Ferdowsi.

After decades of Russian hegemony, Tajikistan's Persian identity has been reignited.

"It was a living hell," said Bahriddin Aliev.

Plump and swarthy skinned, he was seated in his office in central Dushanbe over a table scattered with papers and scripts from his different jobs as journalist, radio playwright, political analyst, and historian—as if the table itself were illustrating the chaos he was describing.

"It was Tajik against Tajik," he said. "We had the Islamic movement and the nationalist movement against the Communists against the Uzbeks. You couldn't go outside for fear you'd be beaten up or killed by the looters. They even came into our houses. Once—you remember?"

He turned to his colleague—a tall, lean man with little hair and a grave, earnest manner.

"Dr. Qasimi and I were working in my house," continued Aliev. "Soldiers came in. They beat me on the head with a Kalashnikov, so hard I lost consciousness. Then they turned to Dr. Qasimi and put a knife to his neck."

"I couldn't eat for two weeks," chuckled Dr. Qasimi, as if it had been a minor accident.

"But why? Had you written something against them?" I asked.

"No!" Aliev snorted. "They just wanted our money."

"At day they were soldiers," said Dr. Qasimi, "but at night they were thieves."

The cost of the Tajik civil war was still being counted. It told in the city center, in bullet-scored apartment blocks that looked like they'd been patterned on water crackers, in missing pedimenta on the pastel stucco buildings, and in the earth mounds between them, buzzing with construction cranes. Having managed to survive the Soviet era, it was only now—when power was back in the hands of the native Tajiks—that the indigenous culture was being ransacked. As one of the country's most prominent novelists explained, it was left to a few brave individuals to keep it alive.

"They were throwing our books out onto the streets," said Munira Shahidi.

She was a striking woman in middle age with a moon-shaped face where a pencil line of brow ran above her eyes. Her father had founded the Tajik National Opera and her grandfather was a local folk hero who fought against the Bolsheviks before ending his days in a Siberian gulag. This made her a name in Dushanbe, but it was her father's legacy she followed, borne out by the drums and two-stringed *dotars* and the photographs of bards in striped *chapan* coats surrounding her— fragments of the native Persian culture she had fought to preserve:

"When I saw the Melody Music Shop on fire—by maybe Islamic fundamentalists, but I don't like to use those terms—I bought everything in the shop—for nothing, about two thousand rubles. There were translations from Tajik into European languages that were being thrown away in the library, and they were so dear to me, so I collected them."

While the war was being waged, she held poetry and musical gatherings in her father's old house and set up classes for the local children.

"I even had classes for small girls who couldn't go to school," she said. "Many of the mullahs said girls shouldn't go to school, and many of them still say that. Sometimes parents would take their girls away from the classes and when I asked them why, they would give funny explanations like, 'We don't have any shoes.'"

She shook her head as she spoke.

"It is because the mullahs are badly educated," she said, "because the Soviets banned Islamic education. But this is where intellectual Islam was born—here, in Central Asia."*

Spilling out of a lush green valley under the icy peaks of Mount Hissar, Dushanbe belies its setting. Flyovers lunge over the cement mounds and high-rise Soviet concrete blocks soar between them. It's the architectural equivalent of an old hag in a beautiful ball gown. And in this respect, it's a far cry from desert-wrapped Bukhara. Where the latter is a has-been, Dushanbe is the wannabe. It's only been around for eighty-odd years, so it's barely out of infancy, but it really wants to start making some noise, and the best way it's found to attract our attention is its statues. They're everywhere—sculpted from plaster, beaten out of bronze, molded from gold. And guess what era most of them are from. . . .

You walk past the Writers' Institute on Prospekt Rudaki (the former Prospekt Lenina, now named after the tenth-century poet) and you see Ibn Sina with a towel over his legs, Rudaki raising a book, and Ferdowsi himself, twisting his body to face the viewer, with a scroll in his hands. The same characters are enmarbled at the Ferdowsi Library, where the

---

* It was in Bukhara, especially, that many of the early important Islamic scholars resided, such as Imam al-Bokhari, a ninth-century theologian whose work on the *hadiths* (anecdotes and sayings about and by the Prophet Mohammed) are considered the most authentic of all. To many Muslims, his book is second in importance only to the Quran.

poet appears in a bust in the lobby and in a pair of *gabillin* rugs (based on the technique of the Gobelin tapestry-makers of sixteenth-century France), while his turbaned head has been fashioned out of verses from the *Shahnameh* in an ink sketch. And in a park named after Ferdowsi, the statue that once took the place of Lenin now holds his flame over the ice-cream stalls. It's a medieval orientalist's Disneyland.

The most prominent of all the statues is in the middle of Prospekt Rudaki. Framed in a triumphal arch and raising a star-shaped scepter like an Olympian's torch is Prince Ismail, ruler of the Samanid empire in the late ninth century. He soars over ordinary mortals, eleven meters of iridescent gold, looking less like an icon of Persian identity than a Greek god. Water, which couldn't be coaxed out of the taps in the apartment I'd rented for the week, sprays in grotesque abundance from the fountains behind him, spewing over a succession of pools all the way to the Radio Centre. If you step too close, a policeman blows his whistle and ushers you away. It's as if Prince Ismail is a deity (and a double for the Tajik president, Imamali Rakhmonov, whose portrait is set beside the prince's in government buildings as part of a strategy to bask in the glory of the Samanids). But in a country where the monthly minimum wage is barely enough to buy half a sack of flour, the question niggles: How much did the statue cost?

In 1999 President Rakhmonov placed a capsule of soil from Bukhara under the statue of Prince Ismail. This wasn't just a token gesture: According to Khodai Sharifov, a scholar whom I met at the Writers' Institute, members of the Tajik government frequently repeated Prince Ismail's apocryphal slogan—"As long as I live, I am the wall of Bukhara."

"They want Bukhara and Samarkand to be part of the Tajik state," Sharifov said, "because most of their citizens are ethnic Tajiks."*

---

* When the Tajik government asked UNESCO to declare 1999 the "Year of the Samanids," the Uzbeks were apoplectic. A meeting was arranged in Paris to defuse the dispute, in which Uzbek President Karimov's representatives insisted it was insensitive for the Tajiks to celebrate as a "state" an empire that included the best-known cities of a neighboring country.

So the statue is more than just a celebration of the past—more than just a nice old fellow from yesteryear for everyone to look at on their way to work. It's a needle to jab at the Tajiks and keep the conflict with the Uzbeks alive.

"I have a pain in my heart!" said Davra, a young Tajik scholar, sitting next to me in Bahriddin Aliev's office. "The Uzbeks, they organized the civil war here so the Tajiks in Uzbekistan would not want to join us. But Bukhara is ours. It belongs to the Tajiks."

He clenched a fist and held it over the table.

"Why did God create the Turks?" he hissed. "They aren't even human; they are more like wolves!"

I was intrigued by the Uzbek-Tajik conflict. The ghosts of the region's past were being harnessed on both sides to help them in the battle for supremacy—a battle in which history and culture were as significant as territory. It was a playground scrap in which two fledgling states were fighting for their identities.

For the Persian-speaking Tajiks, Ferdowsi and the *Shahnameh* were essential to this identity: Hence I came across the poet's image—carved in busts, painted in murals, erected in statues—in all sorts of unexpected places in Dushanbe. But there was a sinister shadow over this Ferdowsi love, and when I met the scholar Ustad Valli Samad, I learned about the mighty superpower that had cast it.

"I dedicate my life to Ferdowsi!" he announced.

To reinforce his claim, an image of the poet, in his trademark tufted turban, was pinned to the lapel of his jacket. But this small, stooped Tajik scholar with a round, gnomelike head wasn't just a Ferdowsi-phile. He also had a surprising affection for the Russians.

"When the Tajik republic was created in the 1920s," he said, sitting at a cloth-covered table in a café in downtown Dushanbe, "Stalin telegrammed the Tajik government and said the *Shahnameh* was the source of Tajik culture and tradition. The *Shahnameh* saved our culture and our language, because if it didn't exist, the Turks and the Arabs would have destroyed the Tajik nation. This is why, when independence came in 1991, the people took off the Lenin monument and put Ferdowsi in its place."

His bulbous head dropped down as he dug into his satchel and pulled out a proof copy of a book he was writing: *The Shahnameh in the Destiny of Chernishevsky.*

"It is based," he said, "on my research in many cities. Chernishevsky was one of the first great Marxists. He wanted to save the Russian nation, and he saw a way to do this in the *Shahnameh* because it explains how to fight foreign invaders. When Chernishevsky read the story of Rostam and Sohrab to his students, he had tears in his eyes, his students too. When he was exiled to hard labor in Siberia, he wrote a poem about Ferdowsi. And under his influence, Karl Marx also became an admirer of Ferdowsi."

"Marx?"

They hardly seemed natural bosom buddies. However much Ferdowsi might criticize the shahs, it's not for having too much private property. But Ustad Valli had "proof."

"Do you know what Marx called his daughter?" he said. "Eleanor Tussy. After Tus, Ferdowsi's hometown."*

If Ustad Valli was trying to suggest the founding fathers of Bolshevism had a genuine admiration for Persian culture, then another scholar insisted it was more about realpolitik.

I had met Azim Malikov in Uzbekistan, in the city of Samarkand, the extraordinary metropolis built around the great blue tiled *pishtaqs* of the Timurids. An expert on ethnic identity, he criticized many of his fellow Uzbek historians for their obedience to government ideology. Unlike many of them, he acknowledged the Persian/Tajik identity of the scholars who flourished in the Samanid era, and pointed

---

* This was the nickname "by which she was to be known even outside the family" (according to Eleanor's biographer, Chushichi Tsuzuki, who suggested that it "seems to have been derived from pussy, for she was very fond of kittens"). However, Marx was certainly known to have studied Chernishevsky's writings and to be fond of epic literature (the tales of Homer, Shakespeare, and the *1001 Nights* were among the bedtime stories with which Eleanor was entertained as a child).

out that Turkic tribes were only beginning to push into Central Asia in this period, sparking battles with the Samanid army.

"After the fall of the Samanid empire," he said (which happened at the very end of the tenth century—many of its lands were sucked up by the Ghaznavid empire of Sultan Mahmud), "Tajiks and Turks were starting to assimilate. By the end of the medieval period they were mixed up and getting on pretty well."

Blood was no longer being shed because blood was being mixed.

"But in the nineteenth century," he continued, "Persian- and Turkic-speaking people fought together against the Russians. So the Russians decided to split them. They encouraged the idea that Persian speakers had a different culture and the Tajiks had been robbed by the Turkic people. So they encouraged the Tajiks to celebrate their culture—especially any parts of it that were different from the Uzbeks."

A similar tactic was used by the British in India, to divide the Hindu and Muslim populations under their control, with similarly disastrous long-term results. I thought of Sadriddin in Bukhara, who had spoken angrily about the Uzbek "Turks," and of the many Uzbeks I'd met in Tashkent a few days earlier, who derided the Tajiks as "without culture." The Russian policy had clearly been effective.

According to Malikov, it was this desire for divide and rule that prompted Stalin to praise the *Shahnameh*. The same tactic led, in the 1960s and '70s, to the Soviet regime championing a trilogy of films based on Ferdowsi's epic. They were directed by Boris Kimiyagarov, a former student of the great Russian auteur Sergei Eisenstein. Although Kimiyagarov died many years ago, I had heard that his assistant director, Zuad Dokteh, was still alive and living in Dushanbe. If I could talk to him, perhaps I would learn a little more about the politicization of culture in the region, so, on my last afternoon in the city, I set out to a metal-gated office complex to meet him.

"You have seen those films?" he asked, leading me to a round hardwood table under a map of Tajikistan. "If you had seen them when they came out—the impact they had! When they were shown at the Moss Studio in Moscow, there were so many famous people watching and they were in awe—because it was so wonderful!"

A plump, easygoing man in slacks, he sat back in his chair, nodding contentedly as he remembered the complicated shoots, which
took the production team as far as the Balkans in search of the right
castles for their scenes. Not only had he been the director's technical
assistant, he was also his general factotum—organizing the shooting
schedule, carrying out the director's research in the libraries of Moscow, and, on one occasion, teaching one of the actresses how to use
a bow with her left hand.

"We hardly ever had a weekend off!" he said breezily. "But Kimiyagarov got results—even if you only watch a few scenes, you will
understand. When they first came out, everybody wanted to see
them, and they loved them—in fact, they still do."

I did too. Thanks to a kind employee at the state TV studio, I had
secured a copy of the third film in the trilogy, *Under the Banner of
Justice*, about the life and death of Prince Siyavash, and back in London a few weeks later I lapped up the slightly dated spectacle. To see
Rostam on screen, wearing his tiger-skin cape and swaggering under
the flame torches of the court; to see hundreds of cavalrymen, with
lances outstretched, charging off to battle against the backdrop of
the sawtooth mountains; to see Prince Siyavash, dressed in white
with a gentle, beardless face, riding through the crackling fire to disprove his lusty stepmother's slander, was to see the Persian miniature
paintings bursting to 16mm life. You didn't have to imagine it anymore. You could *hear* it—the birdsong as the Iranian army passed
through a wood, the thunder of the enemy Turanian hooves, the rattle of the chariots' wheels. It might have lost that extra charge the
imagination can conjure, but it was the most vivid realization I had
encountered so far of Ferdowsi's tales.

As soon as I asked Dokteh why the films had been made, however,
this historic live wire fizzled out. I winced at his words, proof that even
this beautiful film had been a propaganda tool, which, in the end, is
the only explanation for all the money the Russians poured into it.

"The films were recorded," he said, "because the Tajik nation has
a relation with the Iranian people, and we have the right to this
place—we have lived here for thousands of years. Uzbekistan and

Turkmenistan are Turan,* but Tajikistan is part of Iran. So the legends of Iran are our legends too."

In the *Shahnameh*, Ferdowsi describes Iran and Turan as "fire and water, they rage with each other / Deep down in their hearts." Kimiyagarov's films helped to make sure they still do. For all their visual brilliance and epic scale, they were grist to the mill of divide and rule: cinema as a wrench—to keep the squabbling nations of Central Asia apart.

⁓

WHEN I THINK OF CENTRAL ASIA, I THINK OF . . .

A pair of fat-tailed sheep looking over the Oxus—the fabled 1,578-mile river where Rostam and Sohrab fought their legendary battle, where Alexander's phalanxes floated across on blown-up tent skins and Sultan Mahmud's platoons built a pontoon bridge with iron chains and cowhide. I stepped between the sheep, gazing across the river's breadth—almost still except for a faint ripple, the water curdling at the banks and lapping with a murmur at the stones. Here, on the banks of Turkmenistan, the Oxus hasn't yet been bled dry.

---

* This association of the mythical land of Turan (the kingdom of the Iranians' great enemy in the *Shahnameh*) with the Turkic peoples of Central Asia was shared by many of Ferdowsi's contemporaries. Mahmud of Kashgar, who compiled the first Turkic dictionary in the eleventh century, identified Alp er Tonga, ancestor of the Turks, with the great Turanian king of the *Shahnameh*, Afrasiyab (the same king who slays Siyavash and has Bizhan imprisoned in a pit). In the early twentieth century, in the wake of nationalist movements around the world, the concept of a motherland for all the Turkic-speaking peoples, from Istanbul to China, was pinned to Turan. "The country of the Turks is not Turkey, nor yet Turkestan," wrote the Turkish ideologue Ziya Gökalp. "Their country is a broad and everlasting land—Turan." Although nowadays more commonly known as "pan-Turkism," the notion of a united Turkic nation still has plenty of support, especially in Central Asia. "We Turks have to be united," said a prominent Uzbek writer called Alishir Ibadinov, whom I met in the Fergana Valley, "if we don't want problems with our borders, economy, and security. Maybe in the future we will have a confederation of Turkic countries."

An old man on a donkey cart who rode me out to the copse of minarets and conical roofs where the scholar Biruni once lived—the ruins of Old Gurganj. His eyes were nearly hidden by the fabulous curls of his black lambswool hat, but he could see well enough to direct his steed and dig out a plastic sachet of *nas*—Central Asia's narcotic of choice. He smeared the sludge across his gums, his gold teeth catching the sunlight as he waved me off.

A Tajik wedding in Khojand, in a hotel still pitted with bulletholes from the civil war. Women in ceremonial gold headscarves shimmered as they swayed their arms in the air, taking care not to bump into the men, who executed manly fist-shakes on the other side of the dance floor. Long brass *karnai* horns (a frequent feature in miniature paintings of ancient battles, usually depicted in gold leaf) poked out of the mouths of apple-cheeked musicians, as if they had sprouted elephant trunks, while on a dais above them the groom pressed a hand to his tuxedo and the bride, in her sugary dress and veil, gazed mournfully into her lap.

A "white-hair" in Panj Rud, the Tajik village where the poet Rudaki is buried. He was sitting among his fellow elders, with their sickles hanging behind them on the wall of the village shop. I knew this region was famous for its hospitality ("on the arrival of a stranger," reported the tenth-century geographer Ibn Hawkal, "they contend, one with another, for the pleasure of taking him to their home"), but I was still overwhelmed when he invited me back to his homestead. A wooden gate swung back to reveal a square structure like a Scottish steading, with a goat nodding above a long drop loo and a set of stirrups draped beside his spare turban on the washing-line. We drank tea and ate fresh yogurt, courtesy of the goat, while he showed me a Cyrillic copy of the *Shahnameh* and lamented the decline of his former powers. "When I built this house I was as strong as Rostam," he exclaimed, "but now my beard is white and my strength is ruined!"

Perhaps, I wondered as I stretched out on my stiff bedding on the train back to Iran, his words could be taken as a lament for the region as a whole.

~~

I came back over the Oxus even more conscious of the importance of the *Shahnameh* in the psyche of the Persian-speaking people—but aware, too, of the ease with which Ferdowsi's epic can be manipulated. And something else had been reinforced—that Persian culture is more than just Iran. There was still one more piece of the Persian puzzle to explore—the last piece. The piece that frightened me more than all the others put together. It was time to head to the unruly land to the east, billowing out of the cat's behind—Afghanistan.

I didn't want to go there just to complete a personal Persian set—a quick pop over the border, like driving to Calais to stock up on booze. If I went to Afghanistan, if I was really going to cross the old Persian badlands, there was a specific route I wanted to take—to follow Ferdowsi's own footsteps on an arc through the south of the country, ending up in the city where he presented his epic to Sultan Mahmud. There could be no more appropriate endpoint for my journey.

The image of Ferdowsi—the old, broken-backed poet, his life spent putting together his treasure trove of stories—had been gnawing in my mind for months. The farmer in his seventies, setting out across the wastes of Afghanistan, hoping for a grand reward befitting his extraordinary work. With each new discovery, each new community of people who stored his epic in their hearts, this image had taken on more texture. I felt desperate for Ferdowsi—for the pain and rage consuming him as he stumbled out of Ghazni, for the sense of grievance that must have poisoned his final years, and for the doubts it must have sown, the fear that his life's work would come to nothing and would be forgotten after his death.

Over the past six months, I had been listening to Ferdowsi's echo, hearing it around me—not only in the vitality the *Shahnameh* still has today, but also in the way other writers, struggling to pull together their own lives' work, have been mistreated throughout this region. As the Professor had told me more than once: "Ferdowsi was not the only one." To set out in his footsteps would be my own way of paying tribute to the tenth-century poet; but it would also, in a tiny sense, be a way of paying tribute to all the writers in this part of the world whose lives have been wrecked by the authority figures around them.

But I didn't simply want to offer homage. If I had learned anything about Persian culture over the past few months, it was this: Under the immaculate structure, the orderliness and refinement, there is blood and dirt and darkness. There is Shapur II, cutting off the Roman emperor's nose, or Rostam, tearing off a doorman's ears when he gets in his way, or the "dagger-strikers" in Tehran, slicing their heads with their blades. Afghanistan embodies the wilder side of the Persian myth, which is why it would make an appropriate setting for an act of revenge. If I ever reached Ghazni, if I ever found myself standing in front of the tomb of Sultan Mahmud, I vowed to myself that I would do something to avenge Ferdowsi, something to set me squarely on the poet's side—not only against Sultan Mahmud but against all the other tyrants who have scuppered so many writers' hopes in this part of the world.

I told the Professor what I was planning, imagining he would thoroughly approve. After all, it was he who'd started me off, when he recited Ferdowsi's satire all those months ago under the poet's statue.

"Ha!" He lit up a Bahman and blew out a cumulus of unimpressed smoke. "You think you can turn up in Ghazni and inform these people their hero is the son of a whore?" His furrows were showing as he flashed his owl-like eyes. "Child, they are Afghans! They will tear you to pieces!"

PART FOUR

AFGHANISTAN

"And separation has kept on driving us to a remote destination, buffeted this way and that, in all possible directions."

— ABU DULAF AL-KHAZRIJI,
ODE OF THE BANU SASAN

11

The Adventures of Abbas

Herat. September.

Dawn at Herat's cavernous terminal. One "Abbas," with a thin beard, wearing *shalwar qameez* and a checkered turban, is pushing a bundle into the trunk of a 4X4. Unfortunately, the driver notices that Abbas's eyes are hazel, his skin is fair, and his accent isn't very Afghan, and announces his conclusion—"Foreigner!"—in a voice loud enough to raise a lynch mob.

"Take your luggage," hisses Hassan-Gul.

He grabs my arm, guiding me down the aisle between the cars.

"You spoke! You spoke! Why did you speak? You have to understand, this cannot happen again. Never! How can I protect you if you speak?"

Shouts are looping through the air, mixed with air-horn honks and punctuated by the odd squelch when a sack of grapes falls off an overloaded roof rack. There is a sparkle as a flashlight swings in front of me, and for a breathless moment I think someone is going to shout "Foreigner!" But the light arcs away to shine on an old jalopy where there's a kerfuffle over jumper cables. Hassan-Gul nudges me into the front passenger seat of a Corolla, having dealt this time with the inquiries himself, and once our bundles are in the trunk he squeezes in beside me, tossing a greeting to the passengers in the back. Fists are gesticulating in the windshield mime-shows around us, engines buzzing like we're in a hive that's just waking up.

Traveling in Afghanistan makes one think a lot about death: both the risk to yourself and the regularity with which it's visited on the locals. So it's appropriate that the stony plain south of Herat is full of tombs—made of pebbles with masts wrapped in green Islamic cloths, occasionally encircled by a dry-stone wall to denote a popular Sufi, and guarded by a pollarded willow. The city is shrinking behind us but the mountains are growing. On one side pale and blue, they seem to float on a mist-shrouded lake; on the other, they are muscling across the vista, humpbacked and huge. We dive between them, snaking into the Paropamisus (literally the "peaks over which eagles cannot fly"), through a craggy gorge suited to banditry and sharpshooters.

At Shindand, we stop for breakfast. Bells tinkle on camels trotting beside a mud-brick wall, while an old man struggles to load a sack of roots onto the back of his donkey. Behind them is the Afghan version of a motorway diner. Long-bearded men sit around the teapots and aluminum spittoons, cross-legged on the carpeted tiers—except for one of them, who is slumped beside his prosthetic leg. A thigh of meat is swinging behind them, in front of a wall-hanging of the *Ka'aba* of Mecca, dripping its juice onto a fringe of rug. As we settle onto the top tier, a drop splashes onto the shoulder of Hassan-Gul's blazer. Although he's dispensed with his polished black brogues (replacing them with a pair of rubber sandals) and has left his signet ring in Herat, that doesn't mean his standards have slipped. He twists his neck to see the blemish, wrinkling his nose at it, and tweezers out the spotted handkerchief from his top pocket to rub it away.

The men on the tier below are asking him questions. If we'd been in Herat, I might have been able to scramble for an interpretation, but now we're in the land of the Pashtuns, so it's impossible. I wouldn't go so far as the nineteenth-century British officers who called Pashto "the language that would be spoken in hell," but it's certainly less easy on the ear than Persian. It means that for most of the journey to Ghazni I will be effectively deaf, as well as dumb, depending on Hassan-Gul for interpretation.

"They said your skin is fair," he tells me later, "but I informed them your father was a Nuristani.* Thanks to God they did not ask any more questions, because I told them your father passed away, so they are all going to pray for his soul."

I must have creased my brow or shown some other sign of confusion, because Hassan-Gul leans closer, pressing down on my shoulder.

"Don't you remember, Mr. Nicholas? It was the story you decided at my father's house."

Of course! Yesterday evening, Hassan-Gul took me to meet his parents in a concrete box on the outskirts of Herat. His father was a great admirer of the last king, Zahir Shah, as well as his successor, President Daoud (who toppled Zahir in a coup in 1973), and after showing me his hunting rifle, he spoke fondly of that time.

"I say the time of Zahir Shah was a golden age," he declared. "We had peace, work, the prices were low. In President Daoud's time also—he was progressive. Benzes were imported, we had television, a railway was started. But the Communists killed Daoud and his family—they brought destruction; they are the cause of all the disaster."

Although Hassan-Gul's mother was fretting in the kitchen, his father talked about our impending journey with excitement and reminisced about a boyhood hunting trip to Kandahar.

"But you must have a story," he said, gesturing for me to dip my hands into an enormous bowl of rice, bright with red radishes and cheese. "You must say you are on a pilgrimage."

"Yes!" I replied. "We could say I am asking for my voice back."

"But they will want to know how you lost it. You will say you are from the north, because most people you will meet have never been

---

* Nuristan is a province in northeastern Afghanistan, where many of the inhabitants have blue eyes, fair hair, and light skin. Traditionally this has been attributed to Alexander the Great and his men, who camped here in the fourth century BCE, although the arrival of the Aryan tribes several centuries earlier is just as likely a source. By calling myself a Nuristani, I wasn't really fibbing—well, not entirely, if we're to go with one Afghan theory (recorded by Doris Lessing in *The Wind Blows Away Our Words*). According to this point of view, the ancient "Angles" or "English" originated in Nuristan and only left the region because of the pressure on grazing.

there. And tell them your house was destroyed in the war; that will pull their hearts! You understand? It must be something sad, so the hearts of the people turn toward you."

While Hassan-Gul is narrating my new biography to our fellow tea-sippers in Shindand, I sign that I need the toilet. I've work to do.

Because of my disguise, I can't write in my notebook. It's not that I'm worried our fellow passengers will turn hostile if they work out I'm from a little farther away than Nuristan. But I do fear it being mentioned at a teahouse or in one of the towns where we stop. I've no idea how easy it might be for such information to slide its way to someone who's hankering for one of the Taliban's free motorbikes, and under the circumstances it seems like a good idea to be cautious. So I stroll to a scrub field behind the teahouse and squat in a dip—an Afghan spending a penny. Slumped over my lap, I scribble down the mnemonic word-strings I've been keeping in my head to help me remember the details from the journey so far:

Sultan Mahmud Was a Greedy Motherfucker
(Stony plain, Masts, Willows, Gorge, Mountains)
and
Crazy Dippy Tourist Killed by Cunning Sniper
(Camels, Donkey, Teahouse with *Ka'aba* Carpet
and Spitoons).

Back by the jeep, Hassan-Gul is on the back end of a conversation with a man in a sheepskin coat.

"This man is a doctor," he tells me. "He saw you in the teahouse and asked about your disability. He says you have a problem with your neurons."

He is saying this for the man's benefit, and also I think for our fellow passengers, since he adds a few words in Pashto. They look at us with empty expressions, but they are listening. The man bids goodbye, offering "God's blessing" to us both as he steps toward his car. Opening the door of his Corolla, Hassan-Gul is shaking his head.

"We were also talking about the road," he whispers, in English this time. "He has come from Ghazni and he says there are bandits. He says one in eight cars is being attacked."

After Shindand, the journey becomes increasingly sinister. Standing beside a truck is a long-beard with a Kalashnikov. He doesn't look like he has an official function, but he conforms to a pattern in which every man we see is holding a shaft—a shepherd's crook, a whip for goats, a Kalashnikov or a telescopic pole attached to a disk hovering inches off the ground. The latter are carried by men in blue protective suits, with ropes and trowels: a mine clearance team. Some are placing white painted rocks where an area has been cleared, while others are holding on to dogs on leashes.

The road is tarred, but terrible. We tack across it, driving sideways to avoid cracks, ruts, and pond-sized potholes, and sometimes we dive off altogether, to overtake a gaudily painted long-haul truck, jangling with chains to ward off the *divs*. North of Farah Rud, we pull to the side and stop. I watch Hassan-Gul pull our luggage out of the trunk, trying to work out why he is doing this, because there's no sign of our destination anywhere in the vicinity. I can feel an unpleasant shifting in my stomach, a sense that this journey isn't going to turn out quite as I anticipated.

"What are you doing?" I whisper.

"Abbas!"

He gives me a look of warning as the passengers in the backseat turn around. I've forgotten again: my lips should be sealed.

"I am taking the luggage," he continues. "This car is going to Farah Rud. But *we* are going to Farah. It is a different place."

He is already striding onto the wasteland. If I don't follow him soon, he'll contract into one of the pebbles with which it's speckled.

"You aren't? . . . Hassan-Gul, you can't be! . . ."

What kind of lunatic is he? Heaving my pack behind me, I jog until I am alongside him and reconsider. It wasn't Hassan-Gul who asked to come here.

Hovering over the horizon is a bulky gray mountain, the sort of place where ogre-kings live in fairy tales. Its peaks seem to watch over us, and as we wander on in silence I imagine them whispering about what they might do to us.

"Mr. Nicholas," says Hassan-Gul, "if we meet anyone, you must be sure to be quiet."

I gesture toward the mountain—between us there isn't a sign of a single living creature:

"Who are we going to meet?"

The answer comes an hour later, when the silence is broken by the rumble of a tractor engine. It's half a mile away, but Hassan-Gul races across the plain until he's flagged it down. How much we will pay is less a concern to the driver than whether we are carrying any weapons.

This is the snail's pace of transport, complete with the slug's trail of the herringbone pattern printed by the tires in the sand. What it lacks in speed, though, it more than makes up for in the opportunity to see the world around us. Men are squatting in the shade of their domed mud-brick houses or sitting on wooden bedsteads hooded by burlap canopies. Many of them are nursing cups of tea, but I spot a couple with flutes of rolled-up paper in their hands. They hold these to their mouths, leaning over a paraffin stove in the lee of a hut: opium smokers. A castle rises alongside us, bursting with round towers and frilled with battlements, light seeping through a gash in its curtain wall, and as we roll on, the driver starts whistling. I want to ask why he's driving a tractor across the wasteland, but since I can't speak, I concentrate instead on imagining what I would think if I were an alien.

Imagine: You're from some distant galaxy and you've crash-landed on the Afghan plains. What would be your first impression? The modern traveler is saddled with so much psychological baggage that it's difficult not to see potential death everywhere you look. Ordinary men become terror-in-a-turban because their beards are long and their headwear black; a motorbike is morphed from a practical way of crossing the dunes into Taliban ahoy! Even the mastiffs prowling in the ditches look fearsome, and they don't sound any better. But for an alien, unprejudiced by extra meaning, I wonder if they would find

Afghanistan any more frightening than if he were to land instead on
Clapham High Street.

Nervous of the motorbike men and their Taliban-length beards,
I wrap my turban tight around my face, which at least keeps out the
dust. Men holding shafts—farming hoes and sickles, occasionally
Kalashnikovs—peer at us from the plains, their guarded expressions
burned onto my brain as we jitter over a dry riverbed where an old
shepherd is coaxing his flock. Behind him are domed houses and
high-walled homesteads, which grow more abundant until there are
hundreds of them. A policeman is directing the traffic from a roundabout, chickens are squawking in their plastic yellow cages, and
pomegranates are tumbling out of a handcart. They reappear, as flattened skins, on the tires of the tractor, their juices dribbling between
the grooves. We have reached Farah.

Like most of his neighbors, Hassan-Gul's friend Nasrullah lives in
a fort—a house on stilts surrounded by a mud wall and barred by a
metal gate, with an army of chickens charging around the yard,
pecking at your fingers if you step too close. Nasrullah was a *mujahid*
in the war against the Soviets, and with his broad, bearlike frame, it
is easy to imagine him in warrior mode. But he has a softer side, signified by a red cardboard heart glued to his gate. Not that this allows
for any contact between the women of the house and the foreign
guest. When light footsteps sound outside, and his wife or daughter
(her *chador* is too tightly wrapped to distinguish which) stands before us with a tray and a cloth full of bread, he takes it off her before
I can offer a salaam and sends her away with a flick of the hand.

"You are looking very tired, Mr. Nicholas," says Hassan-Gul. "You
must rest."

"Actually, I'd quite like to have a look around," I say, reaching forward to taste the bread. "Isn't there a famous fort in Farah?"

"No, no, Mr. Nicholas!" Hassan-Gul edges toward me, carefully
studying my dust-caked face. "Don't you think he looks tired?" he
exclaims to Nasrullah.

"Oh yes," replies our host. "Guest! Be comfortable."

I have no choice. The afternoon vanishes in the languor of the guest room, nudged along by regular offerings of tea. Having been informed of my exhaustion, I *am* starting to feel fatigue creeping up on me, and what little energy I have left is sucked away by the chief activity of the afternoon.

It centers on a paraffin stove. Nasrullah sets it in the middle of the guest room, kneeling over it like an acolyte at an altar. He breaks up a mud-colored tablet, impaling it on a stretched-out safety pin; while Hassan-Gul raises a needle that's been burning on the stove. Smoke rises like incense, and they both lean forward, with flutes of rolled-up paper bound with sticky tape, to inhale the holy essence. Islam might have its place in Afghanistan—but this afternoon at Nasrullah's, opium is the religion of the masses.

"Guest!"

Nasrullah addresses me by the name he'll give me for the duration of my stay, making a cross of his fingers to signal his invitation. I lean forward, exhaling a bitter, rubbery-smelling miasma.

"Do you smoke opium?" he asks me.

"Not as a habit."

"Don't be afraid! In Sistan we smoke it all the time. That is why nothing is ever done!" He points to the tray of green tea he's set between us. "Drink, or your throat becomes dry."

His own voice is so raspy as to imply it's already too late for him. I take the glass and glug. The rolled-up flute of paper passes into my hands and I can feel myself sinking, slowly and unstoppably, into dreams and the gentle hug of the bolster.

12

How to Walk Like an Afghan
Farah. September.

"You mustn't talk about Ferdowsi—not in front of Nasrullah," says Hassan-Gul, whispering over the stove in Nasrullah's guest room.

The opium has run out, so now the stove is being used for a more humdrum purpose—to boil the tea.

"Why not?" I whisper back.

"Well, he is a Pashtun, of course—they are not the same as us! Their hearts never soar when you speak of the *Shahnameh*. They have their own heroes."

Nasrullah has been out in the yard, deciding on which chicken is going to be slain for tonight's supper, but his hearing is acute.

"What is this?" he exclaims, plodding back into the room. "Our guest doesn't know about the Pashtuns?"

I'm pretty sure he isn't offended—because he is speaking in Persian, for my benefit. He delivers a defiant snort, followed by the seventeenth-century verse of Khushal Khan Khattak, a warrior-poet who fought against the Mughals:

> *The very name Pashtun spells honor and glory,*
> *Lacking that honor what is the Afghan story?*

From the beginning, the best way of acquiring that honor was by fighting. When the tenth-century scholar Biruni writes of the "Afghans"

(a word related to the ancient Persian for "noisy"), he means the Pashtuns who lived in the mountains east of Ghazni: warrior tribespeople
who burst into the area in the first century BCE.* There were "Afghans"
(i.e., Pashtuns) in Sultan Mahmud's army as early as 1008, although
that didn't stop other Pashtuns from plundering the frontier district
of the sultan's empire and blackmailing merchant caravans returning
from India. What with silks, furs, pearls and paper heading across the
trade routes, it was as good a time and place as any to be a highway
robber—and the Pashtuns were cornering the market. According to
the court historian Utbi, they waylaid Mahmud's troops on the way
back from a campaign in India. So incensed was the sultan by their
cheek that he marched against the Pashtuns, surrounded their mountain haunts, and "did terrible execution among them." If they could
trouble the best army in the region, then for a solitary traveler like Ferdowsi, this tribe of Butch Cassidys would have posed an even more serious threat.

By the fourteenth century, the Pashtuns' power had expanded.
"They hold mountains and defiles and possess considerable strength,"
wrote the traveler Ibn Battuta, "and are mostly highwaymen." The introduction of firearms only increased their influence, enabling them
to dominate their sedentary Persian-speaking neighbors. From the
rise of Ahmad Shah Durrani** in the eighteenth century, the Pashtuns have been the most powerful force in the country. They were so

---

* Some legends trace them back to the Bani Israel, one of the lost Jewish tribes
expelled from Jerusalem by Nebuchadnezzar. Others associate them with the Sakai,
who beat the Greeks in the second century BCE and who have been linked by some
scholars to the feats of Rostam.

** He was known as "durr-e durran"—"pearl of pearls," because of a looted pearl
earring he was fond of wearing. Like many a Pashtun ruler, Ahmad Shah liked his
rocks shiny—among his stash was the Koh-i Noor diamond, which would later
famously come into the possession of Queen Victoria. His other adornments
included a silver nose mask, to cover up a wound caused by a piece of flying brick
in a gunpowder explosion. The wound, which would eventually kill him, grew so
gangrenous that maggots fell into his mouth when he was eating—so his dining
companions, as well as Ahmad Shah himself, must have been grateful for the mask.

disruptive to the Raj that the British diplomat Sir Mortimer Durand divided them in two when he drew the borders between Afghanistan and India in 1893. It's a division that is still being contested.

"You know about Pashtunistan?" asks Nasrullah, spreading out a large map across the rug. "This should all be part of Afghanistan. All the Pashtuns want to be in Afghanistan, the ones in Pakistan included. And we should have more of Iran, and parts of Tajikistan and Uzbekistan too."

Hassan-Gul is standing behind him, windmilling a finger beside his head to indicate what he thinks of his friend's idea.

"Maybe Nasrullah has a heart like a lion," he tells me later, "but his brain came out of a donkey. Afghanistan was always a Persian-speaking country—the kings of our country, even if their tribe was Pashto, the language of the court was always Persian. But in the 1950s President Daoud made the Pashtun issue for political reasons, so he could claim a passage to the sea, even though he always spoke Persian when he was with his family."

This is the Dari or Persian-speaking perspective, contradicting the Pashto point of view, as is the case in just about every matter of importance in Afghanistan. Nasrullah and Hassan-Gul might be friends but, like the country at large, there is no political subject on which they can find a common line.

"Well," says Nasrullah, finally conceding his territorial ambitions for the Pashtun empire might be a little bit excessive, "at the very minimum we should certainly have double what we have so far."

I am warming to Nasrullah. The idea that a country as troubled as Afghanistan could even consider extending its borders is insane, but it provokes plenty of laughter, which rolls on throughout the afternoon. At least—until Nasrullah's war experiences come up, when the conversation takes a more somber turn.

"We had to fight them," he says—I have just asked about his experience as a *mujahid*. "Who will permit a foreigner to rule his country? But when we drove the Russians out, I put down my gun. I didn't want to fight anymore. I wish I hadn't fought."

"I thought you said you had to?"

He looks at me, his calflike eyes gently probing. "When the Taliban came," he says, "they accused me of being a *mujahid* and they came to my house—to punish me. But I wasn't here. My brother was here and they beat him. They beat him very hard."

Hassan-Gul touches his friend's shoulder, a terrible silence articulating what happened to his brother.

Over the next couple of days, I get the easy job: hanging around with Nasrullah. Hassan-Gul, meanwhile, is scouring Farah for the needle in our haystack—someone who will actually be prepared to drive us to Helmand.

Nasrullah's friends live in gated mud-brick forts like his own, and their guest rooms are just as foggy. We cross our legs on the rugs, waiting for the rolled-up flute of paper to be passed, or a carved wooden pipe, or a beaker with a straw at the top. Nuggets the size of kidney beans are rubbed between our hosts' fingers and stuck to the tips of red-hot wire, while everyone makes a point of offering me tea—"so your throat doesn't become dry"—poured out of large metal pots and thick with sugar. The smell of the roasted poppies floats in the air and another portion of the afternoon is carried off with the swirls of smoke.

Farah isn't the first place I've come across opium—a few months ago, in the eastern Iranian region of Sistan, I met a self-styled traveling salesman who told me he was there to sell socks. For some reason he had an enormous supply of the brown stuff too, which he heated over a paraffin stove while reciting from a dog-eared copy of the *Shahnameh*. Since opium is one of the oldest things mentioned in this book, I suppose I could argue that it was all part of my research.

It was known by the Sumerians as the "joy plant," while the Babylonians mixed it with licorice, the Greeks crushed its pods in wine (Helen of Troy mixes one such cordial in the *Odyssey*, serving up an early form of laudanum), and the Roman doctor Galen made it an apothecary's catch-all, encompassing headaches, deafness, epilepsy, asthma, and leprosy in its vast orbit of cures. As the Dark Ages descended and Europe fell into the sort of forgetfulness that opium can induce (but forgot opium too), it became a trading commodity in the Islamic caliphate, which was how Europe renewed its acquaintance, during the Crusades. The favor was returned a few centuries later, when the British showed the East how to get high on it. Men in Persia, India, and China fell into slumbers, and the British made a lot of money. Since then, opium has been connected in the Western imagination with the East, distributed by Fu Manchu gangsters, white slavers and—currently—Afghan warlords.

Sitting on the floor of someone's guest room, with Nasrullah beside me and the sickly sweet smell of the opium around us, I'm not exactly bombarded by chatter. But there are occasional attempts at conversation, some of which are provoked by curiosity about my origins.

Much to my delight, a number of Nasrullah's friends connect my fairer skin with Nuristan, the region to the northeast where Hassan-Gul has been saying I'm from. Someone else rubbishes this and insists I'm from Azerbaijan.

"I met others like you," he declares, talking of encounters on "business" in Iran (although Nasrullah later tells me this man has never been there—he was just trying to look sophisticated in front of the others).

Whatever his reasons, it takes a good five minutes before I can wipe the smile off my face—for a few people, at least, I'm not immediately identifiable as a Westerner, which is surely a good thing! But I haven't been congratulating myself for long when I'm brought back to earth by the bizarre attribution of another of Nasrullah's friends.

"He wants to know if you are from Pakistan," explains Nasrullah. "It's because your skin is soft. He thinks you are a Taliban agent."

Naturally, I should find this association alarming, but for some reason I'm feeling strangely detached from it all. . . .

"You shouldn't smoke this rubbish, you know!"

A tall man with a waxed mustache and several gold teeth is standing over me, his large, leathery face scored by a frown.

I don't know how many rugs I've sat on, how many different paraffin stoves I've crouched beside, how many squeaking gates I've stepped through. But I remember Rishad's, because the air is clear and books are piled against the walls.

"Most people here have no interest in books," he says sadly, stroking his mustache. "They say, 'Why do we need books? We can learn our wisdom from the elders.' But elders need to sleep, don't they? Books you can read whenever you want!"

He picks out a volume, drawing it gently off the shelf with a hand on each side of the cover. It's the poetry of Rahman Baba, a seventeenth-century Sufi dervish who lived in Peshawar, in what is now Pakistan.

"We call him the Nightingale," says Rishad. "You know, when I meet Tajiks in Kabul (i.e., the Persian-speaking population), they tell me the Pashtuns have no poetry. But there are more than three hundred poems in this book! And we Pashtuns have no poetry?"

As I sit, cross-legged on the carpet in front of him, it's as if I'm still among the Persians: sitting on a rug, drinking tea, listening to poetry. Except the rug is a little more frayed, the tea a little less sweet, and the poetry a little harder to understand. Rishad may not represent all the Pashtuns, but I suspect from listening to him, and from the verses quoted by Nasrullah, that there is the same poetic spirit I enjoyed among the Persians.

Even the ideas suggest a link. When Rishad reads out one of Rahman Baba's most famous verses, in which he declares, "Humans are all a single body, / He who tortures another is wounding himself," it recalls the medieval Persian poet Sa'di, who wrote a similar verse that currently adorns the lobby of the UN building in New York: "The people of the world are limbs from one body, sharing one essence. / When a single limb is oppressed, all the others suffer agony." Given the ethnic fighting that's torn this country apart, both poets are expressing an apposite idea.

Rishad's is a larger house than the others I've visited, with a mound of cement in the courtyard and an obstacle course of planks and buckets to negotiate before you reach the guest room. There's still space for two pots of red geraniums, although I doubt they're going to last very long, what with all the poles piled above them.

"Please excuse all the mess," he says as he leads us through. "I am having renovations."

In the early nineties, soon after the Russians withdrew from Afghanistan, he left the country and made a fortune for himself in China.

"Now," whispers Nasrullah (who is filling me in on Rishad's status as one of the local "big men"), "he has seven houses in this district."

Before Rishad set off for China, he was a teacher. He lived in Kabul and taught Pashtun literature at the university. A gentle sigh creaks out of his mouth as he remembers this time, and I'm itching to learn more. Why would a man leave his country soon after the invaders had been expelled?

A wife appears at the door with a tray: rice doused in sheep's fat, with raisins and shredded carrot and a bottle of Pepsi. I'm surprised she isn't wearing a burka—I can see part of her face. Her hair might be hidden, and her figure is lost in the shapelessness of her long black gown (the ends of which she has to grip between her teeth to hold the tray), but after the concealment elsewhere in Afghanistan, her appearance has an erotic intensity to it. She disappears behind all the clutter in the courtyard, but as I listen to the clanking of the planks and buckets she has to move among, I can understand why Nasrullah is stirring, his face slightly redder than usual, beside me.

Sitting in such close proximity with Rishad, I feel comfortable enough to tell him where I am from (unlike some of Nasrullah's other friends, he knew straight away I was a Westerner) and trust him not to go spreading it around town. He returns my trust, by telling me about his own personal experiences, and why he left Afghanistan after the Russians had been defeated.

"You have to remember, I was in Kabul," he says. "And at this time it was taken by the Northern Alliance. Well, it is okay if you are a Tajik, but I am a Pashtun; for me it was a dangerous place to be. One day they took me out of my car, they covered my eyes with a scarf, and on the way to the jail they beat me with the butts of their rifles. Before I was even in my cell, they had already broken my teeth."

He ended up in an underground pit at Kabul's Northern Palace, just a couple of meters square, and stayed there for three months.

"They tied my legs and hands with chains," he says. "Occasionally they would give me boiled water with sugar and bread, but many times I would go for two whole days without anything to eat at all. They called me 'Afghan *ghol*' [or "ogre"]. It's an insult; they are saying I am mindless! Ha! And the man who took me, you want to know what happened to him? Now he is a professor at Kabul University!"

He takes a mouthful of rice in his hand and swallows it down.

"So you see," he mutters, "between Pashtuns and the Persian-speaking people here, there are many problems still."

⌒∕ℓ⌒

Rishad has been so generous with his rice he might as well have shoveled it into my mouth, and a couple of Nasrullah's other friends have offered food as well—so by the evening I'm finding it hard to raise an appetite. But Nasrullah has specially slaughtered one of his chickens: I can see by the droop in his calflike eyes (not to mention the grease and blood on his fingers) that he'll be put out if I don't put away.

By the end of the meal we're all bloated. Nasrullah calls it a night early, but Hassan-Gul and I stay up, smoking in the guest room (we're only on cigarettes now—after Rishad's ticking-off, I've decided to go cold turkey; my half-a-day addiction is over). It's good to be able to speak in English again—the different languages have been making my head spin—and we lie on the floor, with bolsters under our heads, exchanging stories about our lives back home.

"You don't have a girlfriend?" asks Hassan-Gul.

I tell him about a girl I stepped out with a few times in Tehran. We'd walk up Valiasr Street in the center of the city, occasionally stopping in a coffee shop and a couple of times we went to the theater, where thanks to the Iranian hospitality code (extended to foreigners in general) we were given some of the best seats in the house.

"She was only interested in you because you're a Westerner," says Hassan-Gul.

"Oh, thanks!"

"It is true. Iranian women, they are interested only in money."

"Well, thanks for the vote of confidence!"

"You know," says Hassan-Gul, twisting round and propping himself up, "I once had an Iranian lover."

"Lover?" I wriggle closer: This sounds like a story I want to hear.

"She was from Shiraz. Her lips, I am telling you, Mr. Nicholas, they were like the petals of a rose. It is true what they say: The daughters of Shiraz are the most beautiful girls in the world! We discovered each other in Mashhad; she was a student."

"What were *you* doing there?" I ask.

Hassan-Gul nods solemnly, a streak of sadness crossing his face. "It was when the Taliban attacked my city," he says, "a lot of people went to Mashhad at that time. You know, I was only eighteen years old."

He reaches out for his cigarettes and lights two in his mouth, then passes one of them across.

"We did many nice things together," he says. "We walked in Malek Abad park, we visited the shrine of Omar Khayyam and the Martyrs' Cemetery. I wanted to marry her, but she said her family will not accept me because I am from Afghanistan. I said, 'Well, *mine* will say you are sandwich-eaters!' She laughed when I said that. She had a nice laugh."

As I listen to him, I want to reach out and give Hassan-Gul a consoling pat on the shoulder, to touch him somehow in the way you would with a friend. But my fingers are still greasy from the food—and I know better than to make a mess on his blazer. *That* would be a definite faux pas.

"Goodnight," he says a few moments later.

I can hear the bark of a dog outside and the tinkle of water. Perhaps one of Nasrullah's womenfolk is doing some washing-up. I fall asleep easily, imagining Hassan-Gul, in his polished black brogues and his shiny-buttoned blazer, strolling through Mashhad's central park with the beautiful girl from Shiraz.

"Be careful," says Hassan-Gul, stepping cautiously beside me the next day. "There may still be mines here."

"Mines?" I gasp. "But we're not in a military zone, are we? I mean, this place, it's . . . medieval."

We have just crept inside the gateway of Farah's principal landmark—the fort. From a distance, it looks like it's made out of giant sponge fingers arranged in a ring. As we draw closer, they resolve themselves into stocky pillars of mud, melting into the ground and shoring up the barbican. I wipe the sweat off my forehead (the author of the medieval *Regions of the World* was right when he described Farah as "a town in the hot zone") and point to the mounds ahead of us. With each step we take, it's becoming increasingly clear they aren't mounds at all.

They're tanks and armored personnel carriers. A dozen are clustered together like giant toads whose legs have been ripped off and their eyes gouged out. Their skin blistered, their side-skirts dribbling, their tracks and tires torn off and their gun turrets shattered, they are melting, slowly, under the firepower of the sun.

There is more. At the back of the keep is a mud-brick hut, with a rusty rocket tripod on its roof. A sniper's bandolier is dangling beside it, and as I spin around to the crumbling fortress walls behind, I realize this is just the tip of the iceberg. Bullets of every shape and size, for assault rifles and mountain guns, some of them gathered in a mound, with a couple of bandoliers strewn among them; two hundred or so mortar shells, laid out in neat rows like fish at a market stall, their tail fins sticking under the noses of the row behind; and an enormous tube like a telescope, which I think is a mortar gun. There is enough ammunition here to supply an army.

The reason for the artillery is introduced by a wisp of smoke and a cough. Out of the hut, wearing a tank operator's helmet over his *shalwar qameez* and carrying a bent-out safety pin with resin on its tip, comes a man with droopy eyes and ankles so narrow they look like you could snap them with your fingers. First he offers a flurry of Pashto, then his hand, and finally his opium.

"He thinks," explains Hassan-Gul, "that you represent the Americans."

"What do you mean 'represent'?"

"The army."

"*What?*"

Our new acquaintance is called Reza. His uncle was the *mujahideen* chief in Farah, and gave "those sons of dogs" (the Russians) a whole heap of trouble. Later he turned his arms against the Taliban but was outmaneuvered and forced to flee across the border, before being assassinated by the Iranian Secret Service—which sounds like a pretty standard career pattern for a regional *mujahideen* leader.

Reza himself is a gentler sort of fellow. He shows us the Tower of the King's Daughter, where a dozen clay columns rise out of a basin of weed-choked earth; points out the ancient army headquarters, where shards of pottery are scattered among the foundations; and leads us onto the northern ledge of the fort, where we look down into the stubble fields and grazing enclosures below.

"You see where the fields are now," he says, "there used to be water. People could only get to the castle by boat."

"What happened to it?" I ask.

"It dried up." He sighs as Hassan-Gul translates his words. "In the past this land was green, but now look—it is dying."

Like the thirsting deserts of Central Asia, it is this—more than war and dodgy governments—that's having the most devastating effect: the cruelty of nature as the water recedes from the land.

࿇

We have now been in Farah for three days and it's time to move on. On our last night, I'm eating supper with Nasrullah in the guest room when Hassan-Gul bursts in, panting.

"I have found a driver for tomorrow," he announces.

Tomorrow! The most dangerous journey so far—when we will attempt to make it to Sultan Mahmud's summer palace. But this is no lush, idyllic paradise. It's deep in the Helmand region, near its principal city, Lashkar Gah, which half the people I talked to in Herat labeled the "Taliban capital." The other half said it's where most of the opium is sold.

"He will take us to Helmand and on to Kandahar," explains Hassan-Gul. "But he is worried Lashkar Gah is too difficult. He wants to check the situation when we arrive at Girishk."

"He's worried about taking a foreigner?" I ask.

"Of course, Mr. Nicholas! Of course he is worried about taking a foreigner! You understand this place we are going to? There are warlords and drug chiefs and many people with evil in their hearts. Farah is a garden and we want to enter a pit of poisonous snakes!"

We are eating lamb's fat stew and rice—it will be our last decent meal for a while. Some of the flecks fall out of Hassan-Gul's hand. I look at him but he won't meet my eye. He picks up the flecks one at a time, being especially fastidious when they land on his blazer, and makes a pile on the tray.

"But I must tell you," he continues, "the driver, he is not *very* worried. As far as he knows, Mr. Nicholas, *you* are not a foreigner."

I remember the man who thought I was a Taliban agent and Reza at the fort—one deciding I'm a Pakistani, the other an American. They might not have established my exact identity, but my disguise can hardly be said to have been a roaring success.

"He'll work it out," I protest, "especially if we're his only passengers."

"Well, he told me he will not take any foreigners, so you will have to be Mr. Abbas."

"What do you mean he won't? . . . He's not Taliban, is he?"

"In this area it is hard to tell. But probably it is because he knows it is dangerous to be with a foreigner."

In that case, I feel I need to improve my Afghanness.

"Too many people know I'm a foreigner," I say. "Am I not wearing my turban properly?"

"No, the clothes are fine," replies Hassan-Gul. "The problem, Mr. Nicholas, is *you*. You do not walk like an Afghan."

"*Walk*? How am I supposed to *walk* like an Afghan?"

"In a straight line, for example, and you should take bigger steps. Foreigners look at the floor and their steps are always short. When I look at them, sometimes I think there is a cloud in their minds and they don't know which direction to take."

For epic heroes, putting on a disguise was never this complicated. Rostam might have been eight times the height of a normal man, but in the *Shahnameh* all he had to do was don the enemy's clobber and he could steal into their camp. It wasn't much harder in Ferdowsi's time, when the great physician Ibn Sina disguised himself as a Sufi dervish to steal out of prison. But for me, disguise requires more than just the costume: I need the body language too.

When Hassan-Gul walks, it's with long, regular paces: Perhaps he was a panther in a previous life. Now, as I watch him marching across the room, I'm trying to mimic his movements.

"Yes, congratulations! That's right!"

Nasrullah is clapping at me from the doorway, cheering me on as I point my chin to the ceiling, push back my shoulders as far as they will go, and make large, purposeful strides.

"You became an Afghan!" he exclaims, laughing.

"Now," says Hassan-Gul, "all you must do is practice."

The oil lamp is flickering, an hour or so later, as I sit on the carpet scribbling in my notebook. Usually I jot down the main events of the day and try to remember all the little details. But tonight I'm blocked by anxiety. All I can think about is what lies ahead, and my entry is full of doubts about my purpose. Up until now, I've been faintly aware there is something ridiculous about what I'm doing—but only faintly. I've been in thrall to Ferdowsi's world. It's as if I could hear his voice all around me, urging me on. I'm in a land of big gestures—a romantic, impractical, extraordinary land—where a great poet, rather than accepting a significant but unsatisfactory payment, tossed it away and scribbled a furious satire against the sultan. To feel I've fully immersed myself in Ferdowsi's world, I need a big gesture of my own—and traveling in the poet's footsteps is the only one I'm capable of.

But now, out of earshot of the Persian language, Ferdowsi seems more distant than ever. His voice has gone quiet for the first time since I flew to Tehran. Now, just two days away from the target of my quest—my Dark Tower or Emerald City—doubts are buzzing in my head like flies around a corpse.

I step outside and light a cigarette on the stoop. A stray dog is having what sounds like an altercation with the wind, as tempestuous as the thoughts in my head. I try to block them out, peering into the shadows, tracing a figure who's darting across the ground. The silhouette and the braided hair swinging behind her shoulders suggest a girl—one of Nasrullah's daughters, I assume—on her way to the outhouse toilet. Tiptoeing back, she seems to stumble, the ground being rocky and uneven, stops and sees me and freezes. I press a hand on my chest; she bows her head. Then, as fast as a hunted deer, she is off.

13

A Holiday House in Helmand

Farah. September.

"Nicholas!" Hassan-Gul is whispering, in the tone of a jailor leading a convict to the gallows. "It is time."

It is, to be specific, twelve past four in the morning. A Corolla engine is buzzing outside Nasrullah's gate, waiting for us to come out. I have one last task to perform before I join Hassan-Gul—I must say a final decade of the rosary, my third of the morning.

Since coming to Afghanistan, all the religious beliefs knocked into me over five years at my monastic boarding school have burst back to the surface. I can't go for half an hour without offering a "Hail Mary" and every time I hear an unexpected noise it inspires a "Glory Be." Religion is like a branch you cling to when climbing up a mountain, and it makes the strength of religion around me all the more understandable. You need something to hold on to for fear that otherwise you'll fall.

The driver only speaks Pashto, so I can't understand anything he says; still being mute, I can't say anything back. He is in his mid-twenties, with a checkered turban over a cotton jacket. He asks Hassan-Gul something in Pashto, and after he's replied, Hassan-Gul speaks to me in Persian.

"He asks about your parents. I am saying how your father was killed by the Russians."

He speaks again to the driver, whose voice drops to a softer pitch when he replies.

"He says that is sad," explains Hassan-Gul.

I catch the driver's eye in the rearview mirror and exchange a fleeting smile, before I nervously look down. There is something strangely ironic about his name: Haq or "Truth."

The sun is breaking out of its hiding place to paint a golden halo around the castle we passed a few days ago. Apart from the odd oasis of trees, the land is a pebbled wasteland, like the dried-up aftermath of a volcanic eruption. This is the Desert of Death, named after the fate it's dished out to the invading armies audacious enough to attempt a crossing, from Cyrus the Great to the Soviets.

Haq has a bag of dry lentils, which he cracks between his teeth, and for most of the morning this is the only noise I hear. The combination of official muteness and my anxiety isn't exactly a great conversation prodder, but Hassan-Gul isn't talking either—he stares out of the window, as if he's been hypnotized by the sullen wasteland around us.

A couple of hours in, we hit a metaled road and spin across a bridge spanning a flat, rocky valley as gray as the moon. To our right, the mountain sits behind a shroud of white sky that sucks all color and reduces it to an outline. To the left, it is closing in on us—craggy sinews and high muscular walls, with lumps of rock scattered around them like giant clots of blood.

But nature's hostility is less alarming than the increasingly regular toll booths, pulling us to a stop with a length of rope stretched across the road. The toll police might nominally claim government patronage; many of them, however, wear no uniform other than combat trousers and turbans, and they swing their Kalashnikovs with the casual confidence of men who haven't been trained but know how to use them. Several times they peer into the Corolla and shoot questions at Haq.

Once, there are two of them, neither in uniform. One is stocky and black-bearded; the other is thinner and has a sallow complexion, lit by the flame-colored henna in his hair and the kohl around his eyes. He dangles his Kalashnikov loosely over his shoulder, catching the sun on the raised edge of the gunmetal, and stares at us through glazed, empty eyes.

The black-bearded officer is addressing Haq, who laughs. He speaks again. Hassan-Gul leans across and says something. This time there is no laughter. The henna-dyed officer rests his beard on the lip of the window, muttering to Haq. Hassan-Gul dips into the inside pocket of his blazer, counts out some banknotes, and hands them over. They are taken by the black-bearded officer, but when his colleague tries to snatch them, he pushes him away. The henna-dyed officer turns back to the car, exchanging an angry word with Haq, then reaches in and turns off the ignition. Haq tries to turn it on again, but his forearm is seized, as the officer's glazed expression transforms with startling elasticity into a tiger's snarl. He leans farther into the car, pricking my nose with the bitter smell of his addiction, and settles his angry expression on me.

THIS MUST BE IT.

He's going to recognize I'm not an Afghan, demand a thousand dollars or some ridiculous sum, and when I can't produce it he'll shoot me.

How lucky I am! No, *really*—how incredibly lucky! We're being held up by the sort of brigands who would have accosted Ferdowsi when he came this way all those years ago. This, at least, is what I'm telling myself; it's the only way I can think of to block out the sound of henna-hair's Kalashnikov. . . . And opium has an honorable pedigree in this region, after all—it was recommended by Ibn Sina, as "the most powerful of the stupefacients."* And . . .

But the sound of the Kalashnikov is too regular, too loud, too insistent . . .

It's actually not an unpleasant sound, a rhythmic beat against the driver's door. If it weren't for the circumstances, it would be quite

---

* Although he might not have been so keen to endorse it if he'd known that an opium overdose, administered by a treacherous slave, would lead to his death.

musical, even soothing. Now it's growing fainter, and I realize it is only knocking against the officer's leg, because he's being pulled back by his colleague, the percussion of his weapon drowned by the rumble of the engine. There is an outtake of breath in the front passenger seat. Hassan-Gul is smoothing down his blazer.

We drive through Delaram—which amounts to a few houses and shops, though like many such places it merits capital letters and a large circle on my map. Lavishly decorated trucks pass us in convoys, with trees and streams painted on their gunwales, as if to distinguish themselves from the landscape around them. I'm always pleased when trucks are near: Traffic is a reasonable assurance against bandits, as are the mine-clearance teams working in the fields.

I am feeling very nervous now. After the toll booth incident, every time I see another human being, I sink lower in my seat. The fact that more and more of them are wearing black turbans and riding on motorbikes, as the Taliban are famous for doing, isn't exactly pushing down my heart rate. In fact, there is only one way to keep myself calm.

Every so often, when the tension of the journey is especially thick, I pick up the green-jacketed copy of the *Shahnameh*. I'm not sure if it's the discipline of translation or the content of the stories, but one way or another they distract me from my fear of the world outside the Corolla.

Mostly I turn to stories about journeys. There is the tale of a knight called Giv, who sets out in search of Prince Kai Khusrau, the son of the slain hero Siyavash, and frets that his quest is like "throwing walnuts at a dome," before eventually finding the prince and guiding him back to Iran. There is the leech Borzuy, who is sent off to India in search of the Elixir of Life, and instead comes across a book of fables much like the tales of Aesop. Best of all are the adventures of Rostam. It's amazing what a sense of perspective can do for your fear—I might be worried about Taliban informers and Kalashnikov-wielding opium addicts, but at least I don't have any dragons to deal with. Compared with Rostam, I'm in the comfort zone.

THE TALE OF ROSTAM'S SEVEN COURSES

*The shah has been captured! The evil divs are holding him in the king-
dom of Mazanderan and there is only one knight who can rescue
him—Rostam. Saddling up his jet-bellied horse, known as the Rakhsh,
he rides out to the cave where the king is held, bracing himself against
a series of obstacles along the way.*

*First there is a lion. Rostam has fallen asleep after feasting on a wild
ass, but the Rakhsh does his work for him, bringing down its hooves on
the lion's head and tearing it to pieces. Next the hero must cross a desert
where the heat is so intense it turns the birds to powder, before slicing
off the head of a dragon. After all this activity, Rostam is feeling under-
standably weary, not to mention hungry, so when he spots a feast of
roasted sheep, sweetmeats, and a bowl of wine, he settles down and
tucks in. A fair maiden appears, but he works out she's a witch and
cleaves her with his blade.*

*Now close to the stronghold of the divs, Rostam binds the local
marchlord, slays a few of the local chieftains, and scatters the divs, before stepping inside a murky cave, where he finds the terrifying White
Div—a gigantic pasty-faced monster with hair like a lion's mane. They
charge at each other, hacking and ripping "till all the ground was pud-
dled with their blood"; but after lopping off a foot and one of its hands,
Rostam raises the beast above his shoulders and dashes it to the ground,
before stabbing it in the heart and plucking out its liver. The shah is
now free, and the divs will never pose so great a threat again.*

At the edge of Delaram, we stop at a teahouse to check out the situation in Lashkar-Gah, the town where Sultan Mahmud's summer
palace is located. A black stove rumbles at the back and carpets stretch
across raised tiers for us to sit on. Hassan-Gul orders tea and a bowl
of fava beans, which we crush with a pestle and eat with soggy bread.

A couple of men come over to our tier, apparently to ask where
we're from and if we have any news along the way—bandit incidents
or gunfights. One of them, who has an alarming mass of thick black

beard, looks at me several times and eventually addresses me, but Hassan-Gul steers him away, explaining I'm incapable of speech. I press a hand to my chest and bow my head—grateful for all the formal gestures that make it possible to communicate here, even if you're mute.

"They said the situation in Lashkar Gah is okay," explains Hassan-Gul as we make our way back to the car. "Less than ten people have been killed there in the last few days."

The river Helmand is trickling beside us now, running toward the summer retreat of the Ghaznavid sultans. This is the country of Bost, where, according to the tenth-century *Regions of the World*, the "inhabitants are warlike." Medieval guidebooks can be strangely resonant.

But they also underline how badly the decline has set in. In Ferdowsi's time, the geographer al-Maqdisi declared, "In all the countries of the earth which I have traveled through, I have never seen one superior to Bost in beauty, healthiness, abundance of provisions, dates, sweet-smelling herbs and cultivated vegetables." What is surrounding us now is a different world.

It's total desert—a vacuum of sand and pebbles where once or twice a car approaches, whipping up a dust cloud through which it takes several seconds for us to be able to see. A hamlet of mud farmsteads rises out of nowhere, though apparently with nothing to farm. In a few more weeks, Hassan-Gul later tells me, they will plant opium seeds here—the only crop resistant enough to thrive in this parched soil.*

The absence of any other plant life is, visually, the greatest change this land has undergone since Ferdowsi was traveling here. It isn't a modern phenomenon—it goes all the way back to the thirteenth century, to one of history's most famous military sweeps—the invasion of Genghis Khan and the Mongols. "With one stroke," wrote the

* According to the White House Office of National Drug Control Policy, the area of poppy cultivation in Afghanistan had grown from 7,606 hectares in 2001—when the Taliban reduced it with harsh penalties—to 131,000 in 2004. Many of the Afghans I spoke to insisted that in an arid land it has a practical value. "You don't need so much water to grow opium," said Nasrullah, "so it is easier to grow, and in some places it is not possible to grow anything else."

contemporary historian Juvjaini, "a world which billowed with fertility was laid desolate, and the regions thereof became a desert and the greater part of the living dead and their skin and bones crumbling dust." The Afghans' resilience worked against them: So hard were they to subdue that the Mongols tired of conventional tactics and destroyed their irrigation works.

A century later, another conqueror came marching down from Central Asia—Tamerlane. Any chance the Afghans had of recovering from the Mongols was shattered: Not only did Tamerlane inflict his own damage on the region's fragile water sources, but he wasn't especially nice to the people either. When he left the town of Sabzawar, he probably thought he was being generous: After all, he hadn't actually *killed* most of his prisoners. He'd just piled them on top of each other—a tower of prisoners—and cemented them together with bricks and mortar.

Once at the center of East–West trade routes, Afghanistan was about to be wiped off the merchants' maps. With the discovery of sea routes to India and China a few generations later, it would be consigned to its current position of commercial—if not political—obscurity. Ferdowsi, riding toward Ghazni with his freshly finished epic in the early eleventh century, was approaching the fulcrum of his world. For us, driving across Helmand, we aren't just in a different era—we're on a different planet.

Close to Lashkar Gah now, dust clouds are veiling the landscape, sometimes drifting apart to reveal fields of shriveled crops and the long-beards in black turbans riding motorbikes between them. They might as well be riding the skeletons of Western aid workers, because I am convinced their steeds have all been earned through the Taliban method. Every ten minutes I am struck by the thought that if I say a decade of the rosary I will be okay, which gives me sufficient reprieve to scribble down:

This Country Seriously Scares Me
or: Trees, Courtyard houses, Shrines made from sticks
and Stone Mounds pierced by green flags.

We drive under a metal arch and past a machine-gun emplace-
ment marking the boundary of Lashkar Gah.* Donkeys plod through
the sand beside us, while long-bearded men race past them, some
with guns over their shoulders. But I start to forget about those
sinister-looking men, their turbans and Kalashnikovs: because behind
a plain filled with nomads' tents—stitched pavilions of colored cloth
surrounded by camels and tribesmen with waist-length beards—rises
the mud-brick shell of Sultan Mahmud's summer palace.

The structure swelling in front of us looks like a giant beehive.
Crumbling walls of sun-dried brick stretch behind it, pockmarked
and sunk in pebbles and sand as if they've been sucked into the
ground.

"It is beautiful, no?" says Hassan-Gul.

"Yes! Oh yes . . ."

I would say more, but I button up after a glance from Haq, who's
watching us from the car. For the first time I can see him frowning
at me, looking at me more carefully than before. I throw my shoulders back and take several giant strides, mimicking Hassan-Gul until
we're far enough away to lose ourselves in the wonders around us.

It's like an army of beasts rising out of the sand, with their
mouths as the arched doorways, gaping in front of the mounds of
risen earth as if they are fighting over who will get to gobble them
up. Sometimes the walls cave in, sometimes they soar two stories
high, with blind keyhole-shaped windows and lines of dog-tooth
serrating the cornice. There are thick buttresses, swinging out like
peg-ropes to pitch the walls to the sand, and huge stocky brick
columns that make the pillars of Persepolis look as flimsy as reeds.
This is the best available glimpse of Sultan Mahmud's world—of a
time when Helmand was the Balmoral of the region. I wonder what
the Professor would think of it. He would probably say it's not what

---

* Which takes its name—"Soldiers' Place"—from the eleventh-century Ghaznavid
barracks on which the city was founded.

it was, it could have been better preserved, it looks a lot more impressive in the books. But there would be a gleam in his eye as he crossed his arms behind his back and stomped about, acknowledging that yes it really is remarkable.

There would have been a mosque and a bazaar behind us, a harem to the west and palace baths served by running water. Sultan Mahmud and his family came here on hunting-trips, bringing their cup-bearers and clowns to entertain them on the après-hunt. Beardless guardsmen in brocade robes with gold and silver maces would have flanked them, and there would have been a few of the sultan's favorite vehicle—the fighter jet–cum–sports car of his era: his elephants. When they weren't sticking their arrows into the backs of gazelles on Bost's vast plains, the sultan and his boon-companions would have been sitting on elaborate barges on the Helmand River, hung with gorgeous Esfahani silks. Given Helmand's current reputation as Afghanistan's fiercest battle zone, it's hard to see it as the setting for a sultan's holiday home, but as I run my hands across these brittle walls, I think of Ferdowsi, imagining him exactly where I am now, his last major rest before Ghazni.

It is here, as you take in this tiny glimpse of Sultan Mahmud's court, that you realize how false the media comparison has been. In the run-up to Operation Enduring Freedom, every half-baked journalist rushed to brand the Taliban as "medieval." Because of their book-burning and their misogyny and their rule that a man's beard must be long enough to stick out of a fist. And sure, if you compare them to a medieval dynasty like the Ghaznavids, there are plenty of similarities. Both were Orthodox Sunnis and iconoclasts, as well as lovers of the hunt (the Taliban leader Mullah Omar liked fishing with dynamite and went on deer-hunting expeditions with Osama bin Laden, while Sultan Mahmud and his kinsmen preyed on gazelles). But what did the Taliban ever build? They tore things down, they didn't raise them—the similarities they share with a dynasty like the Ghaznavids are vastly outweighed by the differences. Sure, the Ghaznavids could be grisly, but they had an appreciation for culture that puts the Taliban to shame. To call the Taliban "medieval" is an insult to medieval times.

Figure 2. Ghaznavids and the Taliban

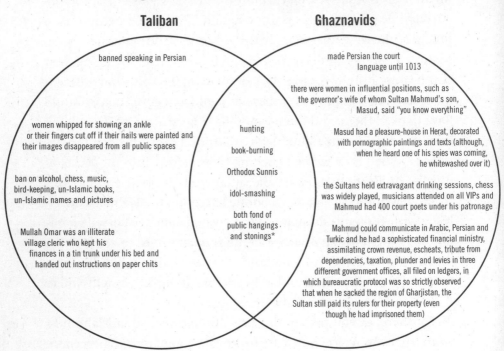

Taliban

banned speaking in Persian

women whipped for showing an ankle
or their fingers cut off if their nails were painted and
their images disappeared from all public spaces

ban on alcohol, chess, music,
bird-keeping, un-Islamic books,
un-Islamic names and pictures

Mullah Omar was an illiterate
village cleric who kept his
finances in a tin trunk under his bed and
handed out instructions on paper chits

hunting

book-burning

Orthodox Sunnis

idol-smashing

both fond of
public hangings
and stonings*

Ghaznavids

made Persian the court
language until 1013

there were women in influential positions, such as
the governor's wife of whom Sultan Mahmud's son,
Masud, said "you know everything"

Masud had a pleasure-house in Herat, decorated
with pornographic paintings and texts (although,
when he heard one of his spies was coming,
he whitewashed over it)

the Sultans held extravagant drinking sessions, chess
was widely played, musicians attended on all VIPs and
Mahmud had 400 court poets under his patronage

Mahmud could communicate in Arabic, Persian and
Turkic and he had a sophisticated financial ministry,
assimilating crown revenue, escheats, tribute from
dependencies, taxation, plunder and levies in three
different government offices, all filed on ledgers, in
which bureaucratic protocol was so strictly observed
that when he sacked the region of Gharjistan, the
Sultan still paid its rulers for their property (even
though he had imprisoned them)

Now most of this medieval world has disappeared: stolen or smashed up or swallowed by the sand, or in the case of the most precious of all the artifacts found here—the frescoes uncovered by a

---

* For example, when they took Kabul, the Taliban seized ex-president Najibullah from his hiding place in the UN compound and strung up his castrated body on a traffic post; while stonings replaced soccer in the city's main stadium. The best-known Ghaznavid execution was suffered by the ex-minister Hasanak and is described by the chronicler Baihaqi: "He fastened the string of his trousers," narrates the historian, "and tied up his drawers. He took off his coat and shirt and threw them away, and there he stood naked with only his turban and trousers on, and his hands clasped together. . . . The executioner fastened him tight and the robes hung down. It was proclaimed that he was to be stoned, but nobody touched a stone. . . . At last a band of vagabonds were hired with money to throw stones; but the man was already dead, for the executioner had cast the rope around his neck and suffocated him. . . ."

team of French archaeologists in the 1950s—destroyed by the *mujahideen*. In a mile-long soldiers' bazaar excavated from the ruins in front of us, they revealed beardless Turkic guardsmen—4,000 of them in total—in brocaded tunics with jeweled daggers and feathered plumes. The frescoes lasted until the 1990s, one of Afghanistan's many historical treasures to be destroyed by the recent fighting.*

I can feel the air, dry and sticky, as we drive through a gateway and park beside a monumental horseshoe-shaped arch. Terracotta arabesques swirl across its surface where they haven't been nibbled away by the wind, and among the strapwork and chevron patterns there are swastikas—suggesting the input of Hindu artisans culled from the Ghaznavids' invasions of India.

Shouldering over the arch is the fort—a giant mound crested by chambers and bastions. Oval niches inch into the crumbling flanks of the walls, where lamps could have been set, and at its back a round tower spirals more than a hundred feet down a pockmarked cavity, into the Helmand, which winds under the citadel's rump like a moat.

A man is standing by the banks of the river. He's looking into the water, presumably to perform his ablutions before prayer. Then he does something surprising. He pulls off his shirt, undoes the drawstring of his trousers, slips out of them, and stands by the bank in his birthday suit. In a moment he's disappeared. The surface of the river is rippling with bubbles; it breaks with a splash and out of it comes a head of black hair and a torso glossy with water, so his barklike skin looks like it's just been varnished.

There is no one else on that side. But when I stroll back into the ward, Hassan-Gul is talking to the fort's guardian. His face is patched with goatlike tufts of hair, which make me think of Mr. Tumnus, the

---

* I hoped to see these frescoes at the National Museum in Kabul. But when I was there a week later, the acting manager explained that they had been destroyed in a fire caused by fighting between rival *mujahideen* factions. These murals cast a beam of light on the world of Afghanistan's greatest empire, a light extinguished by the infighting of the civil war.

gentle fawn in *The Lion, the Witch and the Wardrobe*. Hassan-Gul introduces me as a Tajik—a Persian speaker (or, more precisely, a Persian listener, since I'm still dumb). The guardian smiles, taking hold of my arm and leading me back up the slope. In his free hand are a couple of coins and a clay stamp press.

"These were made in the Ghaznavid time," he says. "You can sell them on Chicken Street in Kabul. I ask only for 150 (about $3.50)."

I take the stamp press and hand him some Afghani, but as he accepts the money, he holds onto my wrist.

"Your skin is like milk," he says.

I notice a wrinkling above his eyes and become conscious that mine aren't brown. I can feel the electricity between us, the sense he is working something out. But we are distracted by a noise behind us: a humming sound.

A tractor.

Three men are strolling into the keep, barefoot and long-gowned, one of them fiddling inside his robes. As they step closer, I see he is holding a Kalashnikov.

What are they doing here?

If I need to hide, the obvious place would be the fort. I climb back up the slope, trying to look as if I'm acting out of pure architectural curiosity—hmmm, interesting niche up there, on the inside of that half-collapsed wall, I wonder if that's where they put their candles . . .

"You wish to know about the fort?" says the guardian. To my surprise, he's following me up the slope.

I spread out my palms, tipping my head up and down—I feel for a moment like the mime-artist Marceau Marceau, transmatted off the streets of Paris.

"It was built by Shah Anushirvan,"* he says, "more than one and a half thousand years ago."

---

* He appears in the *Shahnameh*, as one of its wisest and therefore most boring rulers, who fills up dozens of pages with his aphorisms and judicial decisions. "Praise be the Sun and the Moon," writes Ferdowsi, who shares the reader's eagerness to get past him, "that at last I have escaped from Buzurjamihr (Anushirvan's minister) and the King."

And why are they looking at us?

"He was the Aryan king. In this time, all the people in Afghanistan were Aryan. It was before all the Turks came . . ."

Is it because they're after a free motorbike?

" . . . The Ghaznavis and the Seljukis and the Mongols, all ruining our land. You know before they came, sir, you know all this land was green?"

Or they've been sent here by the Taliban?

"I heard President Karzai is digging wells. God willing, our land will become green again."

The man with the Kalashnikov has laid it on the ground. Which is reassuring. He is pointing at us, which is not.

"You are a child of where?" asks the guardian.

He is looking at me differently, looking through me as if he is seeing the real me behind the *shalwar qameez*. As if he is adding up the facts: the color of my eyes, my skin, my inability to talk.

"You are not from here," he says.

My hand drops and he steps away, the crunch of his footsteps ominous in the sand.

Behind the arch, Hassan-Gul is standing by the car, deep in conversation with Haq. At least, I thought it was a conversation. From Haq's jerking arms and the submissively outspread hands of Hassan-Gul, I realize now it's an argument. And I have a sickly feeling I know what it's about.

"Abbas!" shouts Hassan-Gul.

Haq is behind the wheel and the engine is growling. He's driving off without us! I start moving toward the car, but I'm blocked. The men from the tractor are coming toward me. One of them is shouting, but I've no idea what he is saying.

Haq is trying to drive while at the same time pushing Hassan-Gul, who has muscled inside the door and is being dragged backward. It's a mercy the car's traction is being slowed down by the sand. One of the men repeats the question in Persian, but I'm not thinking quickly enough and my attention is distracted by the car. We are in the open air, but I feel like I'm in the most claustrophobic of caves, surrounded by thirty men, not three. I edge back, and one of the men steps toward me. I can feel my turban slipping. I try to shift it into place, but he grips the end and it comes away from my head, unwinding as it falls.

I see this moment as if I'm watching it from outside: the turban spiraling on its descent, me stooping to pick it up. A look passes between the men, and I can imagine the anxious expression tightening across my face. I see the car, Hassan-Gul straining to keep inside the door, Haq pointing. Now I can follow the direction of his finger to see who he's pointing at: me. A burst of sound, and I can hear the word he's repeating, over and over again. It's unmistakable, its meaning registered in the eyes of the men surrounding me—the one word that frightens me more than any other:

"Foreigner!"

I run. I leap between two of the men and race to the car.

"Get in," exclaims Hassan-Gul, throwing open a door.

The men are a couple of yards from the car, peering through the window. Hassan-Gul speaks sharply to Haq, who is still glaring at the dashboard. They are nearly against us, they could reach out and yank open the doors.

Then they step back. An arm is flung across their chests like a cordon, and at its end stands the guardian. There is a kindness in his eyes, gleaming through the windshield as we reverse out of the gate. We turn around, skidding back through the sand to Sultan Mahmud's palace, and there Haq stops, smacking his head against the wheel.

"What's he saying?" I whisper—there's no point in acting dumb anymore.

No one answers. In fact, no one speaks until we are past Lashkar Gah, driving along the desert back to Girishk, with only the sound of Haq's lentil-cracking to break the silence between us.

"He wanted to leave us there," says Hassan-Gul eventually. "He was very angry. He said he would be safer if he went back on his own. But he *couldn't* leave us."

"Why not?" I ask.

"Because how was it possible when I was standing in the door?"

I remember wheat and barley fields, a cemetery where Afghan flags wave over mounds of stones, the long, fractured, crater-filled roads and the slow accumulation of city detail—auto-rickshaws, pony traps, clusters of iron rods poking out of apartment blocks peppered with bulletholes, buildings with signs advertising "rehabilitation program," and the onion domes of silver-nosed Ahmad Shah Durrani's mausoleum. We have reached Kandahar. After the tension of Helmand, arriving here, in the former Taliban capital, there is the atmosphere of a relative haven. A very relative haven.

A rush of sound—horses' hooves, the *vroom* of rickshaws, a smelder's whirring. Vendors cry for custom outside the Nur Jahan Hotel, named after the wife of a Mughal king. I pay Haq and offer my hand.

"Thank you," I say, "and . . . sorry."

He's about to get back in the car. He turns toward me, pulling himself up to his full height, looks me squarely in the eyes, then, to my surprise, says something in Persian:

"*Khoshal Shodam*"—*I became happy*. More loosely: "I'm glad we met."

Until Bost, nervous of him working me out, I avoided eye contact with him; since Bost, angry at the danger to which I've exposed him, he has been avoiding eye contact with me. Here, for only the second time—and the last—we share a smile.

PART FIVE

cover

IRAN

"The season of drinking and kissing and hugging
  has come again . . .
O saqi, open the door of the wineshop for me . . . "
—AYATOLLAH KHOMEINI, *A JUG OF LOVE*

14

The Bird in the Coffee Cup

Tehran. August.

"Tahmineh!"

Khanom was getting no response, so she marched into the corridor, rapping on her daughter's door. Over in the sitting room, Sina and the Professor shrugged. It was par for the course these days: I'd come back from Central Asia three weeks earlier, and not once had Tahmineh turned up for supper when she was summoned.

"Well," announced the Professor, "if madame insists on making us wait, we must find something to do with our time!"

He opened up his green-jacketed copy of the *Shahnameh* and turned to the back. Over the past few months, I had read many passages with him. Snake-shouldered Zahhak had gobbled up the brains of the Iranian youth. The armies of Iran and Turan had clashed their maces, with Rostam in the goriest patch of the fray. Siyavash's throat had been slit and his widow had scratched her cheeks in grief. Alexander the Great had filled the Persian battlefields with headless trunks and seized "the crown of shahs." And the Sassanian dynasty—inventors of backgammon, the banker's check, and the squinch—had loosened their grip on power, leading to their final defeat by the camel-riding army of Islam's first holy warriors. This climactic event—"the catastrophe," as the Professor called it—was the focus of our reading tonight, as we waited for Tahmineh to come out to supper.

It begins with a catfight. The commander of the Persians sniffs at the Arabs for "drinking camels' milk and eating lizards." Well, what about you lot, retorts the Arab general: "You call yourselves men, but instead you appear / In colors and shapes such as women might wear."

Which are pretty much the same accusations Iranians and Arabs have been leveling at each other ever since.

The battle at Qadisiya was arguably the most significant three days in Iranian history. Outnumbered four to one, the Arabs blinded the Persian elephants with their arrows, causing them to run back into their own lines. The fate of the Persian army—and their empire— was sealed. It was a turning point even more significant to Iranian history than the Battle of Hastings is to Britain.* It changed the religion, language, and system of government, and destroyed the symbol of national identity—the shah—for several centuries. The poet Nader Naderpour compared this earlier "Islamic Revolution" to the events of 1979, arguing that both shattered Iran's integrity. It also resonated in the Iran-Iraq war of the 1980s, which Saddam Hussein declared "a new Qadisiya," building a pair of triumphal arches in which his hands were linked with the crossed swords of the Arab general, Sa'ad bin Wakkas. For many Iranians, the mere mention of Qadisiya sends a shiver up the spine. Far more than just another historical event, it's remembered as a national calamity, the effects of which are still being felt.

In the aftermath of the battle, the last shah, Yazdagird III, flees to the city of Marv and hides in a mill. But the miller stabs him with a dirk and flings his body into the river. "Well done, / Thou crooked-back sky!" exclaims Ferdowsi. It's as if, stricken by the calamities he is describing, he's gone mad with grief. He can think of only one consolation:

---

* Both are etched into their respective national consciousnesses, and just as Ferdowsi sought in the *Shahnameh* to bring back to life the culture Qadisiya swept aside, so in Britain an antiquarian epic writer would also rail against the influx of foreign culture after Hastings, and seek to imagine the world that was lost, albeit with a heavy dose of fantasy—J. R. R. Tolkien, in *The Lord of the Rings*.

All men who are pious and prudent will praise
My name when I'm gone in the far-future-days.
For so I shall live as my word's seed extends
All over the earth and my fame never ends.

There was a thud as the Professor let 1,500 pages drop. The expression on his face—his furrows stretched and his brow creased, his owl-like eyes flashing with anger—was just as I imagine Ferdowsi's to have been when he composed those lines a thousand years ago.

"So now," said the Professor, "you know the story of our people."

He pushed the green-backed volume across the table. "It is for you," he said.

"Really?" I was stunned. "Oh, but I can't! It's . . . well, it's just too kind. I don't think I can accept it . . . can I?"

"Of course you can!" said the Professor. "Now take it with you and may God help you in that dreadful place."

I picked up the book. For a moment it felt as light as one of Tahmineh's fashion magazines, until reality expressed itself in the ache in my wrists.

"I don't know how I can thank you," I said.

The Professor was pulling himself out of his Louis XVI. He patted my arm and led me to the kitchen.

"Come on," he said, "let's eat."

There were only a few days before I would be heading off.

"You really must go to that country?" asked the Professor with a terrifying snort, one evening after supper. "You don't know what an uncivilized people they are?"

"Baba is right," said Sina, turning away—at least for the moment—from the telly. "There are too many Afghans in Tehran and whenever there is a murder on the news, it's always one of them."

They would have tried to discourage me wherever I was heading: Before I set off for Central Asia, they'd been preparing me for the "donkey-brained" Turkmen and the torture practices of the Uzbeks (such as removing people's fingernails and boiling them to death—although the techniques of Iran's prisons are hardly any better), and if I'd been turning west there would have been plenty of invective about the wildness of the Arabs.

Still, there's one thing you can say for all this jingoism—at least it's consistent. Iranians have always enjoyed throwing barbs across their borders. In the *Shahnameh*, the Turks are described as "household slaves," while the Arabs are "wretched ugly crows." Jingoism has no place in the Islamic perspective—to the true Muslim, there is no such thing as national borders. It's survived because the *Shahnameh* has survived, because so many Iranians still identify themselves, first and foremost, by their nationality.*

The Professor was pouring us glasses of vodka. But there were creases on his brow as he asked why I needed to go there.

"Well, that's where Ferdowsi went," I said, "and I want to follow him—you know, when he traveled to Ghazni to give the *Shahnameh* to Sultan Mahmud."

"You wish to experience what it was like for Ferdowsi?"

"Yes, I think so."

There was a rip beside me as a new packet of Bahmans was torn open and the Professor tapped the bottom so the ends of a couple of cigarettes poked out.

"And still you intend to go to the tomb of Sultan Mahmud?"

"Yes. With Sultan Mahmud I am very angry!"

I looked up from the sofa at the smoke rings blowing toward me from the other side of the table. The Professor was studying me, running his owl-like eyes over my face as if there was a verse written across it.

---

* Ayatollah Khomeini underlined the "Islamic" perspective on nationalism in a speech on Radio Tehran on December 17, 1979: "There is no difference between Muslims who speak different languages," he said, "for instance, the Arabs and the Persians. It is very probable that such problems have been created by those who do not wish Muslim countries to be united. . . . They create the issues of nationalism . . . and such-isms which are contrary to Islamic doctrines." This is the exact antithesis of Ferdowsi's point of view—and of the point of view of most of the Iranians I met.

"So you must go," he said finally. "But I do not wish to hear that you were killed."

His head tipped downward, his eyes looking up—as if he were issuing a stiff warning against any such occurrence. I wasn't quite sure how to frame my reply—but fortunately I didn't have to. The clatter of wooden counters drew my attention to the floor, where Tahmineh was sitting cross-legged behind the backgammon board.

"Nicholas, you are ready? I hope you have been practicing!"

On my last evening, Khanom dragged a sack of rice out from under the sink.

"You won't get any decent food from those Afghans," she said, "I can promise you."

She sprinkled turmeric into the pan, diced the mutton, and mixed it with onions to conjure up okra stew—one of my favorite dishes.

There was a lively atmosphere at the table that night. Tahmineh had been cast as Lady Macduff in a semiprofessional production of *Macbeth* and she regaled us with stories about her fellow cast members— "the guy who's Macduff plays with the same sex; he's always hanging around at the park by the City Theatre!"; "the king who Macbeth kills, before the revolution he went on tour to Paris and they say he has a child there with a French actress!"

"So," exclaimed Sina—like his sister he was in high spirits— "Queen Elizabeth gave Nicholas his orders!"

He was repeating a joke often made by a friend of the Professor's— that I was really a spy in league with both the mullahs and the British government (at least, I *think* it was a joke).

As for Khanom, she rounded off the meal with one of her favorite rituals, filling up a skillet with water and setting it on the stovetop.

"Before you go," she said, "we must know you will be safe."

Once I had finished my coffee, she took the cup, placed the saucer on top, and tipped it about, and after a few moments had passed she made a careful study of the grounds.

"Oh yes, it is good," she announced.

I couldn't see anything to warrant her appraisal. Just two muddy blobs. One stretched wide across the inside of the cup, the other hovering over it, with a tapered protuberance.

"It is a bird," announced Khanom, her lips rising in a smile so warmhearted I would remember it for weeks afterward. "A great bird," she said.

"Like the *simorgh*?"* I suggested.

"Oh yes," she replied, laughing, "like the *simorgh*. A great bird, flying all over the world."

---

* The *simorgh* is a magical bird that appears several times in the *Shahnameh*, providing a home to Rostam's abandoned father Zal, and when Rostam is injured in a battle with a metal-plated evangelist-warrior called Asfandiyar, he rubs his wounds with the *simorgh*'s feather to heal himself.

15

Drinking Arak Off an Ayatollah's Beard

Mashhad. September.

More than any other city in Iran, Mashhad has a heart. A beating, bead-clicking, prayer-chanting, chest-thumping heart. It bursts out of the market streets and the peeling-plaster apartment blocks in a fountain of blue faience and gold, catching the afternoon incandescence and glistening at night under strings of golden baubles. It explains all the pilgrims flowing along the streets, stopping at the kish-mish stores, getting themselves photographed in the "Fast Photo" shops, and buying posters of the imams off the pavement: men in checkered headdresses and long gowns, brushing against waistcoated long-beards in knee-length shirts and woolly *pakol* hats shaped like Yorkshire puddings; others in sheepskin busbies floating past men in gathered drawstring trousers and women in blue and white burkas or floral-print *chadors*. They are Arabs, Turkmen, Pakistanis, and Baluchis, and they're all heading to the country's holiest shrine—the martyrdom place of Reza, the eighth Shia imam and the great-great-great-great-great-grandson of the Prophet Mohammed, who was murdered in ninth-century Khorasan by a bunch of poisoned grapes.

I spent many afternoons sitting outside the shrine. The patter of pilgrims' footsteps rang through the marble courtyards and you could hear the hum of men reciting from the Quran under the mirrorwork alcoves. But to me it was like the castle of Bluebeard;* as a non-Muslim, I was officially forbidden from entering its innermost precinct, and it wasn't time to trespass there . . . yet.

So I went elsewhere. I needed to waste time—and not just to delay going to Afghanistan. . . . Well, not *entirely*. I actually had a good practical reason for my dawdling: I'd decided to grow a beard. If I wanted to get myself through Afghanistan, if I wanted to fit in with the locals on the other side of the border, there was one essential accessory—my chin would have to be as furry as a billy-goat's.

So I tramped around Khorasan—the region in which Ferdowsi lived—delaying my trip each day as I sought out another tenuous link to the poet's world. There were the old ramparts of medieval Tus, where you could climb under the webs of scaffolding poles and the bastions wrapped in sheets of plastic, and burrow among the streets of the medieval city. You could spot a barrel-vaulted house here, a shop in the recess over there, the pavestones where Ferdowsi himself might once have set his feet. These were the moments when the poet's world would flicker in front of the eyes. You could squint and imagine a beggar shuffling toward you, with legs and arms tied in a bandage, while a nobleman rides past on a silk-frill saddle; and you could hear what sounds like the clatter of hammers in a coppersmith's shop—only to realize it's the wind rattling through the scaffolding above you.

A couple of hours' hitchhike away was the shrine of Sang Bast, officially the resting place of Arslan Jadhib, one of Sultan Mahmud's most favored generals, who saw action from Central Asia to India. He was very much a man of his time, who recommended cutting off the fingers of the Seljuk Turks to stop them from using their arrows but was also an admirer of poetry, who is said to have built Fer-

---

* Or, more appropriately, the Caliph Mansur's storeroom. In a similar story to the tale of Bluebeard, he gave a key to his daughter-in-law and told her that it could only be used when he was dead. Unlike Bluebeard's wife, she bided her time, but when she opened it up, she too found a chamber filled with dead bodies—in this case, the caliph's Shia enemies, each with a label in the ear providing their name and ancestry.

dowsi's first mausoleum. Like many political figures of the era—among others, Sultan Mahmud—he balanced a keen ear for beautiful verse with the brutality you would expect of any self-respecting medieval military bigwig.

"You think this is the tomb of Arslan Jadhib?" asked a farmer in a yellow turban.

He was knitting his thick brows several dozen feet underneath me, as I climbed up the minaret behind the shrine. Quranic writing scrolled around its shaft, up to the cracked top, out of which I was popping my head to look over the scree and the brick dome of the shrine below.

"Oh yes, this is what you strangers always say," the farmer continued, "you say it is the tomb of Arslan Jadhib. But you are wrong—it belongs to Ayaz!"

He was referring to Sultan Mahmud's number-one slave—the man whose relationship with the sultan was the inspiration for mystic poems about "true love." The reason for his high status in the sultan's private chambers is suggested by the scribe Nizami of Samarkand. Ayaz, he tells us, was "mightily endowed with all the arts of pleasing; in which respect, indeed, he had few rivals in his time."

"They say," the farmer explained—now in a small muddy hut next to the village mosque, "Sultan Mahmud's wife had a problem with Ayaz."

I wasn't surprised—if any of the rumors were true, she had good reason.

"She wanted the sultan to kill him and Ayaz was sure he would die. So he fled to this place, built the minaret you see outside, and he called out from the top to Imam Reza. And the imam listened to him and saved him."

Now, the farmer told me, people visit the tomb when someone in their family is ill.

"They place a stone on the tomb and walk around," he said, "and often they take a sheep and cut its throat so the imam will hear their prayers."

Here was another figure from Ferdowsi's time—like the Sufi poet Ansari of Herat or the physician Ibn Sina in Hamadan—to whom people still turn today in times of trouble, a sign of what a resonant era the poet inhabited. But there was one slight problem with this story. Sultan Mahmud was a strict Sunni, and Imam Reza was as Shia as they come. It's almost inconceivable that Mahmud's favorite slave would have been a Shia. But I would soon find reason to believe the sultan had a closer relationship with the Shia than is traditionally assumed—which is tied up inextricably with Ferdowsi's journey to Ghazni.

Wherever the day took me, the evenings would find me under a shopping street near Imam Reza's shrine, at the "Thousand Stories" teahouse. A pair of parakeets sang on top of an empty wine barrel, in duet with a fountain gurgling at the center. Men and a few women sat cross-legged on carpet-covered bedsteads, and one evening, one of them nodded as I came in with Jahangir, a geology student at Ferdowsi University. I had befriended him on the Simorgh Top-Train (named after the mythical bird in the *Shahnameh*) on which I'd traveled to Mashhad, and he was putting me up in his dorm.

"That's my friend Piruz," said Jahangir. "He's a poet."

The teahouse certainly fitted someone of that description. A small boy was fumigating the air with a pan of wild rue, while a waiter in a brightly colored stripy *chapan* coat, like a courtier in a miniature painting, was carrying a tray of tea and a plate of *faludhaj*—a sweet of wheat and honey enjoyed by the Sassanian shahs. But this particular poet wasn't the kind you'd expect to find in a Persian teahouse: He looked like he'd be more at home at a hip-hop night on Whitechapel Road.

"Hey, man, it's cool!" said Piruz, in English—before asking in Persian who I thought was better—Eminem or the Iranian rapper Sandi. He had all the right gestures: His thumbs were tucked inside the waistband of his tracksuit and his baseball-capped head nodded even when there didn't appear to be anything to nod to.

"Hey man, it's cool!" he said again. "I'm not a poet, exactly. I'm a musician. When I read my verse," he added, chiming on his tea bowl with a spoon, "I do it with a drum."

He recited one of his songs, using the teaspoon to count the beat. Although he had shied from calling himself a poet, a lot of his imagery was familiar from medieval Persian verse: a girl with a "moon-like" face whose lips are "a rose" (he rhymed the Persian for flower, "gul," with "bulbul," the word for nightingale, a common rhyme in classical Persian verse), while the use to which he was putting his lyrics wasn't exactly uncommon way back when.

"Do you know how we find girlfriends here?" he said. "We go to the library. *You* have the discobar, *we* have the library! If we see a girl we like, we ask her, 'Hey, pass us that book,' and we write our telephone number in it. Sometimes I put my verses in the book."

I had a vision of shelves full of Piruz's scribblings—entire sections of biography or perhaps (as this was his subject) mechanical engineering, with a couplet hidden in every textbook.

"Do you have much success?" I asked.

"Hey, man, of course! Because I say nice things about them—and girls like that."

Given the romantic content of Piruz's lyrics, we were in an appropriate setting. The water pipe had passed to me, and as I closed my lips around the fipple, I gazed across the room at someone I recognized. Her hair was long, brown, and out in the open (which proves she wasn't real, but painted onto a pillar) and she was leaning out of a crenellated tower. She was Rudaba, the princess of Kabul, waiting for her lover in a scene from my favorite of all the stories told in the *Shahnameh*.

THE TALE OF ZAL AND RUDABA

The story takes place early in Ferdowsi's epic. Zal is the son of a great warrior, but his father doesn't think much of him when he's born, because he has a lock of white hair, and to avoid the ridicule of his peers he exposes him on Mount Alborz. Fortunately, the mystical giant bird, the Simorgh, takes pity on Zal and rears him as one of her own, at least until his father relents. Now that he's a grown man and clearly of able parts, his father is prepared to overlook the aberration of his prematurely white hair, but what he isn't prepared to overlook is Zal's choice of a mate.

It all goes wrong when Zal turns up at the city of Kabul. Hearing a description of the king of Kabul's daughter, he is smitten, while she, receiving an equally florid account about Zal from her handmaids, is of the same mind. A meeting is arranged: Zal steps up to the tower where Rudaba lives and decides to climb to the top. But it's several stories high, far too lofty for him to mount it with his hands and feet. Rudaba offers a solution—she happens to have extremely long hair, so she takes off her wimple, lets out her locks, and offers them as an alternative to a rope.

This is the moment recorded in the painting on the pillar: when Zal climbs up to meet Rudaba. But he's more of a gent than Rapunzel's prince (proof that politeness isn't only a modern-day Persian attribute), so instead of using her hair, he flings his lasso and does a Spider-Man job on the pinnacles.

"Oh silver bosomed cypress!" he declares as he clasps her in his arms. "I swear by God I'll never break my troth to thee."

Unfortunately, their parents get along about as well as Romeo's and Juliet's. Zal's father is so angry he decides to wage war against Kabul. If he can grind it into the dust, then his son won't have any rancid Kabuli to hanker after. There's only one way around this dilemma: Zal must ride to the royal court and appeal to the shah.

The current royal incumbent is no softie, so rather than accept Zal's request, he puts him to the test of his high priests. His request will only be granted, says the shah, if he can solve their riddles.

Their questions are not exactly transparent. "What are the dozen cypresses erect?" they ask, and "those two steeds moving rapidly . . . Each one to catch the other, but in vain?" And what is "the meadow-land . . . To which a fierce man cometh, in whose hand/There is a scythe?"

Fortunately, like any decent mythic hero, Zal is a master when it comes to a conundrum. It takes him just a few moments of head-scratching to work out the answers. The dozen cypresses, he decides, are the twelve moons of the year, the steeds are night and day, the meadow is man, and the scythe is time. He's right: The shah has no choice now but to grant his blessing.

"So the war is stopped," said Jahangir.

"And for Zal and Rudaba," added Piruz, with a cheeky grin, "finally it's . . ."

He didn't finish the sentence. Instead, he drove a fist into the open palm of his other hand—a signal for what would happen once the lovers reached their marriage chamber.*

"You see," said Jahangir, as we turned away from the pillar, "Ferdowsi is important for us, because he isn't given importance by our government. So we want to celebrate him even more."

"The boy says it right," added Piruz, who had been swaying over the pipe like it was a microphone. "You know what I say? The mullahs, they don't know love."

Which was what my new friends were hankering for. Zal found it, but the riddles he'd faced were nothing to the obstacles imposed on young Iranians today.

At the "Thousand Stories" we drank tea; back at Ferdowsi University, something stronger was located. Jahangir's roommate, Hamid, had a friend known as *taa'min kanandeh*—"the Provider." This was because he had a large supply of arak, which he provided in plastic bags to anyone with the cash. One night, Hamid burst into the dorm, holding the knotted end of a bag in his fist, like a boy holding a goldfish at the fairground. Careful measures were poured into plastic

---

* The fruit of which, delivered by cesarean section (with a steel dagger for the surgeon's knife and wine as the anesthetic), is the greatest of all the epic's heroes—Rostam.

cups and a newspaper was spread on the floor. The front page showed a black-and-white photograph of the Supreme Leader, Ayatollah Khamenei, who would play the role of a doily as we rested our cups on his face. A toast was raised—

"To your health!"

"We drink," announced Piruz, "to the Supreme Leader!"

"No, no," said Hamid, "we drink *on* the Supreme Leader!"

We all pressed a hand on our chests and made ceremonial bows to the photograph of Khamenei, then necked our drinks and slammed the cups back down. Something I'd never thought I would do: drinking arak off an ayatollah's beard.

It was only later, when I was traveling in Afghanistan, worrying my way across Helmand, that I would think about the significance of that moment. Not just *that* moment but many others—the scribbled phone numbers Sina would pass through car windows in Tehran, the "London" gin Reza served at his parties, the poetry meetings at the Professor's, when his friends would recite from banned under-the-counter books. Like the *Shahnameh* itself, they were ways of fighting the homogenization of the mullahs' regime. Too private and secretive to be protests, they were proof, at least, that the government couldn't force its citizens into its own narrow straitjacket. They were small sips of freedom.

But inevitably, it was the lack of freedom that my friends talked about most—in particular, the restrictions when it came to girlfriends. That night Piruz bragged, to howls of disbelief, about a girl he'd kissed one night at the back of the women's gym.

"He is a cunt-ogre!" cried Jahangir.

"He only says that," retorted Piruz, "because he knows it never happens to him!"

But when Hamid started talking about his experiences, the atmosphere grew heavy.

"I was walking with my girlfriend in the street," he said, "and the police took us. I was in prison for a day and a half and I got beaten twenty lashes with a whip. The police were very angry and her parents said she must never see me again."

He poured out another measure from the plastic bag and raised a toast: "To the girls!"

It didn't take the students much to get drunk. Soon they were kicking out their feet, spidering their arms, peeling off their shirts, and unzipping their trousers, then wheeling around the room in their underpants. So this is what it's like to get mashed in Mashhad.

"Request golden liquor if goblet is near," wrote Ferdowsi in the *Shahnameh*, "For that is no sin if it gives the heart cheer." Hardly a sentiment that would meet with the approval of Iran's regime today. Yet in the poet's era, the Ghaznavid rulers were as fond of a drink as anywhere in the medieval world: represented by such figures as the general Ariyaruk, who "had the habit that when he once sat down to drink he would continue boozing for three or four entire days."* Sitting on the floor of the dorm, it felt like the thousand-year-ago poet was more in touch with the people I was meeting than the old men in power.

Pulled back to the present by a refill of the Provider's arak, I have a vague memory of being part of an all-singing, all-dancing merry-go-round. Piruz was our axle, cross-legged in the center, sticking out his fingers like Eminem as he chanted his verses:

> *So down this road I'm riding in my Peugeot 206*
> *I see this girl so hot it's like I went to paradise!*
> *She's driving on the other side her lips they're like a rose*
> *She's singing to herself, her voice it's like a nightingale . . .*

That was my last night in the dorm. The university police burst into the room in the morning and insisted that foreign guests were forbidden.

"It's an insult!"

"The police have no idea about hospitality."

"You must stay with Piruz."

---

* According to the contemporary chronicler Baihaqi.

At my slightest mention of a hotel, Jahangir and Hamid were practically tearing their hair out. But the university police were a nudge, reminding me that it was time to move on. The Afghan border was calling.

My beard wasn't exactly what you'd call full. Patchy at best, in several spots it was turning an alarming shade of ginger. But it was thick enough to rub out my one remaining excuse for waiting. I spent my last couple of nights in Mashhad at a shabby hostel where the lobby had a familiar, acrid smell and the manager wandered around with a flute of rolled-up paper and a bleary-eyed expression. My association with the students, however, wasn't over just yet. I would meet up with Jahangir one last time, on my final evening in Mashhad. First I wanted to embark on a short but essential pilgrimage, to an obscure village called Pazh.

It was hot, but the wind was impressive. It rattled in the rooftop water tanks and sent dust spirals over the road. Even the clouds were struggling against it: torn rags of cirrus clinging to the mountains. It picked at the black rayon *chadors* so the women were gripping their ends more tightly between their teeth, waddling into their mud-brick farmsteads like the penguins to which Iranian men often compare them. A motorcyclist *vroom*ed past my bus, wrapped in a turban so he exposed no more flesh than the women. But in his case, it was to keep out the dust, not disgrace.

"You came for Ferdowsi?" asked a man called *Hajji* Mohammed.

He had stubble on almost every part of his face and big brown eyes darting around like a squirrel's. He had come out of his shop— a flat-roofed mud-brick building like most of the others. Striding ahead of me as if we had made an appointment, he guided me up the tapering hillock at the center of the village, past battered medieval ruins gaping around us like eggshells. Nudged by the wind, we found ourselves at the top in no time at all, standing under a two-tiered house of sun-dried brick: like a tower made out of nutmeg.

"Is this," I asked, "where Ferdowsi lived?"

Hajji Mohammed nodded. "He wrote the *Shahnameh* here."

Flat-roofed and thin, the house was pincered between its neighbors, as if to keep it from flying up into the clouds. The wind held back as we climbed a ridge to the doorway, but it welcomed us in with a ruffle of our hair. Dust and soil were threading a carpet under our feet, and there was more dust on the niches sunk into the wall, which spun around us before being sucked out through a row of empty arched windows.

"I take it nobody lives here now," I said.

Hajji Mohammed turned his squirrel eyes on me. "Of course not! This is Ferdowsi's house."

Down in the courtyard underneath us, a fat-tailed sheep was sticking its head into a trough, and two boys were dueling with a couple of sticks. Dipping and swelling far behind them were the mohair caps of the mountain peaks, known locally as "the Thousand Mosques." I breathed in the dusty air, feeling the sun on my neck and the wind on my nose, and tingling with the excitement of where I was standing.

"You have read the *Shahnameh*?" said *Hajji* Mohammed later that afternoon, squatting over a paraffin stove in his shop.

"I've been trying," I replied.

"Then you know. You heard of Zal? Huh? You must have heard of Zal! He was one of our great warriors, he grew big in a bird's nest. And his son Rostam—the greatest warrior of all! Ha! One swing of his mace would kill a thousand men. And Asfandiyar, of course, he was made from metal so you could never kill him, not unless you shot him in the eye. And . . . "

Living just down the hill from where Ferdowsi grew up, it was no wonder *Hajji* Mohammed was so proud of the poet. But when I mentioned Sultan Mahmud, his pride transformed into a terrible fury—a stretched mouth, arched brows, and eyes like gimlets. The squirrel had become a tiger.

"Son of a dog!" fumed the *Hajji*. "You know what he did? What that son-of-a-dog sultan did?"

He narrated the same story the Professor had told me, many months earlier, sitting under Ferdowsi's statue in Tehran: how the poet labored on the *Shahnameh* for more than three decades, how he took it to the sultan in the hope of a spectacular remuneration, how he was given a single sack of silver for his pains.

"*One* sack of silver!" exclaimed the *Hajji*. "Ha! Well, we all know what Ferdowsi thought of that, don't we?"

The anger rushed out of his face—and in its place emerged a look of bitter triumph. He sipped his tea slowly, before reciting the same words I had heard from the Professor, all those months ago in Tehran:

> *If only your father a true king had been*
> *Then wouldn't your gold on my head have been poured?*
> *And as for your mother, if she'd been a queen*
> *Then I would be sunk to my knees in your hoard.*

I took a Dictaphone out of my jacket. "Can you repeat that?"

Sitting in my room in the shabby hostel, later in the evening, I listened to those verses again. The reels of my Dictaphone were turning, *Hajji* Mohammed's voice crackling through the grille: the words of Ferdowsi's thousand-year-ago wrath, repeated at different ends of my time in Iran. They summed up the anger felt by people toward the sultan for rejecting their poet, toward *all* the sultans and authority figures who have rejected *all* the poets in this part of the world—the perfect weapon for my mission of revenge.

Sultan Mahmud was a fanatical Sunni—this much is attested in the annals. He slaughtered the Shia in numerous battles and burned their books. So why would a Shia poet like Ferdowsi have traveled all the way to the sultan's court at Ghazni with a poem in which there are numerous references to Shiism?

This was the last thing I needed to find out before I set off for Ghazni. I wanted an explanation for why the poet ventured there. If I was to travel across Afghanistan, I didn't want to be following a fairy tale—I needed evidence for the historical facts. If I really *had* to go to Afghanistan, if that really *was* where Ferdowsi went, I needed something tangible to tell me *why*.

Which led me to Professor Haidar Reza Zabat. A jovial scholar with a rich, thick beard, he worked at the Islamic Research Foundation, an institute near the shrine of Imam Reza. He was an expert on Iran's medieval religious history who believed, contrary to the image of Sultan Mahmud as a die-hard Sunni, that the sultan was in fact much more ecumenical.

"We have a story," said Dr. Zabat, "that Sultan Mahmud saw Imam Reza in a dream and after this he became a lover of Imam Reza and built the shrine to the imam here in Mashhad."

There was a practical explanation, he added:

"Mahmud's most important projects were his invasions of India, and it was from there he gained the wealth to enrich his empire. In order to attack India, he needed manpower, and many people in Iran had a great love for Imam Reza, especially in Tus. So Mahmud constructed the shrine here and said he had seen Imam Reza in a dream and the imam supported his actions."

But the medieval shrine was knocked down by the Mongols in the thirteenth century and the present-day structure dates from the seventeenth. The sultan's rapprochement with the Shia has, apparently, been wiped out.

"Well . . ." said Dr. Zabat. "There is *something*, in fact. You can still see it—it's an oratory built by Sultan Mahmud—it is still there, in the shrine of Imam Reza itself."

He paused, nibbling the end of his pen.

"But of course," he added, "you are not a Muslim, so unfortunately you are not permitted to see it."

I nodded respectfully from the other side of his desk.

"Oh yes," I said, "I realize that would be . . . very wrong."

When the lights are as bright and blurring as at the shrine complex that night, the effect is like emerging from underwater. Pigeons roosted on a cupola like seagulls on a rock and men clung to the silver grille outside the shrine, like they couldn't let go for fear of being sucked away. A golden dome rose ahead of us, light spinning off its rim and gleaming on tiles that smeared the portal in the ninety-nine names of God.

"Hopefully they won't notice you," whispered Jahangir, "because you look a little like us."

Our shoes slipped off and floated beside us in the bubbles of plastic bags, while a guard turned the other way just before we dived through the cranny of a doorway behind him.

We were sucked in among them: surfing on a thump of bare feet, down a mirrorwork corridor, through a succession of glass-framed gilded doorways; choked sobs, breathless gasps, hysterical cries, chanted prayers, and the echoes of hundreds of bare feet—surging together, threaded with the smell of sweat and of smoke winding in a watery spiral above a tin thurible. A man tripped and the shoals of worshippers hurtled against his back. Others swept forward, squeezing through the gaps and spurting over the marble, as the golden cage of Imam Reza's shrine keeled into view.

It was like some fabulous casket at the heart of a whirlpool, hauling men against its sides, forcing them to cling to its gilt bars and rub their hands against the cornice, while on the other side of a glass screen that made them look like they were in an aquarium, women flung against the shrine with so much feeling a female guard had to yank them away. Lamentations were pulled out of the pits of their stomachs, screams blasted in our ears, and a chorus of Quranic recitation floated up, up to the vault of colored glass.

The excitement of being within touching distance of Mashhad's holiest of holies was all the stronger knowing I wasn't supposed to be there at all. Prohibitive edicts are a godsend for the modern traveler. With the world becoming so much more accessible every day, it's great to have a few spots that are still, officially, off-limits. When you sneak into a shrine like Imam Reza's, you get a tiny whiff of what it must have been like for travelers of the past—men like Sir Richard Burton, stealing into Mecca disguised as an Afghan.

But it wasn't Imam Reza's shrine I was looking for. Avoiding the glances of the worshippers around me, I was hunting for the oratory of Sultan Mahmud, the structure mentioned by Dr. Zabat. It was like trying to find a treasure in a storm, what with all the bustle around me, and I was swept too fast by the crowd to be sure if the simple glazed-brick structure I spotted was actually a thousand-year-old relic—the last tangible evidence of Sultan Mahmud's rapprochement to the Shia.

Was it really made under the auspices of the sultan? The experience of being in the shrine was too fast and dizzying to tell. But it didn't really matter—I needed something to believe in, a talisman to cling to, just as the men around me needed to believe in Imam Reza. The oratory was rare evidence of a softer approach to the Shia by Sultan Mahmud, an explanation for the hope a Shia poet like Ferdowsi could have invested in this Sunni monarch.

Mahmud was "the world-lord," as Ferdowsi puts it in the *Shahnameh*, "bright sun in light, / A lion with scimitar ready to fight." Setting off for Ghazni, the poet was convinced he would be set free "from every want on earth" by this mighty king—the new incarnation of the ancient Persian shahs—"whose treasuries groan / With his munificence." He would turn out to be sorely mistaken, but the oratory at Mashhad underlines why he believed he was about to be rewarded beyond his wildest dreams, and why he set out on his ill-fated journey.

According to the great physician Ibn Sina, before you set out on a journey you should purge yourself by bleeding, rub your body with oil, and wind a binder around your loins. Sound advice, no doubt, but on my last night in Iran, I was looking for emotional, rather than physical, comfort, which I suppose is why I found myself loitering around the *Haram*.

The evenings always brought groups of men together in the courtyards around Imam Reza's shrine. Their hands struck their chests and their voices croaked as they recited the mourning songs. One group was standing behind a wire fence, in a nest of concrete slabs and scaffolding poles where a new mosque was being constructed.

"You think America will attack Iran?" asked a young man called Mohammed. He wore a blazer over his jeans like a brand of sophistication, and his mobile phone was clipped to his belt.

"I hope not," I said.

"So let them attack." He hunched down beside me on a pipe. "They think because they occupy Iraq they can take Iran! They surround us on every side, but they cannot occupy us. Remember— Iraq is Sunni and Shia, they are divided. But in Iran, we are all Shia. We are brothers!"

One of his friends joined us. He was a soldier called Mustafa, still in uniform, and after the previous conversation I expected more military discussion, so I was surprised by the question he asked.

"What can you tell me," he said, "about love?"

"Well . . . " I racked my head for something really profound. "It's . . . good, isn't it?"

"Good?"

"Um, beautiful?" No, no, no, this really wouldn't do. Right at the moment, love was the last thing on my mind. "Well . . . " I reached for the ultimate cop-out. "I suppose it depends on what *kind* of love."

Mohammed nodded sagely, and Mustafa rapped my knuckles.

"What is the most important kind?" he asked.

"I don't know; there are so many. What do you think?"

"Love," declared Mohammed, "of Imam Reza!"

In front of us, a dozen men were standing in a circle, rhythmically beating their chests while one of them sang. Others hunched against a wall, one sobbing into his hand, which was cupped as if to catch his tears, while his friend's arm was gripped, consolingly, on his shoulder.

"You know," said Mustafa, "if we ever want anything, we pray to Imam Reza."

"You can do this too," added Mohammed.

"Whatever you want," said Mustafa. "If he likes you, Imam Reza will make it possible."

As they stood in the circle, they cupped one hand over their mouths to stifle their sobs, at the same time beating the other hand against their chests. The chanting dropped, fading through the air like a falling leaf, and they kissed each other three times on the cheeks.

"Do you feel God here?" asked Mustafa.

"Yes."

I was trying to please him, but I wasn't lying—I *did* feel something. It was hard to rationalize—an electric current of faith. With my head full of Afghanistan, I think it was fed by my fear of the coming journey, which had prompted me to say the rosary every morning for the past week.

"God is everywhere," announced Mustafa.

"And he is in all of us," added Mohammed.

"Even in me?" I asked.

"Yes, he is in you," said Mohammed. "But . . ."

"But I won't be saved unless I become a Muslim?"

"A *Shia* Muslim," said Mustafa. "The Sunni, they will also go to hell. In fact, they are even worse than the Christians!"

The lights around us were shining gold on our skin and sparkling on the marble courts in flashes of magenta. Ahead of us, the light formed vertical strips on the silver bars of the grille where men were tying ribbons outside the shrine. Some dabbed handkerchiefs on their cheeks to mop up their tears, while others let out soft melancholy sobs.

"Why don't you make a wish?" asked Mohammed.

I had never prayed at a Muslim shrine before. Yet here, a Muslim who believed I was bound for hell was inviting me to pray at his country's most important shrine.

The touch of the bar was warm on my lips where so many other lips had pressed, and as I prayed to Imam Reza I felt swept up in something. *Please please please*, I prayed, *pleeeeease help me get through Afghanistan.*

I stepped back to my companions, blinking away a tear.

PART SIX

AFGHANISTAN

"The homes that are the dwellings of today
Will sink 'neath shower and sunshine to decay,
But storm and rain shall never mar what I
Have built—the palace of my poetry."
—FERDOWSI, *THE SHAHNAMEH*

16

The Road to Ghazni

Kandahar. October.

"Mr. Nicholas!"

Hassan-Gul whistles in my ear as he pulls back the blanket.

"Aren't you ready yet?" he asks.

"No!"

He is already in his *shalwar qameez*. As I sink my legs into the baggy depths of my own, the dawn *azan* is calling through the window, rallying the faithful to prayer. I zip up my waistcoat, making sure my Dictaphone is in the inside pocket. Today, if everything goes to plan, we will follow Ferdowsi to the capital of Sultan Mahmud's empire. It's time for the poet's revenge.

"You became an Afghan!" exclaims Hassan-Gul.

He's nodding approvingly, noticing my pantherlike stride to the door. He presses a hand on my shoulder and gives me an encouraging smile.

"When we place our feet in Ghazni," he says, "your heart will fly like a bird."

Oil lamps flicker from the doorways of mud-brick huts as an auto-rickshaw putters down Kandahar's main street. They light up an old man arranging his gown on a stoop, a couple of boys slapping roundels of bread on the wall inside a shop, and men hunched over their sacks at the side of the road. In front of a metal shipping container, another lamp is raised by a small boy as he warms a turbaned ticket seller. The rickshaw drops us beside him, and we climb into the bus.

Safe from scrutiny, thanks to early morning fatigue and the lack of sunlight, I scribble in my notebook. It's the first time I've done this in public since leaving Herat. Even so, I keep it out of the attention of the other passengers, and when they try to talk to me, I still have to act dumb, pressing a hand on my chest and gesturing to Hassan-Gul to act as intermediary.

Cones of rock are rising on one side of the bus, and low-slung fleshy banks of hill on the other, while ahead of us sprawls a sandy plain as gray and monochrome as the sky above it. The most dangerous part of the journey is behind us—in theory, at least. Although, since the UN High Commissioner for Refugees removed all its staff from this part of the country just a few months ago, after a shooting in Ghazni, it's hardly as if we're moving into Munchkin-land.

Revenge—that's what it's usually about. Or so Hassan-Gul told me last night as we lay in the dark, swatting away the insects that had chosen us for their supper.

"If someone wants to kill you," he said, "it is because his heart has turned black from all the people who died. In our culture, it is blood for blood. Maybe you will say this is not right but it is how things are."

As the impetus for my journey, there could be nothing more appropriate.

It's certainly not exclusive to the Afghans—the importance of blood for blood among the Persians is illustrated in the *Shahnameh* itself. It's a driving force throughout Ferdowsi's epic—from the start, when the first shah's son is torn apart by the evil Black *Div* and an army of beasts gathers to avenge him; to the killing of King Fereydoun's son Iraj, which leads to an everlasting war between the ancient Iranians and the Kingdom of Turan; to the battles that follow the murder of Prince Siyavash. It's the dark side of Persian culture, bleeding out under the rugs and books and fluffy cats. How better to honor the author of those stories than to set out for revenge on his behalf?

But something is scratching at the back of my head, telling me it isn't going to be so simple. When it comes to traveling in this part of the world, it never is.

With nature being so spare, it's up to the people to supply the color. Camel herd-boys have green cloths turbaned around their heads, while the women who cross the plains are wearing bright red and blue skirts and black headscarves. The camels' heads are raised high on erect necks, replicating the posture of Afghan men, as if one has learned their stance from the other. But the women bend low— sometimes back-breakingly so, like those sweeping with handleless twig brooms in their courtyards. On the radio, a female singer is caroling a love song based on the twelfth-century romantic tale *Layla and Majnun*. The confidence of her voice, like the bare ankles of the women on the plains, is surprising in "Taliban country." But it raises no objection from the men in the bus.

We are in the medieval geographers' Zabolistan, the highlands of Kandahar watered by the Upper Helmand. It's a scorching, hellish land, where they say you can grill a fish just by holding it out to the wind, but these things are always a matter of perspective, and after the Desert of Death anywhere would look like a wonderful place to live. Men are moving rocks around a stream that claims the unusual advantage of actually having water, and at Moqor we see mounds of green and yellow melons. The sky grows brighter, while the earth is healing after the lunar plains, softening and sprouting the odd patch of grass. Fruit hangs in nets outside the shops and dangles from trees on the edges of the villages: grape and almond groves where sheep wander about as if to inspect the produce; a pomegranate tree providing shade to a family of Kochi nomads, dressed in bright colors like Romany gypsies, who are sitting outside the black hitched-up skirts of their tent. Near the city of Sultan Mahmud, nature is coming back out.

It's as if we've turned the page to a citadel scene in an illuminated manuscript. The stone walls of a round-towered fort soar ahead, and rooks squat on the walls like Afghan men at a teahouse. The scenes

around us—women invisible under their veils, men with baskets and
sacks, their turbans showing tufts at the back like Ferdowsi in every
single painting or statue I've seen of him—all these could have been
viewed through the poet's own eyes.

A rusting rocket launcher sticks out of a hilltop, reminding me of
which era I'm in, while the Afghan tricolor flies above us (instead of
the emblem Ferdowsi would have observed—the Ghaznavid lion
and sun). The tricolor is everywhere—swaying above the fort, dangling out of the rods of new buildings, hanging over the side mirror
of a truck. Men are sinking axes into wooden logs, some sawing
them or boring holes with gimlets; and behind them auto-rickshaws
are gridlocked with yellow taxis in front of the marketplace. Like
Ferdowsi a millennium before us, we are on the threshold of Sultan
Mahmud's capital.

If Ferdowsi had turned up in Ghazni when he was a child, he would
have found a backwater. But a generation later, it was the most daz-
zling city in the Muslim East. A general called Alptigin escaped there
in the 960s, after he'd botched a coup against the prince of the
Samanids, the ruling dynasty in Central Asia, and made the city his
bolt-hole.* He was followed by a series of short-lived successors until, in 977, a military council elected a pagan-born Turk called Sebuktigin, whom Alptigin had bought at a Central Asian slave depot.
Under Sebuktigin the empire of Ghazni swelled, with considerable
help from his eldest son.

That son was Mahmud—a man who, in the words of the medieval historian Nizam al-Mulk, "was not handsome; he had a drawn
face, his skin was dry, his neck long, his nose high, and his beard was
thin. Because he always ate clay, his complexion was yellow."

---

* It is said, in the *Collections of Stories* by Mohammed Awfi, that Alptigin was given
an opportunity to show his leadership skills when some villagers pressed him to
punish the thieves who had stolen their fowls. He had the thieves' ears bored and
the birds suspended from them by strings, with the result that whenever the birds
flapped their wings, blood gushed out of their ears. This, apparently, was exactly
what the people of Ghazni were looking for, so they decided to make him their ruler.

Clearly he was no pinup—but it didn't matter. Because Mahmud happened to be the military genius of his age. Expert swordsman and lance-fighter, he loved nothing more than to lead from the front, throwing himself into the fray and in one battle (at Multan, in what is now Pakistan, in 1005) notching up so many killings that his hand stuck to the hilt of his sword with congealed blood. He was also an expert tactician, adopting counterfeit movements to surprise the enemy. When things weren't going well against the Ghurids of Central Afghanistan in 1011, Mahmud faked a withdrawal, drawing the enemy out, then flipped his army around and put them to a rout. It was this combination of cunning and chutzpah that made him the most terrifying conqueror around. In a world where princes were little more than tax-squeezing mobsters, Mahmud was the don.

The effect of his military prowess started to tell in Ghazni itself. Booty came back by the elephant-load, turning the ex-backwater into a regional powerhouse. Palaces and lavish villas sprouted like the apple trees for which the city was famous, along with a spectacular Friday Mosque funded by Mahmud's numerous conquests in India, made of marble and granite and known as the "Bride of Heaven." The caliph of Baghdad, keen to share in the triumphs of Islam's latest superstar, dispatched his messengers with precious gifts and gave Mahmud the title "God's Shadow on Earth." Visitors flocked from all over the region to make the acquaintance of the man who had never lost a battle. Among them, just a decade before Ferdowsi's own visit to Ghazni, was one of his townsfellows, whose description gives us an indication of what the poet would have faced. "I encountered," wrote Abu'l Abbas of Tus in 1001,

> *a vast body of troops, too numerous to be counted, and all fitted out with the most splendid uniforms and outfits, and the finest weapons and equipment, that I have ever seen. . . . I entered, and found the forecourt thronged with wild beasts, chained up on both sides in lines facing each other. I made my way through them, noting first of all lynxes in their natural state, and then panthers likewise, all in great numbers. Finally, I reached Mahmud himself, a fine figure to see, installed in his full*

court, in a hall richly furnished and equipped. He was seated on his
throne with all the great men of state standing before him in two ranks,
all in their finest clothes.

For Ferdowsi it would have been awe-inspiring. But it wasn't only
the sultan's vast retinue that made him difficult to approach.

According to a popular story, on his arrival in Ghazni, Ferdowsi
encountered three poets sitting in a garden: the poet laureate Unsuri,
the lyricist Farrukhi, and another called Asjadi. Although they were
all capable writers, they had devoted most of their talents to oily, ego-
massaging panegyrics for their master.* On seeing a ragged old man,
whose speech they considered old-fashioned and rustic, they refused
to believe he could seriously claim to be a poet of any merit. More to
amuse themselves than as a genuine test, they offered him a challenge.
Sure, they would let him into the court—but only if he was able to
complete a quatrain of rhyming verse. Each of them would recite a
line, matching the rhyme of the first and continuing its meaning. And
since Ferdowsi was the trespasser, his turn would be last.

"Thine eyes are as clear and as blue as the ocean," recited Unsuri.

"Their glances," continued Farrukhi, "bewitch and they charm
like a potion."

Asjadi: "Their wounds can be soothed not by balm nor by lotion."

They knew of no other word to continue the rhyme: the old yokel
was bound to falter. He barely paused, raising his voice as powerfully
as his septuagenarian lungs could manage:

"As deadly as Giv with his spear dealt at Poshan."

The poets were flummoxed: as much by Ferdowsi's reference to a
legendary battle as by his ability to complete the set. Honor de-
manded they admit him to the court, but the defeat rankled. It is
said that both Unsuri and Farrukhi spoke out against Ferdowsi to
Sultan Mahmud: Why celebrate the ancient warriors when there

---

* The sultan's susceptibility to flattery is suggested by a story from one of his conquests in India. Besieging the fort of Kalinjar, Mahmud finally raised the siege
when he was offered (along with three hundred elephants and a promise of annual
tribute) some verses composed in his praise by the Indian prince.

were so many heroes in the sultan's own modern-day army? Perhaps this is what Ferdowsi means when he writes in his satire:

> *A slanderer (oh! On his foul head a curse!)*
> *Interpreted evil from out of my verse.*
> *The credit I'd won with the Sultan he stole,*
> *Extracting the warmth from my hot glowing coal.*

I've been thinking a lot about these verses during the last few weeks—wondering why Sultan Mahmud treated Ferdowsi's epic with such disdain. Why the poet, venturing to Ghazni with such high hopes, was in the end so dramatically rebuffed. By the time I leave the city, I am hoping I will have an answer.

Ghazni at last! The excitement drives me through the market stalls, among Pashtun long-beards and wispy-chinned Hazaras carrying bags of grain measured with stones on tin scales, or women in white burkas bearing reed baskets full of pink rocks of salt; among the sheepskin coats for which Ghazni is famous, as well as the watered yogurt drink, *dugh*, praised by Abu Sa'd of Gorgan in the tenth century, who also recommended the city's apples. "Their juice," he wrote, "is like the saliva of a moon-faced youth." As a taxi steers us upslope to the gray stone walls of the citadel, I can't say the apple I am munching gives me that particular sensation, but perhaps this is because I'm distracted by the tension bristling around us.

Children are filling pails with water from the hand pumps underneath the clay walls of their houses. Bound in torn trousers and bits of rag, they widen their eyes as they watch us pass, while older long-bearded men seem to scowl as we squeeze through the bazaar's narrow backstreets. Their houses huddle behind them, falling in on themselves, snapped in half by shelling, and everywhere the walls are marked by the dot dot dot of the gun—holes regular and big enough for the children to poke all their fingers inside. They underline how precariously peace hovers over Ghazni—teetering like the sheets of corrugated iron perched on the roofs. In November 2003, in this same market, two men on motorbikes shot a Frenchwoman called Bettina Goislard: the first murder of a UN worker in post-Taliban Afghanistan, which led to the withdrawal of the region's UNHCR staff.

"Oh yes, we are having many difficulties," says our taxi driver, Ghulam, addressing us in Persian.

A large blue orb is swinging under his rearview mirror, a talisman against the Evil Eye, and a mini silver Quran dangles underneath it.

"Just last week," he continues, shaking a hand at the splintered windshield, "another mullah was assassinated."

He eyes me through the rearview mirror and speaks to Hassan-Gul in Pashto.

"He said," Hassan-Gul explains, "you have a foreigner's eyes."

Another volley of Pashto.

"I told him," says Hassan-Gul, "you are not a foreigner—only you are suffering from a speech problem."

Another volley.

"He said in that case you must be very weak."

Like the houses, the stone walls of the citadel are swiss-cheesed by bulletholes. But I'm not sure if these are from recent fighting or earlier (so often in Afghanistan, everything seems to melt together in one long, horrific saga of bloodshed), because there was a fierce conflict here in the 1840s, which had a peculiar effect: It brought Sultan Mahmud back to life.

The British had demolished the gates of Ghazni en route to seizing control of Afghanistan: another piece of the Asian jigsaw under Queen Victoria's sway. Placing a puppet king on the throne of Kabul, they established themselves as unrivaled masters of the Afghan plains, but when the challenge came, it would be sudden. Bursting out from the mountains, the warriors of the deposed king hanged the British senior envoy's corpse in the Kabul bazaar and fomented riots throughout the capital. By the time the redcoats had sounded a retreat, it was too late—the Afghans were in no mood for mercy and they ambushed the British in the Koord-Kabul Pass. Those who didn't take a direct hit were finished off by frostbite. Out of 16,500, only a single survivor made it to the safety zone of Jalalabad—a doctor who was saved from a knife wound by the copy of *Blackwood's Magazine* he kept under his cap. The event would make its way into nursery rhymes, to be sung for many years afterward by Afghan children: "Poor Doctor Brydon, his lame donkey trotting, / While under our soil his fellows are rotting."

Returning to Ghazni a year later, the British were still fuming. Proving that the impulse for revenge was hardly exclusive to the locals, their "Army of Retribution" tore down the sandalwood gate of Sultan Mahmud's mausoleum and sent it off to India, claiming it was the same gate seized by Mahmud himself in his most famous campaign—in 1025, when he slaughtered 50,000 Hindus at the Moon Temple of Somnath. "The insult of 800 years ago is at last avenged," declared Lord Ellenborough, in a proclamation to "the princes and Chiefs, and people of India." Set up on show in the fort of Agra, the gate became a symbol of the Raj's policy of divide and rule between the Muslims and Hindus, and of its dubious victory over the Afghans.

But it didn't have exactly the effect the British had intended. Among India's Muslims, a long-buried memory was awakened, and when they established their own nation, they made the sultan one of their mascots. In May 2002, showing how well they remembered Mahmud and his dynasty, the Pakistani army flight-tested its latest short-range single-warhead ballistic missile—the *Ghaznavi.**

---

* This example of history being hijacked for colonial divide-and-rule was underlined a few weeks later, when I continued my travels into Pakistan. "The real founder of Pakistan is Sultan Mahmud," said Professor Homaioun at Kabul University. But according to the popular Pakistani historian Dr. Mubarak Ali, his fame had faded over the centuries. "Mahmud was just a part of history, he disappeared," declared Dr. Ali, as we sipped milky tea under Mughal miniature paintings in his flat in Lahore. "But he was resurrected in the colonial period. The British wanted to show how the Hindus suffered from Muslims and how they were blessed to be rescued from their tyranny by the British." Another historian, Dr. K. K. Aziz, suggested that Mahmud's popularity was symptomatic of Pakistan's present-day troubles. "Mahmud of Ghazni," he said, "is put before Pakistani students from class one as a great general and iconoclast who came to India seventeen times and took a lot of jewelery and all this is applauded as a great Islamic hero. If in the textbooks you wrote that he was a great tyrant, had no business coming to India, and committed a sin because a Hindu temple is a place of worship—well, most probably the government would ban this book."

"What do you think of Sultan Mahmud?" I ask Hassan-Gul, walking along a dusty track cutting through a hill over the citadel.

He steps carefully in his rubber sandals, scouring the grass on either side of the track: According to Ghulam, there used to be mines here, and he's not sure if they've all been cleared.

"People in Herat," says Hassan-Gul, "we have a big place in our hearts for Ferdowsi, and you cannot love them both. But when you talk to people here in Ghazni, you will find their opinion is different."

Every year at Ghazni, Sultan Mahmud held a review. "A splendid pageant drawn up on parade," as the poet Farid ud-din Attar described it, including 1,300 elephants and 54,000 soldiers, covered in mail and armed with all the weapons available at the time—from curved *qalachur* swords, sabers and spears to lances and lassoes, bows, battleaxes, and bull-headed maces.

The sultan was fascinated by anything to do with combat, but nothing swelled his chest as much as the elephants—booty from his conquests in India—made all the fiercer by their metal headpieces, which the *mahouts* would strike to frighten the enemy. When Mahmud defeated the Central Asian Qarakhanids in 1008, one of his elephants lifted up their ruler's standard-bearer with its trunk, hurled him on its steel-clad tusks, and cut him in two, while other elephants threw riders from their horses and trampled them to death. They were noticed by Abu'l Abbas of Tus, who saw "a big group of elephants" accompanied by 30,000 Indian troops.

Now, standing on a hill over the citadel, I'm looking down on a more recent kind of elephant. Their smoothbore guns point up the hill and their glacis-plates are flaky with rust. They're a token of the recent fighting, a striking visual sign that this city—once the crucible of an empire dedicated to war—is still very much in the fray. Is this why I really object to Sultan Mahmud? Because I see him as the symbol of war, destruction, and the trampling of culture? Yet, looming beside me as I sit on the hillside, soaring out of the earth like the trunk of an ancient oak, is a sign of how ambiguous this matter can be—that, in some cases, war can actually *create* culture.

It's one of a pair of victory towers, spearing eighty feet out of an underground pit. The lower trunk is plain, but as it rises the tower umbellates into floral patterns, delicately molded from terracotta, twisting into tendrils and breaking into star shapes, and near its crown the frippery is pushed down for an austere ring of Arabic. There is another tower farther up the hill, smaller, with panels of interweaving lines and elegant wriggle-work, but beautiful too.

Why aren't they ugly? That would make it easier: Art and war could be seen in comforting opposition, perfectly polarized. Instead, they are tangled together, like a pair of lovers who appear to outsiders to be ill-suited, but are clearly head-over-heels in love. They're an example of the muddying of the water, something I will need to resolve if I am to carry out Ferdowsi's revenge.

"Come on, Mr. Nicholas," says Hassan-Gul.

He is standing by the taxi, using his spotted handkerchief to wipe the dust of the track off his trousers. There's a mud stain just above his ankle, and as he wets his hanky to wipe it off, he is shaking his head irritably.

"Your heart wishes to visit Sultan Mahmud?" he asks.

"Oh yes."

I'm ready to do what I came here for. To prove it, my Dictaphone is shaking inside the waistcoat I'm wearing over my *shalwar qameez*.

"So," says Hassan-Gul, "let us place ourselves in the sultan's path."

17

Insultin' the Sultan

Ghazni. October.

"I can't believe it—a swing!"

A short drive from the hill where we visited the victory towers, Hassan-Gul nudges open an iron gate, approaching the only playground installation I will see in Afghanistan. A small boy is whooping as his father gives him a push, and he isn't the only one enjoying himself. On flat-weave rugs laid across the terrace above him, kebab sandwiches are being served by a man humming over a barbecue. Men sit around him, filling up their bellies, while the scent of burning meat and cardamom mixes with the sharp resin of the pines soaring above us. They act like a curtain, hiding the building at the top of the hill.

So leisurely an atmosphere is absolutely fitting: After all, this hill was used by Sultan Mahmud himself, known as his "Garden of Victory." It was here that he caroused with his favorite slave, Ayaz, challenged his ministers to drinking contests, and filled his most sycophantic poets' mouths with gems. Hassan-Gul and I climb the steps, my Dictaphone rattling inside my waistcoat as if it knows its moment is about to come. The curtain of pines draws back, revealing a domed clay building with blue wooden doors. Here, in the spot where so many of his most pleasurable evenings took place, at the time of the evening prayer on April 30, 1030, Sultan Mahmud was put to rest.

"Salaam," announces Hassan-Gul.

He presses a hand on his heart to greet two old men, snowy with turbans and icy with beards, who are sitting cross-legged on the floor inside the doorway.

"These men," he tells me, "are from the Sheikhan tribe. They are famous in Ghazni province."

"We have fifty families in our tribe," says one of them. "And we have been guarding this tomb ever since our blessed sultan died."

"But," I want to say, "that's a thousand years!" I don't say it—as I'm still officially mute, and given the saintly, sympathetic looks they're giving me, I suspect Hassan-Gul is explaining to them my "trouble"—although, as he is speaking in Pashto, I can't understand what he's saying.

"Every day," one of them tells me, through Hassan-Gul's translation, "two members from our tribe come here to clean and guard the tomb for twenty-four hours. Because we are many, it is not a difficult task. And it is a great honor because the sultan was a holy man."

Holy? This isn't exactly the impression I've been receiving from the annals. A lot of Muslims might frown on Mahmud's relationship with his favorite slave, Ayaz, and everyone in Iran appears to frown on his treatment of Ferdowsi. And what about the killing he made, literally as well as financially, on his expeditions to India? On second thought, yes—the last detail is exactly why he is considered to be holy. So says a man with a bifurcated beard, standing in the tomb chamber itself—a dusty, lime-plastered cavern, where the light squeezing through the doorway is flashing on the metal bars around the sultan's sarcophagus.

"Mahmud is so important in the Islamic history," he explains. "He captured up to Uzbekistan and Pakistan, he attacked Iran, and he crushed the Hindus in Somnath."

He announces this last detail with relish, as if it's the most wonderful thing anyone could possibly have done. But there's a softer side to the sultan's popularity, explained by a man dressed in black, who is standing on the other side of the tomb. He's accompanied by a woman in a blue burka, swaying strangely as her hands quiver over the metal bars.

"If people have a problem," he says, "they come here to solve them. I pray here because I have a problem I wish to be solved. I understand Mahmud was a high-character person, a hero for Afghanistan."

"And a *mujahid*," points out the other man, with the bifurcated beard.

"Oh yes," says the man in black, "he was Afghanistan's first *mujahid*!"

I hadn't imagined this—a crowd. A medieval sultan's tomb—I was expecting it to be empty. I thought I could come here, play the satire on the Dictaphone, and be on the road to Kabul after a few minutes. Revenge complete. Instead I've got an audience, and they're addressing me in Persian—so they'll know exactly what the words of Ferdowsi's satire are about.

The thousand-year-old insult.

I remember the Professor, laughing at my plan when I revealed it to him in Tehran a few weeks ago: "Child, they are Afghans!" he said. "They will tear you to pieces!"

So I look at the sarcophagus—the horrible, selfish, miserly sultan's sarcophagus—and, keeping up with the politeness code, I nod in agreement to all the praise the men are heaping on its occupant. *Oh yes, indeed, what a lovely man he was, that wonderful Sultan Mahmud.*

Robert Byron went wild for the "dancing foliage" of the tomb's decorations. Nowadays, it's only possible to sneak a peek by stretching between the metal bars and yanking up the green rugs in which the sarcophagus has been covered, when the guardians aren't looking. Marble embossments swell into dagger shapes and floral lines crawl elegantly around them, as if they are engaged in a debate about which lifestyle the sultan preferred—soft luxury or the sword. But before I am able to undress the tomb any further, I'm stopped by a terrible scream.

It's the woman in the burka. Although her face and body are hidden, you can see the convulsions as she thrashes and throws herself backward, smacking the top of her head with her hand, letting out a husky, drawn-out moan, as if she is finding it hard to breathe. The man in black pulls her against his chest, pressing an arm down on her shoulder. He speaks in a soothing tone, and although there is no question of him removing her burka, he appears to be trying to put her at ease. He guides her slowly outside, a palm pressed firmly against her back.

"She has epilepsy," explains Hassan-Gul, before following them out.

So this is the problem the man in black wished to solve: He's brought her here to pray for help.

Everyone has gone. Everyone except me. Everyone except me . . . and Sultan Mahmud. It's like a sign. Finally—the solitude I've been craving!

I pace around the tomb. I rest my back against its side. I crouch by a carpet hanging from the limestone wall. In the days since *Hajji* Mohammed recited Ferdowsi's satire in his shop near the poet's house, I have thought many times about what I'll do when I finally come head to headstone with the sultan. This wispy-bearded, clay-eating, yellow-faced tyrant, who scuppered Ferdowsi's dreams, sent him out of Ghazni with a single sack of silver, and threatened to trample him under his elephants.

He is the enemy.

The fanatic.

The one who massacred the Hindus and burned the books of rival sects.

The one who hurled Biruni off a roof and chased Ibn Sina around the region.

The one who didn't care for the legends Ferdowsi heroically preserved.

He is the Ayatollahs, Khomeini and Khamenei.

He is the brutes of Dushanbe, ransacking the Melody Music Shop.

He is the Taliban.

He's had it coming.

I take the Dictaphone out of my waistcoat and set it on the ledge of the sarcophagus. I will play the satire, over and over and over again, reminding the sultan he is the "spawn of a slave" and sending his humiliation all the way to his no-doubt-long-established place in hell.*

Except . . .

People come here to pray, to ask Mahmud for help with a woman's epilepsy. The eminent historian V. W. Barthold believed "the system of government in the Eastern Muslim lands reached its full development under him" and it's doubtful Afghanistan ever enjoyed such efficient management again. In a story told in Nizam al-Mulk's eleventh-century *Book of Politics*, a man complains to the sultan about the abuse of a judge, and Mahmud has the judge suspended from a pinnacle of his palace until he's agreed to pay back the money he's taken: proof, as far as the author is concerned, of the sultan's sympathy for the poor.

Another of Nizam al-Mulk's anecdotes demonstrates not only Mahmud's respect for rule-of-law, but also his love of a binge. At the end of a wild boozing session, his boon-companion was in such a "state of giddiness" he warned him not to walk the streets because he risked being thrashed by the censors—the Ghaznavid version of the Morality Police. His companion ventured out nonetheless and, despite having spent the evening with the sultan, he was beaten forty strokes with a stick. "Since the rules of administration and discipline were firmly established in the country," writes Nizam al-Mulk, "the working of justice took this course."

Ever since learning about the conflict that split both Ferdowsi's world and the Persian-speaking lands of today, between "nationalists" on one side and "religious people" on the other, I have seen Mahmud as the other side: the shadow of religious fanaticism, burning books and cutting the throats of the "bright-thinkers," leaving a trail of blood that runs all the way to the present.

But . . . As I've traveled around Ferdowsi's world, I've learned it's not so simple. The nationalists have used Ferdowsi for their own ends—the Pahlavi shahs in Iran exploited him to bolster their iron

---

* Ferdowsi himself declares this is where Mahmud will be, calling on God in his satire to "burn this miscreant's soul in hell."

grip on power. In Tajikistan, President Rakhmonov has been championing the poet, along with other medieval "Persian" figures, to stoke a conflict with the Uzbeks, and the Russians harnessed the *Shahnameh* for their policy of divide and rule. Like the Quran or the Bible, it's a very easy text to abuse.

Conflicting arguments are jostling in my head, hurling me around the chamber in a state of confusion, knocking out another change of mind with every step I take, depriving me of the one thing the revenger needs above all: certainty. And in the middle of all this dithering, something else is calling out, ringing in my ears. It's nothing as wishy-washy as my thoughts: It's a sound, audible and clear—albeit with a slight crackling underneath it—coming from the other side of the sarcophagus. It pulls me away from my thoughts in a voice I remember from hundreds of miles away, just a few days before I set out on the road to Ghazni:

> *If only your father a true king had been*
> *Then wouldn't your gold on my head have been poured?*
> *And as for your mother, if she'd been a queen*
> *Then I would be sunk to my knees in your hoard.*

How has it happened? The Dictaphone is playing out the satire, as if it's lost patience with me and decided to punish the sultan all by itself. As if it's able to operate itself, pushing down the play button and spinning the reels. I step around the sarcophagus, to find myself looking into two pairs of old hooded eyes.

"*She'er!*"

The two snowy-turbaned, icy-bearded guardians are gleaming at me, addressing me with the one word I know in Pashto—because it's the same in Persian: "poetry." The satire stops, but it is followed by more. They are fiddling with the fast-forward button, jabbing their bony fingers at "play," filling up the space between us with sounds familiar from days and weeks and months ago.

We hear the reciter at the mosque in Tehran, whipping up the crowd with the story of the martyrdom of Imam Hossain. Then the

Shahnameh-khwan in the Bakhtiari mountains, telling of Rostam's feats in his butcher's shop. There is a cry of "Agh! Aaagh! Alaghh!" and the Dictaphone drops out of the guardians' hands. But it carries on playing as the Sufis of Herat swing their beards in my head.

Perhaps this is what I was meant to do. To play not just the words of scorn but *all* the words—the poems, the songs, the chants I've recorded, all of which were being recited a thousand years ago. There's a minstrel in Tajikistan, reciting from the tenth-century poet Rudaki, a rendition of the eleventh-century Sufi poet Baba Taher by a dervish in Hamadan, a Zoroastrian prayer intoned by Siyavash at the fire temple in Yazd. It's a variety show of verse, relayed to the guardians who are a living link to Sultan Mahmud's court, just as Ferdowsi or his reciter Abu Dulaf would have recited at the court himself. Here, in the presence of the dead sultan, his living guardians are listening to what's survived from the culture that flourished under his rule. He may not always have encouraged them, but they glowed under his auspices and have never been as bright again.

It's the moment when the flame of Persian culture lit up the world.

Outside in the lobby, I press a hand on my heart to say farewell. The guardians do the same, but before I can move away, one of them leans toward me. His watery eyes sparkle as he nods, tapping a finger to his mouth. I think he wants to know if my voice has come back.

Don't say a word! To disappoint the sultan's guardians—this will be my revenge for Ferdowsi. But the guardian's watery eyes are pulling the word out of my throat and when it comes—the Persian for "Yes!"—it's impossible to begrudge him his smile.

My shoes are on the edge of the threshold. I am still tying up my laces when I hear the sound of heavy boots, crashing against the steps underneath me. My heart thumps. The pine trees seem to split as two men in camouflage uniform burst through the space between them. They are both holding Kalashnikovs, and they are pointing directly at my chest. . . .

So why did it all go wrong? What happened to wreck Ferdowsi's chances with Sultan Mahmud?

We follow him into the sultan's great hall. He kisses the ground in front of Mahmud and recites a verse of praise for the man he considers to be a revival of the ancient Persian shahs—"bright-souled Fereydoun alive again." Perfect start—the sultan is now on the poet's side. As the *Shahnameh* is being recited, he listens eagerly. With his military interests, he especially enjoys the detail of battle and is wowed by a description of Rostam stringing his bow. But something goes wrong—terribly wrong—and when Ferdowsi leaves the court, he is running away from a death threat.

Scholars have come up with all sorts of different theories for Ferdowsi's disappointment. In fact, the subject has more arms than the Hindu idols so ferociously demolished by Mahmud. Was it jealousy? Religion? Egotism? Race? Philosophy? Court rivalry? Ideology? (See Figure 3 overleaf.)

It was none of them. What the sources suggest is something more complicated—a shift in policy driven by the sultan's unquenchable drive for power and glory.

At the beginning of his reign, Mahmud's dynasty was newly established and naturally he looked to Iranian legends to shore up his authority among a primarily Iranian population. So he used Persian as the principal language of his administration, forged a genealogy linking himself to the last Iranian shah, Yazdagird III, and encouraged Ferdowsi to write a poem about Yazdagird and his predecessors. When Mahmud was battling against the Turkic Qarakhanids, who associated themselves with the mythical Turanians, he presented himself as an Iranian shah fighting against the villainous Turks. A poem describing those ancient battles, and comparing Mahmud to the ancient Iranian kings, would be fantastic propaganda, enhancing his support among the Persian-speaking population and (as Dr. Zabat hinted in Mashhad) gaining troops for the sultan's army. It's like George W. Bush casting himself as a Wild West cowboy—appealing to the heroes in vogue with his subjects.

But, like most politicians, Mahmud's interest in these heroes didn't run very deep. In 1008, he defeated the Qarakhanids. So weakened (at least, temporarily) was the dynasty that when they later

3. Religion
The lack of success of the *Shahnameh* in Mahmud's court seems in part to have been because of the poet's apparent shi'i sympathies," writes Dick Davis, one of Ferdowsi's most recent and acclaimed translators, "Mahmud having a notoriously hostile attitude towards any manifestation of religious belief other than the strictest sunni orthodoxy." Perhaps when Ferdowsi recited a Shia mantra—"I am from the city of knowledge and Ali is the door of this city"—his enemies pounced and stoked the Sultan's prejudice.

2. Race
Alishir Ibadinov, a short-story writer I met in Uzbekistan, suggested that Ferdowsi's disappointment was down to Mahmud's Turkic background. "Ferdowsi only appreciated the kings of Iran," he said. "But Mahmud was a Turk. In fact, he created the first Islamic Turkish state, and just remembering him gives a feeling of satisfaction to Turks." The Uzbek scholar Azim Malikov agreed: "Perhaps Mahmud had some pro-Turkic sympathies," he said, adding, "perhaps he disliked the idea of Ferdowsi that Turan would always be defeated by Iran."

1. Rostam
According to the 11th century *History of Sistan*, after listening to Ferdowsi's verses, Sultan Mahmud said, "the *Book of Kings* is nothing but the history of Rostam; in my army there are a thousand men his equal." Ferdowsi replied that "the Almighty Himself never created again a creature such as Rostam," then sensibly he "kissed the ground and left." "To all intents and purposes," said Mahmud to his vizier, "this rascal called me a liar." A search party was dispatched, but the poet couldn't be found.

4. Jealousy

Perhaps the answer is more personal. It is said that Unsuri, the poet laureate, was working on his own *Book of Kings* and had written 10,000 verses already. If that's the case, he wouldn't have been too happy about someone else bringing out the same subject before him, and this may have driven him to the time-honored tactic of the courtly rival. Intriguingly, Ferdowsi himself hints at some such occurrence, when he complains in his satire that "someone painted me black in the eye of the king."

5. The wrong patron

According to Ferdowsi's first biographer, Nizami of Samarkand, the poet was supported by "Abu Hasan the secretary"—that is, the vizier Isfarani. The vizier was a keen promoter of the Persian language and admired Ferdowsi's attempt to sustain it, but he had many enemies at court and his successor replaced Persian as the official court language with Arabic. The vizier's taxation policies were a particular source of outrage against him—he levied so strongly against the people of Khorasan, as the chronicler Utbi put it, that "after water had been thrown on her udders, not a trickle of milk could be extracted, nor any traces of fat."

Figure 3: The arms of Ferdowsi's disappointment.

6. Egotism

Perhaps Mahmud was insulted by the lack of his own presence in the great military victories described in the *Shahnameh*. A scholar in Mashhad, Dr. Abbas Kheirabadi, pointed out that the poetry of Unsuri was mostly about Mahmud. Perhaps the panegyrics interleaved between Ferdowsi's stories weren't enough.

7. Ideology

"There were two groups at this time," Dr. Nodushan Eslami had said in Tehran, "one for the revival of ancient Iran and the other group for Islam . . . Mahmud was the son of a slave and he had a lack of heritage, so he became a fanatic. This is very common—if you are lacking something, you make up for it. They say the *Shahnameh* was shown to Sultan Mahmud but others prevented him from giving a large reward because Ferdowsi was out of real Islam. He was above real religion. He knew God, but he was above all the prophets."

squabbled among themselves, they turned to Mahmud to arbitrate. The battle between Mahmud and the Qarakhanids, one presenting himself as an Iranian, the other as a Turk, was over, and the sultan's attention was turning elsewhere.

If you wanted to get rich quick in the eleventh century and happened to have an army at your disposal, the contemporary alternative to robbing a bank was to head to India. Not only was there no Interpol in those days, but since the caliph of Baghdad was no friend of the Hindus, you were in with a good chance of supplementing your plunder with a bonus from Baghdad. By the time Ferdowsi turned up in Ghazni, Mahmud had already invaded India several times, winning a great victory in 1008 against a super-squad of Rajas, when explosions of naphtha oil caused the chief Raja's elephant to take fright, leading to a mass flight of the Indian troops. The sultan had already collected millions of dinars' worth of gold, unbored pearls, gems and rubies, diamonds as heavy as pomegranates, slaves, elephants, and (if the rumors are to be believed) a collection of the beaten Rajas' fingertips. But this was only the cusp of India's coffer. There was so much more to be reaped from the subcontinent, and now that he was secure on his western flank, the sultan was ready for the big time.

The historian Edmund Bosworth has described Mahmud's empire as "essentially a military machine," and this is how his treatment of Ferdowsi makes sense. His wars in India had no relationship to the Iran-Turan conflict. The propagandists saw them as holy wars between God's *mujahideen*—wagers of jihad—and the Hindu infidels. Endorsed by the caliph, these campaigns helped Mahmud to earn the fame, prestige, and wealth he always craved. They would have a huge effect on later Islamic history—the first major instance of war carried out in the name of Islam, away from the central authority of the caliph. Perhaps the man in black was right: Mahmud and his troops were, indeed, the original *mujahideen*.

The sultan's army was growing with every campaign, not only in numbers but also in ethnic diversity—filling up with Turks and Pashtuns, Indian elephant drivers, Turcoman sharpshooters, and "daredevil" Arab cavalrymen. He took his generals mostly from the Turks, his greatest weapons—his elephants—from the Indians, and his authority from the Sunni Arab caliph. So a poem about Persians by a Shia poet, in which Turks and Arabs were the fall guys, had lost the appeal it once held. If Ferdowsi had finished the *Shahnameh* a few years earlier, his reward would have been enormous. But he had the misfortune to invest his hope in the early Mahmud, only to find his patron in the form his later career would follow. It was a case of terrible timing.

And what happened next? According to the scribe Nizami of Samarkand, the poet "was bitterly disappointed, went to the bath, and, on coming out, bought a drink of sherbet, and divided the money between the bath-man and the sherbet-seller." On the pretense of making some corrections, he lifted the *Shahnameh* out of the royal library, scribbling his satire into the back. Then he left it for all to see, and disappeared.

The men are wearing combat uniforms and black flak jackets. They are hunched, like lions on the prowl, their fingers poised on their triggers. They step toward me, and around me, then somewhat to my surprise they continue their steps until they are inside the mausoleum.

Is there a renegade hiding in the tomb? Watching them as they hunch around it, I don't notice the crowd: a dozen men, with waistcoats and jackets over their *shalwar qameez*, who sweep past me and fill up the mausoleum, where they lift their hands in the air and raise a Quranic chant. One of the soldiers is creeping out. As he scans the pine trees through his gun's rear sight, I tap him on the shoulder and, since this is far too interesting to keep mum (not to mention that Sultan Mahmud has officially given me back my voice), I utter my first public sentence since Herat.

ME: Please tell me who are these people?
SOLDIER: You don't know?
ME: No.
SOLDIER: But this is Assadullah Khalid!
ME: And he is? . . .
SOLDIER: You don't know?

ME: No.
SOLDIER: But he is the governor of Ghazni!

It's hard to tell exactly which one he is, since there's nothing in his *shalwar qameez* to distinguish him from his companions (it would have been a lot easier in Ferdowsi's time—when the governors of Sultan Mahmud's empire always wore pointed hats, girdles, and cloaks to mark them out from the riff-raff). But the soldier nods toward the man at the front as the group proceeds into the lobby, and with one hand on my chest I announce: "Peace be upon you."

"You are a foreigner?" he asks in Persian.

That convincing, huh? I offer a meek nod and press a hand on my chest, to which he responds by asking what the hell I'm doing in Ghazni.

"I am a traveler," I say. "I have come a great distance to . . . um . . . well, to give to Sultan Mahmud . . . my respect. Yes, that's it . . . my respect and great regard."

I'm trying to think of the most flowery Persian words I know: Once again, I'm leaning on code, acting up to get on someone's good side.

He looks me up and down, slowly. "You are mad?"

Now he turns to Hassan-Gul, who is standing beside me. I say standing; in fact, he's bent nearly double with his eyes on the floor.

"You are his guide?" asks the governor.

Hassan-Gul mumbles, "By the will of God."

"And you let him go to these places?"

The governor has pulled himself so high over my guide that I think for a moment he's going to beat him. But he shifts his shoulders back and turns to me instead.

"You do know that two mullahs have been killed in our province in the last two weeks?" he says. "The enemy is attacking anywhere it can."

"Well, yes, I suppose," I say, trying to curry his favor with a smile. "But what about Sultan Mahmud?" This is what I really want to know. "Why are you praying at his tomb?"

For a moment, the governor looks at me with the same ferocity he's shown to Hassan-Gul, and I wonder if he will beat me instead. But his frown melts and his face flattens into the model of stiff-jawed, statesmanlike pride.

"Sultan Mahmud," he announces, "is the greatest person in Afghan history. He is the greatest for religion, and for empire. When he ruled, Ghazni was the capital of a great empire. In India they don't like him because he conquered them, and in Iran because of Ferdowsi, but here in Afghanistan you will find he is liked very much."

The gate swings open and his lackeys usher him toward a jeep with blacked-out windows.

"Now—*you*," he says, turning on Hassan-Gul, "take this foreigner and leave Ghazni at once!"

A cloud of dust sprays us as the jeep sweeps onto the road. Hassan-Gul is pulling out his spotted handkerchief to start working at the blemishes on his blazer. Only when he has tidied himself up properly is he able to throw back his shoulders, lift up his head, and give it a good shake. He is back to his normal height.

"This is an honor for you," he says flatly. "You have met the governor of Ghazni."

"I know."

I look at him from the side, trying to draw out a smile. "Look, Hassan-Gul, I'm really . . ."

"No, no, no, Mr. Nicholas, please! I ask only one thing."

"Anything."

I step closer, looking for reassurance in his face.

"This time, Mr. Nicholas, I ask that we must do exactly as we have been told."

We stroll out toward the market, with Sultan Mahmud's pleasure garden to our backs, and for a moment—for just the shortest of moments—Hassan-Gul presses a hand on my shoulder, the closest he will give me to a smile.

Epilogue

Iran. The Year After.

After fleeing from Ghazni, Ferdowsi went into hiding. Sultan Mahmud had heard his satire and was determined to trample him under his elephants, but his soldiers couldn't find him. As soon as the coast was clear, the poet left the house of his friend Ismail Warraq in Herat and traveled on, offering the *Shahnameh* to the wonderfully titled Sipahbad Shirzad of Buvand, who ruled a fiefdom on Iran's Caspian coast. But the Sipahbad refused. "You are a Shiite," he pointed out to the poet, "and to one who loves the family of the Prophet nothing will happen which did not happen to them." In short: Suffering is a Shia's lot.

Ferdowsi had neglected his estate to work on the *Shahnameh*, and having left Ghazni empty-handed, he was reduced to poverty. A man both broke and broken, he lived out his last days in his home city of Tus, looked after by his daughter. One day, it is said, he heard a small boy reciting a line from the *Shahnameh*. His heart soared, lifted by the hope his verse would survive after all, but it was too much for him, and he dropped dead on the spot.

The boy wasn't alone in quoting from the *Shahnameh*. Thousands of miles east, in India, a line from the epic was recited during the middle of a siege by the minister of Sultan Mahmud.* So impressed was the sultan, he regretted his earlier mistreatment of the poet and decided to make amends. Around the same time Ferdowsi heard the small boy reciting from his work, 60,000 dinars' worth of indigo was being dispatched to Tus.

It was too late. As the sultan's camels were carrying the gift through one gate, Ferdowsi's body was being borne out through another. The poet's daughter, it is said, refused to accept this late reward on her father's behalf, maintaining his proud fury.

It is telling that Ferdowsi's body was buried outside the city. Sheikh Jurjani, the chief religious figure in Tus and a Sunni zealot, had forbidden his body from being interred within the city walls, so he was put to rest in a garden on the city outskirts. Tus itself would fall, but the poet's grave remained, attracting visitors over the years, and in the 1930s, the shah had a new mausoleum fashioned out of marble and decorated with motifs from the tomb of Cyrus the Great. Ferdowsi had truly come out of the wilderness: Once rejected by a king, he was now being celebrated by another, in the style of the greatest of all Iran's kings.

One day in early spring, several months after my journey to Ghazni, I take a train to Mashhad and travel by bus to the poet's tomb. The smell of roses tints the air in a classic Persian garden, where the poet sits on a plinth, wearing a gown with frogged buttons and his trademark turban (with the tuft at the back, like many of the men I saw in Afghanistan). Canna lilies frame a rectangular pool, at the end of which, plump on its steps like a freshly iced cake, is the poet's mausoleum. It's dizzy with decorations—the Zoroastrian *faravahar* spreading his wings at the front, the closing verses of the *Shahnameh*

---

* The verse is a famous one (I heard it recited in Herat, by Abdul Aziz's father) and a motto for political hawks: "And should his reply with my wish not accord / Then Afrasiyab's field, the mace and the sword!" According to the scribe Nizami of Samarkand, on hearing these lines, Mahmud asked, "Whose verse is that? For he must have the heart of a man."

framed between ribbed pillars with double bulls on top. A stairwell pitches underground to the tomb chamber, passing a row of bas-reliefs: Rostam slapping his head as he weeps over a slain Sohrab; the Sassanian king Anushirvan, sitting on his throne surrounded by lance-bearers; a curly-bearded Darius the Great. I am less impressed by Darius's regal pose than the fact he's lost his nose, so I ask one of the curators where it's gone.

"You know about our revolution?" he whispers. "Well, at the beginning, many of the mullahs said bad things about Ferdowsi. They told their followers to attack the tomb, and they did. Look!"

He stubs his finger in front of a panel of writing on the wall facing Darius, which is broken in half.

"They used stones," he says, "and they tried to smash many of the pictures."

There was even, according to a retired teacher I meet in Mashhad, a plan to destroy the poet's tomb altogether.

"In the early days after the revolution," explains Ahmed Ansari, "there was a mullah called Abdullah Hajji who wanted to destroy Ferdowsi's tomb and burn his book in the streets. He said the *Shahnameh* was praising the shahs, so it was the work of enemies, and there was no difference between Ferdowsi's tomb and Reza Shah's. And he would have succeeded. You saw the statue in Ferdowsi Square? He wanted to pull it down and he was coming to attack it. But there was a scholar at the university, called Master Yusufi, who made a speech. He said, 'Was Ferdowsi a *Savaki*?* No! He was a good man and he criticized the bad kings.' So many people came to the square when the mullah was trying to pull it down, and they drove him away."

"What about the tomb?" I ask.

"Well," says Ahmed, "the mullah and his followers came and they damaged some of the pictures, but the people came out to stop them—because they knew Ferdowsi was a great poet and a good person."

---

* i.e., a member of the shah's secret police.

History has repeated itself. Just as a religious leader refused the poet burial in the first place, now religious leaders have been trying to disturb his rest. And just as the ordinary people—represented by the small boy reciting Ferdowsi's verse—saved his reputation the first time, now, nearly a thousand years later, they saved the poet's tomb.

It's all change in Tehran. President Ahmedinejad has introduced a new law to stop two passengers from sharing the front seat in a taxi and half the cars are barred on any given day from driving, after a period of particularly noxious smog. The government's nuclear program is headline news around the world, prompting a million people to demonstrate outside the upturned Y of the "Freedom" monument in central Tehran.

"How can the Americans tell us not to have nuclear power?" exclaims a man called Mehdi. "Do *they* not have nuclear power?"

His four-year-old son is sitting on his shoulders, holding a papier mâché effigy of President Bush. He's about to throw it into a street fire, where Tony Blair is already burning alongside a blue and white Israeli flag.

It's all change at the Professor's too. Tahmineh has let her hair grow back to its natural black, and apparently she has a new boyfriend— although I don't mention this to Reza. I assume Tahmineh is still barred from seeing him, so it's a surprise when the Professor asks if I keep in touch with him. Eventually he has it out of me.

"When you next meet this young man," he declares in his most formal tone, "you must inform him that he is invited."

It's hardly a full-on reconciliation, but it's close. The Professor is organizing a literary event in association with the annual Fajr Theatre Festival, and the artist who was supposed to be designing the poster has fallen sick. I assume Reza will refuse—he's far too proud, I think. But a week later he is back at the house, carrying a brightly colored rolled-up sheet.

This is one of my last evenings in Tehran—and one of the happiest. Tahmineh and Reza joke with each other, laughing about the beard I was trying to grow last summer. There is a serious moment when the Professor holds up the poster—showing a minstrel with a flute in his mouth and a shepherd's crook in his hand—and everyone makes the appropriate noises.

"It's very pretty," says Khanom. "Perhaps we can ask Reza to decorate the living room!"

The Professor smiles. Leaning toward his wife, he whispers something in her ear and plants a kiss on the top of her head.

"Now," he announces, "it is time to give our guests a drink."

Sina has written a song about the president, which he recites as we sip, slicing a finger through the air like a rapper: "You preach to us youngsters like proud old Farun,* / Well, shave off your beard, you repulsive baboon!"

"You think I can get some music for it?" he asks, then raises his glass and declares a toast: "To the president!"

"And," adds the Professor, "to whoever has to clean his bath!"

Late in the evening, the Professor steps over to the walnut bookcase and takes out the *Shahnameh*. It's a new copy, the cover showing the poet's face in white and black swills on a blood-red background. With Tahmineh sitting beside him to turn the page, he starts reading from the tale of Prince Siyavash. At first, Tahmineh is exchanging glances with Reza, while Sina is trying to distract me by flicking my earlobes. But slowly, we all turn toward the Professor and let ourselves be sucked into the story. The light from the lamp is glistening on his hair, and as the hero takes up his horse's reins to ride through the flame of judgment, the Professor looks like he is on fire himself. There is the odd chime when someone puts down a glass, but apart from that, all you can hear are the thousand-year-old words, binding us together as the hero rides out to glory.

---

*Farun is a character in the Quran, famous for his wealth. The Persian rhyme matched "Farun" with "meimun," the Persian for "monkey."

Acknowledgments

Given the political situation in Iran, and the political matter contained in this book, I've decided to stick to first names for my Iranian acknowledgments. I've also disguised the identities of many people in the book, for the same reason. I really hope that no one, in Iran or any of the other countries I visited, suffers because of anything I've written.

For their hospitality, I am especially grateful to Guitti, Amir, Farid, Fariba, and Siyavash and his family. Thanks also to Leila, Vahideh, Reza and all his friends in Yazd, Ehsaan and his friends, Mehmorali, Peyman, Farshid and all their brothers, Vali and Ahmed in Mashhad, Dr. Abbas and his family, Arash H., Mohammed Y. N., Mustafa, Masa, and the dozens of kind people who helped me in so many ways during the course of my travels. Thanks also to my teachers at the Dekhodeh Institute in Tehran and all the staff there. Most of all thanks to Ramin, the kindest and most hospitable of friends.

My travels in Central Asia owed a lot to Habibullah Ibragimov and his family, whose generosity and kindness was extraordinary. I'm also grateful to Professor Bahriddin Aliev, Azim Malikov, Jurabek Sidikov, Dr. Farid Alakbarov, Betty Blair, and Edmund Hayes for his hospitality in Khojand. In Afghanistan, I was very fortunate to meet the teachers at the Afghan English Language Centre in Herat, and I'm grateful to Christina Lamb, Fraidoon Afzali, Vanni

Capelli, Partaw Naderi, Sadiq Osian, Dr. Ghani Barzinmehr, and Professor Homaioun at Kabul University for their kindness. There were a great many other people who helped me during the course of my journey—I'm sorry to anyone I've missed.

Back in London, Ali Tavakolli was my first Persian teacher and gave me a wonderful introduction to the language and culture of Iran. I'm also grateful to Will Shield, Sami Aziz, Shahin Bekhradnia, Tom Wellsford, Daniel Metcalfe, Ardashir Vakil, Aasiya Lodhi, Charles Melville, Mahnaz Badihian, and Eugene Schoulgin for their advice and many kind deeds, and would like to thank the staff of the British Library. Professor Edmund Bosworth was invaluable on the history of the Ghaznavid era, while Bahbak Miremadi was amazingly helpful, as well as a brilliant sounding board, throughout the course of this project. Along with Bahbak and Professor Bosworth, I'm also grateful to Nick Brealey, Arkady Hodge, and Edmund Hayes for their editorial comments and suggestions; to Sally Maltby for designing the beautiful map; and to my family and friends for their support during the long period of time it took me to complete this book.

My agent, Maggie Noach, died soon after I returned from Iran, and I will always cherish the short time I knew this remarkable woman. Jill Hughes and Josie Stapleton stepped into her shoes to sell the manuscript, under difficult circumstances, and for this (along with their editorial advice) I'm very grateful. Jonathan Crowe at Da Capo has been a delight to work with on the publishing side, and I thank him and his colleagues for bringing the book to the shelves.

Finally, and most of all, thank you to Poppy, chief "that"—remover and much, much more—for everything.

Glossary

Ahura Mazda: the supreme god of the ancient Iranians, whose cult was propagated by the prophet Zoroaster.

alam: a standard carried in Shia Muslim processions, used especially in Mohurram ceremonies.

amin: Central Asian custom, similar to the Christian sign of the cross, in which people stroke their hands through the air as a blessing and confirmation of prayer.

ashoura: the tenth day of the Islamic month of Mohurram, when the Prophet Mohammed's grandson, Imam Hossain, was killed along with his family and supporters on the plains of Kerbala.

Avesta: the Zoroastrian scriptures, compiled mostly between 800 and 200 BCE (although they include many texts composed in earlier times). Among them are the *Gathas*, seventeen hymns that are traditionally attributed to the prophet Zoroaster.

azan: the Muslim call to prayer.

barbari: a type of Iranian flatbread, typically crisp on the outside and soft on the inside, with deep ridges and speckled with sesame seeds.

basiji: the brown-shirts of the ayatollahs' Iran, commonly seen on motorbikes tearing down the highways, known for their moral policing and their often violent tactics (not the kind of people to bump into if you're at a demonstration). These paramilitary volunteers belong to the Mobilization Resistance Force, under the authority of the Supreme Leader and the Iranian Revolutionary Guards, and they have a group in every Iranian city.

caliph: often called the "pope" of Islam. Originally the official "successor" to the Prophet Mohammed, the caliph ruled the Islamic community by the sharia. In Ferdowsi's day, the caliph was based in Baghdad.

camancheh: stringed Iranian musical instrument about the size of a viola, made of wood and played with a horsehair bow.

caravanserai: literally a "caravan palace," a roadside inn where travelers took their rest. Usually the *caravanserai* had high walls built around a central courtyard, with a single large gateway and separate stalls for animals.

chador: literally a "tent." A woman's covering, wrapped around her body and covering her head, sometimes kept in place by gripping its ends between her teeth.

chapan: padded coat worn especially in Central Asia.

Dari: the name for the dialects of Persian spoken both by the Zoroastrians of Yazd and the Tajik Afghans, although there are differences between their respective dialects. It comes from the old word for "courtly."

dehkan: originally the head of a village and member of the lesser feudal nobility, who traditionally acted as the middleman between the king and the peasants. After the Arab conquest, *dehkans* continued to be responsible for local administration and largely retained their lands. By Ferdowsi's day, however, their position and influence was in decline. Nowadays, the term is used in Central Asia to denote an individual or family farm.

div: the monsters that appear in the *Book of Kings*, with cloven hooves, sharp teeth, and furry hides. Still used to denote monsters in popular culture today (for example, in the Persian-language version of *Shrek*, the title character is described as a "div"), it is also the root of the Persian word for "mad."

diwan: a book or collection of poetry (although the word can also refer to a register or a governmental office).

dotar: literally "two strings," a plucked instrument like a mandolin.

dhoti: a rectangle of unstitched cloth, wrapped around the waist and legs, traditionally worn in India.

dugh: a popular drink in Iran and Central Asia, consisting of yogurt and water.

duhul: a very big traditional drum, covered in goat hide and beaten on both sides.

faravahar: the iconic image of Zoroastrianism—a winged man with a ring around his waist, holding another ring in his hand. There is debate as to its precise meaning, but it is generally taken to represent the human soul, turning away from evil and toward good.

gabillin: large hand-woven rug common in Central Asia.

hadith: an account of what the Prophet Mohammed said or did, or of his approval of something said or done in his presence; widely considered to be second in authority to the Quran.

Hajji: an honorary title for someone who has performed the *hajj*, or pilgrimage, to Mecca.

Haram: an Islamic sacred compound, coming from the same root as the word for "forbidden."

hijab: literally "cover." A general term referring to a Muslim woman's veil or head covering. For many Muslims, the importance of female modesty is sanctioned in the twenty-fourth chapter of the Quran: "And say to the believing women that they cast down their looks and guard their private parts, and display not their ornaments, except those which are outside; and let them pull their kerchiefs over their bosoms and not display their ornaments."

herbad: a Zoroastrian priest who has undergone the first stage of initiation into the priesthood.

iwan: a large vaulted hall or space, walled on three sides, with one end entirely open.

joob: narrow streetside channels common throughout Iran, which carry water down from the mountains.

Ka'aba: the most famous sanctuary of Islam, located in the great mosque of Mecca, toward which Muslims throughout the world direct their prayers and around which pilgrims make ritual circuits on the *hajj*. The *Ka'aba* is a fifty-feet-high stone cube set on a marble base and covered in a curtain. According to the Quran, its foundations were laid by Ibrahim and Ismail.

karnai: a long brass horn with a flared nozzle, played at weddings and other ceremonial occasions in Central Asia.

korymbos: a globe traditionally worn on the crowns of Sassanian kings.

koshti: a plaited cord worn by Zoroastrians, similar to Jewish tzitzis.

mahout: an elephant driver.

marshrutnoe: a minivan used as public transport in Central Asia.

mobed: a Zoroastrian priest.

Mohurram: the first month in the Islamic calendar, in which Imam Hossain was killed at Kerbala.

mujahid: literally "one who fights jihad." The plural is *mujahideen*.

mullah: a Muslim educated in Islamic theology and jurisprudence, able to lead prayers in mosques and perform ceremonies such as birth and funeral rites. The term is usually applied to low-level clerics in Iran, Pakistan, and Central Asia.

nas: tobacco used in Central Asia, usually cut with spices or lime and chewed inside the cheek.

neyanban: the Iranian bagpipes, an inflated goatskin with a mouthpiece at one end and a reed-pipe for finger placement at the other.

Nowruz: Persian New Year, usually falling on March 21, or the spring equinox.

pahlavan: the name given to the knights or warriors of the ancient Iranian legends, and more recently to the sportsmen at Iranian strength houses.

pishtaq: the screen that rises up in front of the dome in some Islamic buildings, especially prominent in Uzbekistan.

qanun: musical instrument like a zither, played with two plectra on a trapezoidal box.

Qanun: literally "Code"; the name of the medical encyclopedia written by Ibn Sina.

Quran: the holy book of Islam, which according to tradition is the direct word of God, passed down to Mohammed by the Angel Gabriel over the course of twenty-three years.

rawi: a reciter and transmitter of poetry and narrative traditions.

salavat: Islamic blessing, invoking the Prophet Mohammed.

samovar: a metal container for heating and boiling water, used especially for tea.

Savak: the Iranian secret police in the time of the Pahlavi shahs.

Shahnameh-khwan: a "reader of the *Book of Kings*," men who recite verses from the *Shahnameh*, often by heart.

shalwar qameez: literally "trousers shirt." The long shirt and baggy drawstring trousers worn by most Afghan men.

taarof: literally "offer." The custom of humbling oneself as an act of politeness, which is characterized by the tradition of refusing something three times before finally accepting. Practiced widely throughout Persian-speaking society.

zurkhaneh: "strength house," the traditional Iranian gymnasiums, in which men practice sports associated with ancient battles.

Bibliography

Firuza Abdullaeva and Charles Melville, *The Persian Book of Kings* (Oxford: Bodleian Library, 2008).

Soheil M. Afnan, *Avicenna, His Life and Works* (London: George Allen & Unwin Ltd., 1958).

Nasrin Alavi, ed. and trans., *We Are Iran* (London: Portobello, 2006).

Ali M. Ansari, *Modern Iran Since 1921: The Pahlavis and After* (London: Longman, Pearson Education, 2003).

Khwaja Abdullah Ansari, *Intimate Conversations*, published alongside *Ibn 'ata'illah: The Book of Wisdom*, trans. Wheeler M. Thackston (London: SPCK, 1979).

A. J. Arberry, *Classical Persian Literature* (London: George Allen & Unwin Ltd., 1958).

Zahirridin Nasr Mohammed Awfi, *Jami al Hikayat* (London: Luzac & Co., 1929).

W. Barthold, *Turkestan—Down to the Mongol Invasion* (London: Luzac & Co. Ltd., 1968).

Iraj Bashiri, *Firdowsi's Shahname: 1000 Years After* (Dushanbe: ALIS, 1994).

Najmeh Batmanglij, *New Food of Life: ancient Persian and modern Iranian cooking and ceremonies* (Washington DC: Mage Publishers, 1997).

Ibn Battutah, *The Travels of Ibn Battutah*, ed. Tim Mackintosh-Smith (London: Picador, 2003).

C. E. Biddulph, ed., *Afghan Poetry of the Seventeenth Century: Being Selections from the Poems of Khushal Khan Khatak* (London: Kegan Paul/Trench, Trübner & Co., 1890).

Muhammed Ibn al-Bighami, *The Firuz Shahnama*, trans. William L. Hanaway Jr. (Delmar, New York: Scholars' Facsimiles & Reprints, 1974).

Isabella Bird, *Journeys in Persia and Kurdistan* (London: John Murray, 1891).

Abu Raihan Al-Biruni, *The Chronology of Ancient Nations*, trans. and ed. Dr. C. Edward Sachau (London: W. H. Allen & Co., 1879).

Sheila S. Blair, *The Monumental Inscriptions from Early Islamic Iran and Transoxiana* (Leiden, Netherlands: E. J. Brill, 1992).

Martin Booth, *Opium: A History* (London: Simon & Schuster Ltd., 1996).

C. E. Bosworth, B. Lewis, E. Van Donzel et al., eds., *The Encyclopaedia of Islam* (Leiden/London: EJ Brill/Luzac & Co., 1960–2000).

C. E. Bosworth, *The Ghaznavids* (Edinburgh: Edinburgh University Press, 1963).

_____, *Humanism in the Renaissance of Islam—the Cultural Revival during the Buyid Age* (Leiden, Joel L. Kraemer, 1986)

_____, *The Medieval Islamic Underworld* (Leiden, Netherlands: E. J. Brill, 1976).

_____, *Medieval History of Iran, Afghanistan and Central Asia* (London: Variorum Reprints, 1977).

_____, *History of the Saffarids of Sistan and the Maliks of Nimruz* (Costa Mesa, CA, and New York: Mazda Publishers, 1994).

Mary Boyce, *A Persian Stronghold of Zoroastrianism* (Oxford: Clarendon Press, 1977).

Yuri Bregel, *The Role of Central Asia in the History of the Muslim East* (New York: Asia Society Occasional Papers/Afghanistan Council, 1980).

Edward Granville Browne, *A Literary History of Persia* (London: T. Fisher Unwin, 1906).

_____, *A Year Amongst the Persians* (London: Kegan Paul & Co., 1893).

Richard Burton, *Sindh and the Races that Inhabit the Valley of the Indus* (Karachi: Oxford University Press, 1973).

Robert Byron, *The Road to Oxiana* (London: Macmillan, 1937).

Olaf Caroe, *The Pathans* (Karachi: Oxford University Press, 1958).

Jamsheed K. Chosky, *Conflict and Cooperation—Zoroastrian Subalterns and Muslim Elites in Medieval Iranian Society* (New York: Columbia University Press, 1997).

Farhad Daftary, *Medieval Isma'ili History and Thought* (Cambridge: Cambridge University Press, 1996).

Simin Daneshvar, *Savushun: a Persian Requiem*, trans. Roxane Zand (London: Halban, 1991).

Olga Davidson, *Poet and Hero in the Persian Book of Kings* (Ithaca, NY: Cornell University Press, 1994).

Dick Davis, *Epic and Sedition: Ferdowsi's Shahnama* (Washington, DC: Mage Publishers, 1992).

R. K. Dikshit, *The Candellas of Jejakabhukti* (New Delhi: Shakti Malik, 1997).

Louis Dupree, *Afghanistan* (Princeton, NJ: Princeton University Press, 1973).

Nancy Hatch Dupree, *An Historical Guide to Afghanistan* (Kabul: Afghan Air Authority/Afghan Tourist Organization, 1971).

Henry Miers Elliot, *The History of India: As Told by Its Own Historians*, ed. John Dowson (Calcutta: S. Gupta, 1952–1961).

Faith Evans, trans. and adapted by, *The Daughters of Karl Marx: Family Correspondence 1866–1898* (London: Andre Deutsch, 1982).

Hakim Abu'l Qasim Ferdowsi, *Shahnama, on the Basis of the Edition of the Copy Known as the Moscow Edition* (Tehran: Ilm Publisher, 1384/2005).

Abolqasem Ferdowsi, *Shahnameh: the Persian Book of Kings*, trans. Dick Davis (New York: Viking Penguin, 2006).

Ferdowsi, *The Shahnama of Firdausi*, trans. Arthur George Warner, MA, and Edmond Warner, BA, 9 vols. (London: Kegan Paul & Co., 1905–1925).

Abool Kasim Firdousee, *The Shahnameh: An Heroic Poem. Containing the History of Persia from Kioomurs to Yesdejird*, collated by Turner Macan (Calcutta: Baptist Mission Press, 1829).

Gustave Flaubert, *Flaubert in Egypt* (New York: Penguin Books, 1996).

Richard N. Frye, *Bukhara—the Medieval Achievement* (Norman: University of Oklahoma Press, 1965).

_____, *The Heritage of Central Asia* (Princeton, NJ: Markus Wiener Publications, 1996).

_____, *The Heritage of Persia* (London: Weidenfeld & Nicholson, 1962).

Nizami Ganjavi, *Dastan-Khusraw va Shirin* (Tehran: Mu'assasah'i Intisharat-i Franklin, 1974).

Al-Ghazzali, *Book of Counsel for Kings,* trans. F. R. C. Bagley (Oxford: Oxford University Press, 1964).

R. Ghirshman, *Iran: From the Earliest Times to the Islamic Conquest* (London: Penguin, 1954).

Milton Gold, trans., *Tarikh e Sistan* (Rome: Istituto Italiano Per Il Medio Ed Estremo Oriente, 1976).

O. Cameron Gruner, *The Canon of Medicine of Avicenna* (London: Luzac & Co., 1930).

Mohammed Habib, *Sultan Mahmud of Ghaznin* (Aligarh: Cosmopolitan Publishers, 1951).

Hafez, *The Divan of Hafez*, trans. Reza Saberi (Lanham, MD: University Press of America, 2002).

Lt. Col. Sir Wolseley Haig, ed., *Cambridge History of India Vol. 3 Turks and Afghans* (Cambridge: Cambridge University Press, 1928).

Badi al-Zaman al-Hamadhani, *The Maqamat,* trans. W. J. Prendergast (London: Curzon Press, 1915).

Gavin Hambly, ed., *Women in the Medieval Islamic World* (Basingstoke, UK: Palgrave Macmillan, 2000).

Ibn Hawkal, *The Oriental Geography of Ebn Haukal*, trans. Sir William Ouseley (London: Oriental Press/Wilson & Co., 1800).

M. M. Hejazi, *Historical Buildings of Iran: Their Architecture and Structure* (Southampton, UK: Computational Mechanics Publications, 1997).

Herodotus, *The Histories,* trans. Walter Blanco and Jennifer Tolbert Roberts (New York and London: Norton, 1992).

Robert Hillenbrand, *Shahnama: The Visual Language of the Persian Book of Kings* (Aldershot, UK: Ashgate, 2004).

Tom Holland, *Persian Fire* (London: Little, Brown, 2005).

Kathleen Hopkirk, *A Traveller's Companion to Central Asia* (London: John Murray, 1993).

Peter Hopkirk, *The Great Game: On Secret Service in High Asia* (London: John Murray, 1990).

Human Rights Watch, *Iran: Religious and Ethnic Minorities* (New York: Human Rights Watch, 1997).

Ibn Ishaq, *The Life of Muhammad*, trans. Alfred Guillaume (Karachi: Oxford University Press, 1967).

Al-Jahiz, *Epistle on Singing Girls*, trans. A. Beeston (London: Aris & Philips, 1980).

Jane's Strategic Weapons Systems (Internet publication, August 2009).

Yvonne Kapp, *Eleanor Marx: Family Life 1855–1883* (London: Lawrence & Wishart, 1972)

Ryszard Kapuscinski, *Shah of Shahs* (London: Quartet Books, 1985).

Hugh Kennedy, *The Court of the Caliphs* (London: Weidenfeld & Nicolson, 2004).

Mehdi Khansari, *The Persian Garden* (Washington DC: Mage Publishers, 1998).

Stephen Kinzer, *All the Shah's Men: An American Coup and the Roots of Middle East Terror* (Hoboken, NJ: J. Wiley & Sons, 2003).

Edgar Knobloch, *Monuments of Central Asia: A Guide to the Archaeology, Art and Architecture of Turkestan* (London: I. B. Tauris, 2001).

Paul Kriwaczek, *In Search of Zarathustra* (London: Weidenfeld & Nicolson, 2002).

Amelie Kuhrt, *The Persian Empire* (New York: Routledge, 2007).

Robert Lacey & Danny Danziger, *The Year 1000: what life was like at the turn of the first millennium* (Boston: Little, Brown, 1999).

Christina Lamb, *The Sewing Circles of Herat: My Afghan Years* (London: HarperCollins, 2002).

Robin Lane Fox, *Alexander the Great* (London: Penguin Books, 1986).

Doris Lessing, *The Wind Blows away our Words* (London: Picador, 1987).

G. Le Strange, *The Lands of the Eastern Caliphate* (Cambridge: Cambridge University Press, 1905).

Peter Levi, *The Light Garden of the Angel King* (London: Collins, 1972).

Margaret Read MacDonald, *Traditional Storytelling Today: An International Sourcebook* (New York: Routledge, 1999).

Sylvia A. Matheson, *Persia: An Archaeological Guide* (London: Faber & Faber, 1972).

Julie Meisami, *Persian Historiography to the End of the Twelfth Century* (Edinburgh: Edinburgh University Press, 1999).

Homazayar K. Mirza, *Sasanian Zoroastrianism* (Delhi: Delhi Parsi Anjuman, 1992).

Azadeh Moaveni, *Lipstick Jihad* (New York: PublicAffairs, 2005).

Afshin Molavi, *Persian Pilgrimages* (London: WW Norton & Company, 2002).

Shmuel Moreh, *Live Theatre and Dramatic Literature in the Medieval Arabic World* (Edinburgh: Edinburgh University Press, 1991).

Trevor Mostyn, *Censorship in Islamic Societies* (London: Saqi Books, 2002).

Nizam al-Mulk, *Siyasatnama*, "The Book of Government or Rules for Kings," trans. Hubert Drake (London: Routledge & Kegan Paul, 1960).

Abu Bakr Mohammed Narshakhi, *The History of Bukhara*, trans. Richard N. Frye (from a Persian abridgement of the Arabic original) (Cambridge, MA: Medieval Academy of America, 1954).

Mohammed Nazim, *Sultan Mahmud of Ghazna* (Cambridge: Cambridge University Press, 1931).

Reynald Alleyne Nicholson, *Studies in Islamic Mysticism* (Cambridge: University Press, 1921).

David Nicolle, *Sassanian Armies* (Stockport, UK: Montvert Publications, 1996).

Nizami-i Arudi of Samarkand, *Chahar Maqala (the Book of Four Discourses)*, trans. E. G. Browne (London: Luzac & Co., 1900).

Sir Lewis Pelly, *Journal of a Journey from Persia to India through Herat and Candahar* (Bombay: Education Society Press, 1866).

Iraj Pezeshkzad, *My Uncle Napoleon*, trans. Dick Davis (Washington, DC: Mage Publishers, 1996).

David Pinault, *The Shiites* (London: I. B. Tauris, 1992).

Ahmed Rashid, *The Resurgence of Central Asia: Islam or Nationalism* (London: Zed Books, 1994).

A. G. Ravan Farhadi, *Abdullah Ansari of Herat* (Richmond, UK: Curzon Press, 1996).

Everett K. Rowson, Gender Irregularity as Entertainment: Institutionalized Transvestism at the Caliphal Court in Medieval Baghdad, in Gender and Difference in the Middle Ages, ed. Sharon Farmer and Carol Braun Pasternack (Minneapolis: University of Minnesota Press, 2003).

Jan Rypka, *History of Iranian Literature*, ed. K. Jahn (Dordrecht, Netherlands: Reidel, 1968).

Vita Sackville-West, *Passenger to Teheran* (London: L. & V. Woolf, 1926).

Elaine Sciolino, *Persian Mirrors: the elusive face of Iran* (New York, The Free Press, 2000).

Shapur Shahbazi, *Ferdowsi: A Critical Biography* (Cambridge, MA: Harvard University & Mazda Publishers, 1991).

Kamil M. Al-Shaibi, *Sufism and Shi'ism* (Surbiton, UK: Laam Ltd., 1991).

Shaul Shaked, *From Zoroastrian Iran to Islam: Studies in Religious History and Intercultural Contacts* (Aldershot, UK: Variorum, 1995).

Sir Aurel Stein, *Old Routes of Western Iran: Narrative of an Archaeological Journey* (London: Macmillan & Co., 1940).

Rhea Talley Stewart, *Fire in Afghanistan, 1914–29: Faith, Hope, and the British Empire* (New York: Doubleday, 1973).

Stephen Tanner, *Afghanistan* (New York: Da Capo Press, 2002).

Tha'alibi, *The Lata'if al-ma'arif of Tha'alibi* (Edinburgh: University Press, 1968).

Colin Thubron, *The Lost Heart of Asia* (London: Heinemann, 1994).

Habib Hassan Touma, *Music of the Arabs* (Portland, OR, and Cambridge: Amadeus Press, 1996).

W. L. Treadwell, "The Political History of the Samanid State," PhD thesis, Oxford University, 1991.

Chushichi Tsuzuki, *The Life of Eleanor Marx 1853–1898: a Socialist Tragedy* (Oxford: Clarendon Press, 1967).

Arthur Upham Pope, *Persian Architecture* (London: Thames & Hudson, 1965).

P. B. Vachha, *Firdowsi and the Shahnama* (Bombay: MALLB New Book Co. Ltd., 1950).

Geert Jan Van Gelder, *God's Banquet: Food in Classical Arabic Literature* (New York: Columbia University Press, 2000).

Monica Whitlock, *Beyond the Oxus—the Central Asians* (London: John Murray, 2002).

Donald N. Wilber, *Persepolis: The Archaeology of Parsa, Seat of the Persian Kings* (Princeton, NJ: Darwin Press Inc., 1989).

Charles James Wills, *In the Land of the Lion and Sun* (London: Macmillan & Co., 1883).

Michael Wood, *In the Footsteps of Alexander the Great: A Journey from Greece to Asia* (London: BBC Books, 1997).

Ehsan Yarshater, ed., *Cambridge History of Iran* (Cambridge: Cambridge University Press, 1968 onward).

R. C. Zaehner, *The Dawn and Twilight of Zoroastrianism* (London: Weidenfeld & Nicholson, 1961).

Lila Azam Zanganeh, *My Sister, Guard Your Veil; My Brother, Guard Your Eyes* (Boston: Beacon Press, 2006).